D1084226

The Mystery of Numbers

"We don't inherit the land from our ancestors,
we borrow it from our children."
Antoine de Saint-Exupéry

And so, I dedicate this book to
Gaddiël,
Sivane,
Shamgar,
and Nin-Gal.

Cover: *The Proportions of Man*
and Their Hidden Numbers (Cornelius Agrippa:
De Occulta Philosophia Libri II, 1533).

The calligraphy in this work was done by
Marc-Alain Ouaknin.

© 2004 Assouline Publishing for the present edition
601 West 26th Street, 18th floor
New York, NY 10001, USA
Tel.: 212 989-6810   Fax: 212 647-0005
www.assouline.com

First published by Editions Assouline, Paris, France

Translated by Adele Kudish

Copyedited by Margot Ebling and Fredrick Kennedy

Printed by RR Donnelley

ISBN : 2 84323 632 0

Marc-Alain Ouaknin

The Mystery of Numbers

ASSOULINE

CONTENTS

Introduction   8

BOOK ONE: NUMERALS
The emergence and evolution of modern numerals

I. The Indian origins (from the third century B.C.E. to the ninth century C.E.) 20

    1. "Chess and math"   21

    2. Indian mathematics   29

    3. The evolution of Indian writing   35

    4. The five stages of the evolution of Indian numerals   51

    5. The names of Indian numerals   65

    6. *Shûnya, shûnya!* The discovery of zero   73

II. Indo-Arabic numerals (from the ninth to the twelfth centuries)   80

    1. En route to Baghdad   81

    2. *Al-jabr* and algebra   91

    3. Voyage to Arabia…   99

III. How Indo-Arabic numerals reached the Christian West   114

    1. Gerbert of Aurillac, the mathematician pope   115

    2. The importance of the Crusades   125

    3. Fibonacci and the *Liber Abaci*   133

    4. Numerals and the printing press   141

IV. Kabbalah, isopsephia, and the name of Allah   146

    1. Our ancestors, the…   147

    2. Kabbalah, numerals, and letters   153

    3. Isopsephia   159

BOOK TWO: NUMBERS
The great family

I. Crazy about numbers and crazy numbers 164

   1. Memoirs of a mathematician 165

   2. Numbers and number theory 169

   3. Pythagoras and the harmony of numbers 175

II. The classics 186

   1. The wisdom of the irrational 187

   2. Yearning for infinity 199

   3. Odd and even 209

   4. Prime numbers 213

III. Special numbers 218

   1. Perfect numbers 219

   2. The mysteries of 6 and 28 225

   3. "Friendly" numbers 229

IV. Love triangles 236

   1. Triangular numbers 237

   2. The Pythagorean triangle 245

   3. The triangle of Isis 251

   4. Pythagoras, Fermat, and Wiles 255

   5. Pascal's triangle 259

   6. The golden number 263

V. Is God a mathematical hypothesis? 272

 1. Numerical values of divine names 273

 2. The transcendence of π 277

 3. Fermat and the Kabbalah 283

BOOK THREE: **SHAPES**

Magic squares and other talismans

I. Magic squares 292

 1. Lines, columns, and diagonals 293

 2. Chinese origins 299

 3. How do you build a magic square? 305

 4. Faust, Goethe, and the magic squares 309

 5. *Melancholia* 313

 6. Some extraordinary magic squares 315

II. Alchemy and talismans 322

 1. Alchemy 323

 2. The Bible and magic squares 331

 3. Healing and relaxation 335

 4. "The erotic affair between the straight line and the circle" 339

BOOK FOUR: APPENDIXES

Ideas and men

Glossary of common nouns   346

Glossary of proper names   365

Bibliography   377

Acknowledgements   381

Photo credits   383

INTRODUCTION

Oh, how the world is small
Oh, how the cherries are big...
Jean Arp

Numbers and *numerals*

The first question that comes to mind is surely the same I have asked myself for years: What is the difference between *numbers* and *numerals*? We often use these words interchangeably. And to complicate things, we also talk about *figures*.

The numeral is a way of writing, or of signifying, a number. The numeral is a fact of language and writing. On the other hand, numbers exist independently of numerals. Look at this image:

Dignitaries and scribes facing the king, detail from a mural in the palace at Til Barsip (Assyria).
Facing page: Hand reproduced from a digital computation manual;
the original image was published in the fifteenth century.

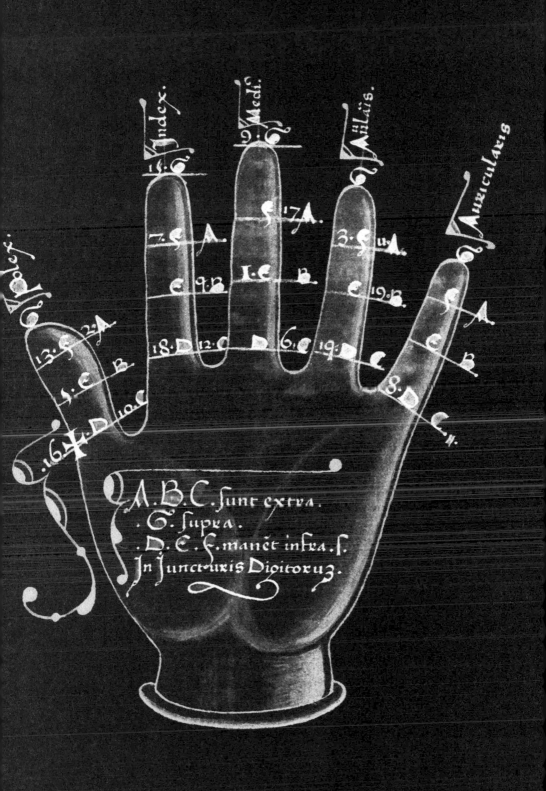

It represents a certain reality that will be interpreted differently by each person who sees it. The fact that there are four characters is certainly clear to any viewer. But the way each person will describe it in writing will depend on his culture, language, and era.

Whether it is "4," "IV," or "Δ," it is still the same number of characters. Only the signs used to indicate them are different. It is these indicators or signs that we call numerals.

It is easy to understand that there may be an infinity of ways of writing numerals. History teaches us that each great civilization offered its own numerals, in other words, its own indicators, its own marks, its own signs. So, there are Babylonian, Egyptian, Chinese, Greek, Hebrew, Mayan, Indian numerals, Arabic numerals, and modern numerals.

The various systems of numeration

We distinguish three broad systems of numeration, according to the era and the symbols used to write numbers.

– Primitive numeration

All this does is repeat a sign made to correspond to an object. Today, we still use the primitive numeration for dice, dominoes, and cards. The clock's repetition of the same sound for hours also constitutes a primitive numeration. This primitive numeration does not use symbols but various objects or simply numerations reflecting a purely oral symbolization.

Rock ball and *calculi* from Susa, circa 3300 B.C.E.

– Ancient numeration

Ancient numeration uses either extremely precise signs and symbols (in which case, we call it "symbolic numeration," like that of the Babylonians, Egyptians, and Mayans), or letters of the alphabet, in which case we call it alphabetic numeration, like that of the Greeks and Hebrews. To emphasize that these are not yet modern numerals, we can use the expression *numerical signs.*

– Modern numeration

Modern numerals are the numerical signs used everywhere in the world today as a universal cultural fact.

0 1 2 3 4 5 6 7 8 9

We must stress, by the way, that zero was met with extreme resistance, as an enigmatic and diabolical creature whose claim was that "nothingness" and a vacuum existed. What a travesty! What insolence! How could zero be possible, if God is everywhere and fills the universe with His infinite glory? Modern numeration has three features that make it superior to all those that preceded it and explain why it prevailed in the whole world as the common numeration.

- the existence of ten numerical signs: 0, 1, 2, 3, 4, 5, 6, 7, 8, 9
- a principle of position according to base 10
- the concept of zero

Position numeration, or *positional numeration,* means that the value of a numeral depends on its position in the writing of a number. The third feature of modern decimal numeration is the use of zero, which is a numeral and a number at the same time, able to take part fully in calculations.
Let us give an example of its importance and function. How should we write the number 6 thousands + 7 tens + 1 unit? The first Indians answered: 671. And how should we write the number 6 thousands + 7 hundreds + 1 unit (what we write today as 6,701)? The first Indians answered: 671.

I II III IV V VI VII VIII IX X XI XII L C D M

Roman numerals.

Modern Arabic numerals, oriental type.

1234567890

Modern numerals.

Egyptian numerals that here represent the number 1,234,567.

Mayan numerals: 5, 15, 8, and 18.

After Peignot, *Du chiffre*, J. Damase, Paris, 1982.

Notched sticks of the Australian Aborigines: numerical aids used since prehistoric times.

How ambiguous is that!

At the dawn of Indian mathematics, scholars circumvented this ambiguity either by using the context or by leaving a blank in the right spot. Thus, the first number was written "6 71" and the second, "67 1." Later, much later, Brahmagupta, a sixth-century Indian mathematician, had the idea that, after all, this "blank" was a number like the others, namely the number corresponding to the quantity "nothing." He proposed to represent it by a little circle. Hence, thanks to the presence of the sign for zero, people no longer confused 6,071 and 6,701.

The notion of base

All forms of numeration have in common, to indicate numbers, the use of a limited amount of symbols called numerals, and the employment of the "principle of grouping by parcels." This is what we call a base. The most widely used base in the world is base 10.

There are forms of numeration in which successive groups are made by powers of a number other than 10, such as the bases 12 and 60 used by the Babylonians, and that we still use to count time.

The mathematical revolution

This book is dedicated to numerals and numbers, to the links between them and with the world. These links lead to the theory of numbers, geometry, and everything that has to do with these two sciences, directly and indirectly. But they evolve in a universe that is even more general, named mathematics.

The word *mathematics* comes from the Greek *ta mathemata*—"that which can be learned" and consequently also "that which can be taught." *Manthanein* means "to learn"; *mathesis* means "lesson," with the double meaning of "that from which one learns" and "that which one teaches."

In reality, mathematics begin when they no longer offer a simple numerical result obtained from a unique, concrete object, as was the case for the Egyptians or the Babylonians, but truths concerning a whole class of beings.

Classification and harmony

This emergence of mathematics made philosophers of mathematics classify numbers according to various special criteria and particular links between them. This research was started primarily by Pythagoras and his school. This signified the birth of the various classes of perfect, friendly, odd and even, triangular, square, cubic, rational and irrational numbers, etc., and the somewhat strange class of immeasurable numbers.

Do "whole numbers" ring a bell? How about "rational numbers"? You don't remember? Don't fret; I don't either. But everything became clear and exciting as I started writing this book. And what most surprised me were the rational and irrational numbers. When I discovered (or rediscovered) them, I became really fascinated.

Irrational numbers: a philosophical metaphor

Irrational numbers are philosophically quite interesting: The irrational is the unforeseeable. "I do not know the day of my death," says Isaac in a famous verse in Genesis (27:3). The irrational means going through life with the assurance that nothing is sure.

What the irrational numbers also tell us is that "thousands of years of rites, thousands of years of transmission of beliefs, do not bring any certitude as to the existence of spirits, the almightiness of God, the usefulness of prayer, that, in any case, there still is a vast area of ambiguity, an irreconcilable breach between the brain and the world of phenomena filled by beliefs, doppelgängers, spirits, gods, sorcerers, and their heirs, the rationalizing theories" (E. Morin, *The Lost Paradigm*).

15

Numbers and psychoanalysis

I had never thought that I would find a link between numbers and sex, or to put it more mildly, between numbers and sexuality. And yet, even the Pythagoreans felt, thought, and decided that even numbers were female and odd numbers were male, which gave this astonishing sexual equation: 2 plus 3 equals 5, where the latter becomes a so-called "nuptial" number, whose symbolism still moves us today. Thus, irrational numbers invite us to build a bridge between the world of numbers and psychoanalysis.

"There is no sexual relation," said Lacan. In this phrase, *relation* is used in the sense of "reporting back." Therefore, this enigmatic expression may mean that one cannot relate anything concerning this relationship because it always exceeds the possibility of telling exactly what it entails. Any word would reduce it. No word can ever relate the infinite complexity of this event.

> "Infinity in the act of the act itself to the extent that it represents the act of exceeding itself. Sex exceeds itself by its very nature, and this is why, also by its very nature, it excites itself. That is why, when satiated, desire does not disappear. The so-called 'ending' pleasure ends only a sequence in a movement that is really without end. The act is consummated by not stopping, it does not make either one or two, it has no result, it never stops beginning, and it does not stop ending."
>
> Jean-Luc Nancy, *The "There Is" of the Sexual Relation*

If I wanted to associate numbers to fields outside of mathematics, it was because the experience of this research made me feel and understand more than ever that thought cannot be imprisoned in a closed universe, but any thought worthy of the name is a bridge toward other intellectual and spiritual worlds.

In order to stress these connections, I delighted in putting in as epigraphs, and elsewhere, poetic or philosophical quotations that illustrate, directly or otherwise, the statements in their various contexts. Perhaps it is a way to hear, in the midst of the "love of wisdom," a little of the "wisdom of love."

This book is the logical extension of my research on the emergence and evolution of the alphabet and the Kabbalah. Like an archeologist seeking the shapes that originated and founded the culture of humanity, I found the world of numbers that came forward in an obvious and unavoidable way.

To conclude, I hope readers will find, thanks to this work—which would obviously deserve to be expanded, including its illustrations, examples, stories, games, and sometimes its humor (since *mathematics* does not mean "solemn")— one of the essential foundations of human intelligence, as well as the pleasures of the spirit.

A few formulas at the core of teaching the theory of distributions
discovered by Laurent Schwartz.

Book One

Numerals

The emergence and evolution of modern numerals

Part One

Indian origins
(from the third century B.C.E. to the ninth century C.E.)

"Chess and math"

Indian mathematics

The evolution of Indian writing

The five stages of the evolution of Indian numerals

The names of Indian numerals

Shûnya, shûnya! **The discovery of zero**

1

"Chess and math"

Books are like spring:
They blossom softly,
just for someone, just when they should.
Philippe Sollers

Let's begin with a story...

This legend is well-known, and like any legend, it dates from a very long time ago. Its many authors transmitted it, adding one or several details every time, always striving to make it more beautiful and more believable.

An Indian master, whose name varies according to the versions of the legend, but whom we will call Sessa, invented a game that posterity would call the game of chess. Some place the story during the reign of the Indian king Balhit, who lived 120 years after King Poros, defeated by Alexander the Great on the banks of the river Jhelum. Others say that the time of this story was the sixth or seventh century C.E.

Throughout the centuries, chess came to us with many modifications. At its beginnings, the game was played with dice and four players. At the time, it was called *chatouranga* (also written as *shaturanga* or *chaturanga*), a word that means "four brothers in arms." One day, the dice and the element of chance that went into it were abandoned, so that the game of chess was born. But it was still not the one we know today. For example, the powerful queen was absent. From India, chess quickly emigrated to Persia, where it took the name *chatranj*, and later *shah mat* ("the king is dead"). Originally, the French word *échec*, "chess," would come from the Persian word *shah*, "king," influenced by an old French word of German origin, *eschec*, that means "spoils of war."

The Arabs brought chess to Spain as early as the eleventh century. The game then spread throughout Europe. We will also specify, that all the pieces symbolized soldiers from the Persian army.

We note that it was by 1485 that the queen emerged on the chessboard, replacing a piece that until then had been the vizier, or the king's adviser. This transformation was attributed to the emergence of female political personalities in Italy. Such female personalities were also present in Spain at the time, if we think, for example, of Queen Isabella the Catholic. Certain chess researchers and players consider the queen to be a consequence of Joan of Arc's fame in Europe since the Middle Ages (cf. Anthony Saidy, The *Battle of Chess Ideas*, R.H.M Press, 1975).

At right: The Indian figurines of the game of chess were sculpted in noble materials such as ivory and precious woods. In the eighteenth and nineteenth centuries, opponents took the form of *Indians* wearing traditional garments with their chariots of war, on the one side, and the troops of the British East India Company, on the other.

23

In fact, it would seem that this birth of the queen followed the linguistic evolution of the word *vizier*, or *fizz*, which in French became *fers*, then *fierce*, then, in French, *vierge*, and then *dame*. A parallel evolution took place for the bishop in French, who from *alfil*, the "officer," became *fil*, then *fol*, then finally, the modern French *fou* (fool).

The primitive rooks were carried by elephants. The names of the pieces are equivalent in all languages, except for the *fou*. The Germans call it the *laufer*, the "runner." The English call it the bishop, and they represent it by a bishop's miter.

At left: *The King of Chess*, by artist Sami Briss.

But let's get back to our story...

The chess master offered his invention to the king of the great kingdom of India. The game was such a revelation for the king, who found great pleasure in it, that he wanted to reward the Indian master as befitting his wisdom. He told him that he could choose his own reward. The king expected the Indian master to ask for something extraordinary: palaces, herds of elephants, precious jewels, lands, etc. But no, nothing like that. The chess master made a humble request.

"I would like," he said, "to receive a few grains of wheat."

"That's all?" said the king in amazement.

"Yes, that's all. In fact, it's not a little thing. I want the quantity of grains of wheat needed to fill all the squares of the chessboard in this way: one grain of wheat for the first square, two for the second, four for the third, and so forth. In each square there must be twice as many grains as in the previous square." The king was insulted by this request, which he found not to be worthy of his wealth. But since this was what the chess master wanted, he would award him according to his wishes.

According to one version of the legend, it was at that precise instance that a broad smile lit up the chess master's face, and he said farewell to the king and left the palace.

The king sent his chief steward to carry out the request of the chess master.

He thought that the calculation of the number of grains to be paid to the chess master was quite simple. Indeed, multiplying a number of grains by 2 was an easy task.

Great was his surprise when his steward told him that the calculations would take longer than expected and would be much more complicated. For these calculations, the king's mathematicians used their fingers and the traditional abaci.

Since the king found that the calculations took much too long, he asked his advisers whether they did not know any calculators living in his kingdom, who would have much quicker methods. One of the ministers answered that he had heard that, in one of the northern provinces of the kingdom, there were calculators who used faster, more efficient techniques than those used by the mathematicians of the court. All the calculations were done simply and promptly, sometimes in only a few hours. The king sent for

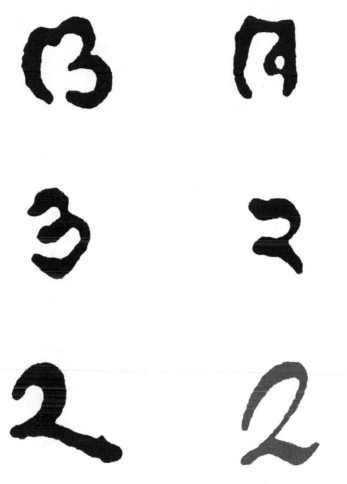

Variations of the numeral 2 in various Indian writings. After Smith, *op. cit.* p. 74.

these talented mathematicians, who solved the problem in record time and gave the king the following astonishing result:

*Churkrum,*or counting board.

"The quantity of wheat needed to reward the chess master is huge. It is exactly:

$$18,446,744,073,709,551,615 \text{ grains.}$$

And if you really want to pay your debt," the wondrous calculators added, "it is necessary to transform the entire surface of the earth into a big wheat field." One version of the legend adds that it would also be necessary to sow seventy-three times this area to obtain the quantity of wheat of the prize. (According to another version, it was seventy-six times.)

The scientific calculations, made much later, specify that it would be necessary to gather the wheat in a volume of almost 12 trillion, 3 billion cubic meters and build for this purpose a silo five meters wide, ten meters long, and 300,000,000 kilometers deep—in other words, with a height equal to twice the distance from the earth to the sun.

Concerning this legend, see Yakov Perelman (1882–1942) in *Figures for Fun*, Foreig Language Publishing House, Moscow, 1985, pp. 98–101. Yakov Isodorovitch Perelman is one of the greatest writers of popular science of the twentieth century. All his books were extremely successful throughout Europe. *Oh, les Maths!* (as the French edition published in 1993 by Dunon is called) is the most popular: It is the work that best represents his talent as a teacher and his creative genius.

The numbers in each square represent the mathematical progression of the number of grains that, when added together, represent the reward to which the inventor of the game of chess was entitled.

1	2	4	8	16	32	64	128
256	512	1024	2048	4096	8192	16384	32768
65536	131072	262144	524288	1048576	2097152	4194204	8388608
1677 7216	3355 4432	6710 8864	1342 17728	2684 35456	5368 70912	1073 741824	2147 483648
4294 967296	8589 934592	1717 9869184	3435 9738368	6871 9476736	1374389 53472	2748779 06944	5497558 13888
1099511 627776	2199023 255552	4398046 511104	8796093 022208	1759218 6044416	3518437 2088832	7036874 4177664	14073 74883 55328
28147 49767 10656	56294 99534 21312	11258 99906 842624	22517 99813 685248	45035 99627 370496	90071 99254 740992	18014 3985094 81984	3602879 7001896 3968
720575 940379 27936	144115 188075 855872	288230 376151 711744	576460 752303 423488	115292 1504606 846976	230584 3009213 693952	461168 6018427 387904	9223372 0368547 75808

Faced with the enormity of this number, the king asked to be initiated in these calculations and these new methods.

The mathematicians then explained to the king the basics of the revolutionary numeration of the scientists of the northern region of India. Thus, the king discovered Indian numerals—the nine signs that would become our 1, 2, 3, 4, 5, 6, 7, 8, 9—as well as position numeration and the existence and use of *shûnya*, this extraordinary novelty: the zero.

They redid the calculations together, and the king received confirmation that the quantity of grains requested by the chess master was indeed exactly:

$$18,446,744,073,709,551,615$$

This legend emphasizes, on the one hand, the presence of rapid calculation methods, the knowledge of a decimal system, and a logarithmic system, while on the other hand a great development of high mathematical sciences. It also shows a special love of large numbers, around which the Indians actually developed a particular poetics, especially with the image of the lotus flower. This flower is equal, depending on the context, to 109 (1 billion: a 1 with nine zeros); 1,014; 1,029; 10,119. (For more on this, see Louis Frederic, *Le Lotus*, Felin Publishers, 1990.)

It is in this scientific universe that modern numerals were born. It was not done all at once, and it was certainly not the work of one person. This scientific knowledge is what we will tackle in the next chapter (as a way of setting the stage), before discussing the history proper of the evolution of the graphic form of letters and numerals in Indian writing, and later their voyage outside this geographic and cultural realm.

2

Indian mathematics

To be alive is to be made of memory.
If a man is not made of memory,
he is made of nothing.
Philip Roth

Overcoming a prejudice

We know very little about Indian mathematics. There are several reasons for this. The main one is certainly that the historians of science have long thought that Indian science lacked originality and was based on borrowings from Greek and then from Arabic science. As for specialists in Indian studies, they were especially interested in cultural aspects, in religions, in philosophies, and they contributed to accrediting among the public at large the idea that, after all, India would be just a nation of philosophers, grammarians, and thinkers. In short, India would have been great by its philosophies and its religions, rather than by its science. More recent research in the history of the sciences and techniques of India show that in fact the country's development was very advanced. There is a huge body of work, manuscripts written in Sanskrit and other Indian languages, that sleeps in Indian libraries. There are hundreds and hundreds of documents that are waiting for someone to read them in a philological, philosophical, psychological, and certainly scientific study.

(For this entire chapter, see Richard Mankiewicz, *The Story of Mathematics*, Orion Publishing, 2001; also, *Le Matin des mathématiciens*, discussions presented by Émile Noël, Belin, 1985.)

Ritual and liturgical mathematics

The first elements of the history of mathematics in India were given to us by the *Veda*: collections, books of hymns, of liturgical chants, of sacrificial formulas, the most ancient pieces of which go back to circa 1500 B.C.E. The attested knowledge in this Vedic literature has an elementary, pragmatic character: It includes elements of geometry used to erect the constructions necessary for the Vedic ritual.

The first Vedic texts deal mainly with religion and ceremonies. The most important ones, from a mathematical viewpoint, are the appendices to the main *Veda*, the *Vedangas*. They are written in the form of *sutra*—brief poetical aphorisms, typical for Sanskrit, which attempt to translate the essence of a thought, as concisely and as mnemonically as possible. The *Vedanga* deal with six subjects: phonetics, grammar, etymology, poetry, astronomy, and rituals. Only the latter two actually teach us about the mathematics of the time. The *Vedanga* of astronomy is called *Jyotisutra*, while the *Vedanga* of rituals is the *Kalpasutra*, part of which, the *Sulvasutra*, deals with the construction of sacrificial altars.

An empirical geometry

The first *sulvasutra* (certain authors wrote *sulbasutra*, the *v* and the *b* being interchangeable, as in *bindu* and *vindu*, the "dot" that signifies zero; see the section on zero, p. 73) were written circa 800–600 B.C.E., before Panini's codification of Sanskrit. Geometry developed to make the dimensions, shape, and direction of the altars consistent with Vedic scriptures.

The oldest of these *sulvasutra*, the one attributed to a certain Baudhayana, states the so-called "Pythagorean theorem." Baudhayana even gives a value close to the square root of 2, correct up to the fifth decimal. He teaches us about the construction of simple polygons, such as the square, the rectangle, and the triangle. He gives various methods for transforming a given geometric figure into another geometric figure: for example, from a square into a rectangle. The *sulvasutra* also have an awareness of the famous problem of the quadrature of the circle.

Sanskrit manuscript. Here we see clearly the difference between the writing of the letters and that of the numbers (in blue). After *Le Matin des mathématiciens*, p. 131.

In addition, these texts give us information on the instruments used by geometers: cords of different lengths, bamboo rulers and compasses, and pieces of cut wood used to delimit or to trace lines on the ground. But this geometry did not evolve at all after the time of the *sulvasutra*, and, intuitively, it remained based on empirical rules, contrary to that of the Greeks, which overcame the empirical stage, replacing it with abstract, general geometric formulas.

The work of Aryabhata

Particularly in the fields of arithmetic, algebra, and trigonometry, the mathematicians of ancient India distinguished themselves, reaching rather early results that were amazingly close to modern conceptions.

The earliest of all these treatises on astronomy to have reached us is that of a famous Indian scientist, Aryabhata (476–550). This scientist's work began at the beginning of the sixth century. He was born in 476, and the actual astronomical observations on which the astronomical canon perfected by him is based go back to approximately the year 500.

He is considered to be the greatest Indian mathematician. His work is written in Sanskrit. To honor him, the first Indian artificial satellite, launched on April 19, 1965, was named Aryabhata.

Aryabhata had a following, and Indian astronomy in its entirety, in the many centuries to come, was based mainly on the canon established by him. Other famous names have remained in the history of Indian mathematics: We can cite Brahmagupta, a commentator on the work of Aryabhata; and another great mathematician, Bhaskara.

It is also in Aryabhata that we find an approximate value for π equal to approximately 3.1416. Nine centuries later, the astronomer and mathematician Madhava (Madhava of Sangamagramma, 1340–1425) achieved the calculation of a circumference for which the approximate value of π is correct to the eleventh decimal: 3.14159265359. A mathematician by the name of Nilakantha, in the next century, used the fraction 355/113, which is one of the relatively correct values of π:

$$3.14159292035398230088495575522124$$

The great revolution of Indian mathematics

In addition to all the mathematical, geometric, and astronomical knowledge we have just discussed, what remains the true revolution of the Indian mathematicians is the decimal position numeration, using the nine unit figures from 1 to 9, as well as the use of the zero, both as a separator in position numeration and as a number. The evolution of these numerals and this numeration are the topics to which we dedicate the next chapters.

Variations of the numeral 3 in various Indian writings. After Smith, *op. cit.*, p. 74.

3

The evolution
of Indian writing

The book one remembers
is the book one would have liked to write.
Edmond Jabès

There is a parallel between the evolution of the letters in Indian writing and that of Indian numerals in the same places and eras. It is important for our general understanding of the birth of numerals to first know and understand the evolution of Indian writing. That is the purpose of this chapter.

First writing of the third millennium B.C.E.:
A script that has not been deciphered

Historians of writing (see, for example, James Fevrier, *Histoire de l'écriture*, Payot, 1948, and Jean-Louis Calvet, *Histoire de l'écriture*, Plon, 1996) consider that the graphics discovered on seals and plaquettes in the ruins of the ancient cities of Mohenjo-Daro and Harappa in the Indus valley (circa 2500–1500 B.C.E.) are the most ancient trace of an Indian script. This script, called "proto-Indian," not deciphered to date, contains between 250 and 400 signs and disappeared by 1500 B.C.E., without leaving a succession.

According to Calvet, Indian script would be derived not from this proto-Indian but from scripts born in Mesopotamia that would have migrated

╲	ﾗ	ﾗ	ﾖ	F	ℰ	ﾂ	S	୨
1	2	3	4	5	6	7	8	9

toward the Punjab, "which would mean that the first Semitic alphabets were the unique source of the alphabets of the world" (*op. cit.*, p. 168).

Books on palm leaves and inscriptions on copper sheets and engraved in stone

The Indian world is rich in terms of written documents, in the form of inscriptions and manuscripts whose remembrance is kept today by contemporary libraries in various printed versions.

(On these issues, see Richard Salomon, *Indian Epigraphy. A Guide to the Study of Inscriptions in Sanskrit, Praktit and the other Indo-Aryan Languages*, Oxford University Press, 1998. See also Jean Filliozat, "Paleographie," in Louis Renou and J. Filliozat, *L'Inde Classique. Manuel des études indiennes*, volume II, Paris-Hanoi, EFEO, 1953 (reprinted in 1985), pp. 665–712. See also Georges-Jean Pinault, Écritures de l'Inde continentale," in *Histoire de l'écriture: de l'idéogramme au multimedia*, Flammarion, Paris, pp. 93–121.)

Although in general the inscriptions are engraved on stone (rough or polished) or metal (copper or bronze), the basic material for manuscripts is the palm leaf, as well as birch bark and aloe phloem. Also found were poplar wood plates or simply sheets of paper. The books made of these various materials all have the same form: oblong sheets pierced by one, two, or three holes, depending on length, and bound with yarn.

The lines of writing are parallel to the length, sometimes divided into columns. The reader progresses by turning the sheet he has just read, parallel to his glance. We must specify that they contain illustrations painted in colors.

The fragile material of these inscriptions on sheets did not allow all of them to be kept in very good shape, especially because of the monsoon climate conditions of the Indian subcontinent. Furthermore, as stressed by G.-J. Pinault (*op. cit.*, p. 93), the oldest manuscripts owe their preservation to the dry conditions of the northwestern and central Asian regions.

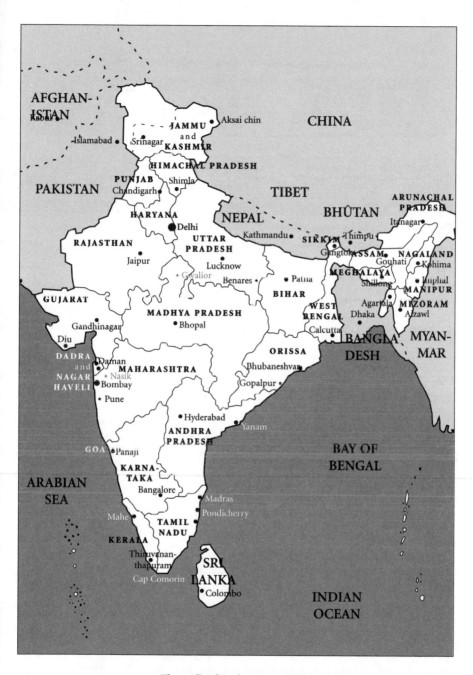

The cradle of modern numeration.
The towns of Gwalior and Nasik are indicated in blue.

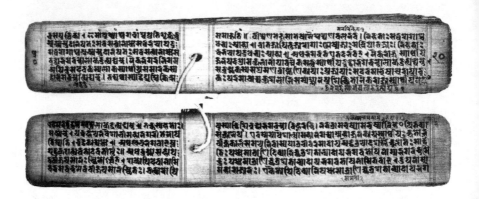

The *Mahayana* Sutra, named "of the five protections" (*Pancaraksasutrani*),
which teaches charms against snakes, demons, diseases, etc. Buddhist text in Sanskrit,
ancient Nepalese script (*nepalaksara*) derived from *siddhamatrka*, Nepal, 1141.
Book with 140 "pages" (30 x 5 cm, six lines on each face). A vertical line separates the
lateral edges and the reserve for the binding hole. Paris, Bibliothèque Nationale de France.

Concerning the inscriptions engraved in stone or metal, the situation
is different and the preservation much better, even though in this case
humidity remains a significant cause of deterioration. We find all types of
inscriptions, but they mainly note circumstantial events such as foundations and royal constructions, donation deeds for villages, monasteries,
bodies of water, explanations and legends of sculptures, and mentions of
the passage of pilgrims (*ibid.*).

The inscriptions of Asoka (circa 260 B.C.E.)

The first written text notations in known Indian languages appeared
rather late in the history of India. These are inscriptions engraved on
pillars and rocks.

They are proclamations or "edicts" of King Asoka (273–232 B.C.E.),
written in the first person and addressed to his subjects, offering them a
philosophy and a morality inspired by Buddhism.

It is relatively easy to date these edicts, because the third edict, for
example, cites various Greek monarchs, such as Ptolemy (285–247) and

Antigonos (278–239). Asoka's kingdom would thus be situated at the time of Alexander's successors, more than fifty years after he crossed the Indus valley.

Detail of the engraved pillar of Delhi-Topra.
After Amulyachandra Sen, *Asoka's Edicts*, Calcutta.
The Indian Publicity Society (Institute of Indology Series, No. 7), 1956.

On these inscriptions, we find two types of vernacular scripts in the form of clearly differentiated syllables: the *brahmi* script, written from left to right, and the *kharosthi* script (some write *kharostri*), written from right to left. These edicts were deciphered by James Prinsep in 1837.

(See James Prinsep (1799–1840), "On the inscriptions of Piyadasi or Ashoka," *Journal and Proceedings of the Asiatic Society of Bengal* (JPSA), Calcutta, 1838.)

Phoenician-Aramaic influence on the *kharosthi* script

The *kharosthi* script was used in northwestern India between the third century B.C.E. and the sixth century C.E.

After being named Indo-Bactrian, then *kharosthi*, according to a Chinese indication from the seventh century, today European scientists call it Aramaic-Indian or simply Indian.

This *kharosthi*, or Aramaic-Indian, script appeared for the first time in the inscriptions ordered by Asoka to be engraved in the middle of the third century B.C.E. in the northwestern corner of India. Asoka's other inscriptions in the rest of India are written in *brahmi*.

Vowels	*Consonants*					*Consonants + vowels*	*Ligatures*
a	ka	ja	ṅa	pa	ra	ka	kra
i	kha	ña	ta	pha	la	ki	bra
u	ga	ṭa	tha	ba	va	ku	rva
e	gha	ṭha	da	bha	sa	ke	sta
o	ča	ḍa	dha	ma	ša	ko	etc.
aṃ	čha	ḍha	na	ya	ṣa	kaṃ	
					ha		

Kharosthi syllabary.. After Février, *op. cit.*, p. 338.

As we stressed earlier, this script is written from right to left like the Phoenician script and the Aramaic script, from which, according to Calvet, it seems to derive (L.-J. Calvet, *op. cit.*, p. 169).

Indeed, it has similarities in tracing with Aramaic, "about which we know that it had reached the Indian borders with the Persian conquest, and that it contains new traits that, by additions or modifications, were used to note phonetic values unknown to the Semite in order to rigorously preserve the pronunciation of the Vedic texts" (cf. *Les Caractères de l'Imprimerie Nationale,* Imprimerie Nationale, Paris, 1990, p. 285).

Section of the roll of *Dharmapada* ("Hemistiches of the law" = *pali Dharmapada*)
of Khotan, Buddhist text in *gandhari* language and in *kharoshti* script.
Birch bark sheets sown together in the lateral edges; lines of writing parallel
to the short side. Paris, Bibliothèque National de France.

The Semitic origin of this script, especially the Aramaic, was definitively demonstrated by Buhlet in 1895 (Pinault, *op. cit.*, p. 113).

The *kharosthi* script disappeared without a succession, and it was *brahmi* that became the source of all of India's various different scripts, up until today.

value	Aramaic	*Brahmi*
ba		
da		
ya		
ra		

After Calvet, *op. cit.*, p. 170.

The *brahmi* script

"With its immense geographic area, India is a place of import and consumption of numerous scripts learned, then forgotten, then replaced: the Greek alphabet, since the conquests of Alexander the Great; Aramaic, used when the northeast of India belonged to Persia; Pehlevi and Avesta scripts, used by the Parsis, the Mazdeans who immigrated to India; several varieties of Arabic-Persian script, heavily used since the ninth century C.E., also used to note Indo-Aryan languages such as *sindhi, kashmiri,* or *urdu;* finally, the Latin alphabet, introduced by the Portuguese and the British, which was used by the colonizers and then by the Indian administration, and which was also used to note languages without script or literature, such as *konkani.*" (G.-J. Pinault, *ibid.,* p. 98.)

In spite of this diversity, we can say that, if we consider a long period of history, with just a few exceptions the major languages of the Indian subcontinent and Indianized Asia were, and still are, noted by derivations of the *brahmi* script.

ꨮꨄꨰꨲꨨꨄꨮꨲ꨼ꨶ꨼ꨂ꨼ꨃꨂꨄꨤꨶꨂꨃꨅꨄꨄꨰꨄꨮꨶꨶꨅꨃꨶꨶꨂꨤꨄꨰꨅꨮꨄꨮꨶꨶꨃ
ꨄꨮꨲꨄꨅꨄꨤꨮꨄꨲꨶꨶꨄꨮꨄꨄꨄꨅꨶꨄꨮꨄ꨷ꨶꨶꨶꨲꨶꨃꨮꨲ꨷ꨶꨃꨶꨶꨶꨮꨲꨄ
ꨄꨮꨃꨶꨄꨄꨃꨄꨮ꨷ꨶꨄꨄꨶꨄꨃꨶꨶꨶꨶꨃꨶꨄꨄꨄꨄꨶꨶꨶꨄꨲꨄꨶꨃꨶꨮꨲꨄ
ꨮꨃꨄꨂꨄꨶꨶꨄꨄꨄꨄꨅꨄꨮꨄꨲꨶ꨷ꨶꨶꨄꨄꨄꨃꨄꨃ꨷ꨶꨄꨄꨄꨮꨄꨄꨄꨄꨄꨄꨶꨄꨄꨄꨶ
ꨄꨮꨃꨄꨄꨶꨄꨄꨄꨅꨄꨄꨮꨃꨄꨮꨲꨃꨶ꨷ꨶꨶꨲꨄꨄꨄꨄꨄꨄꨶꨄꨄꨄꨄꨅꨄꨮꨄꨲꨶꨃꨶꨶꨄꨄ
ꨄꨴ꨷ꨶ꨷ꨶꨃꨄꨄꨄꨶꨶꨃꨶꨄꨶꨶꨶꨶꨃꨄꨄꨄꨃꨶꨶꨄꨄꨄꨄꨄꨶꨶꨄꨶ꨷ꨶꨶꨶꨄꨄꨶ
ꨃ꨷ꨶꨄꨄꨃꨄꨄꨶꨶꨃꨄꨶꨄꨄꨄ꨷ꨶꨄꨶꨅꨶꨶ꨷ꨨꨶ꨷ꨶꨄꨄꨄꨅꨄꨄꨄꨄꨄꨮꨶꨄꨃꨄꨃꨄꨄꨶ꨷ꨶ꨷꨷ꨃꨄꨄ
ꨶꨶꨄꨶꨃꨄꨄꨄꨃꨄꨄꨄꨄꨶꨄꨅꨄꨄꨅꨄꨶꨶꨄꨄꨄꨄꨄꨅꨄꨮꨄꨲꨃꨶꨶ꨷꨷ꨃꨄꨄ

Fourth edict of Girnar, in brahmi script.
After Les Caractères de l'Imprimerie nationale, p. 279.

The *brahmi* script is written from left to right and has simple or compound signs, which vocalization can modify. This transformation is made by adding an element on top or at the base of the letter being traced.

There are several hypotheses as to the origin of the name *brahmi*. Some see in it a link with the god Brahma who would have been the inventor of the script, but this tradition, reported by Chinese and Arab travelers during the first millennium, has no historic or philological grounds.

In the beginning, the term "*brahmi* script" was reserved for religious texts noting the language of Brahma, Sanskrit, the language of the Brahmans of the northwest Indian subcontinent. By extension, the term *brahmi* was applied to all scripts noted from left to right.

Modern philology chose to apply the name *brahmi* to the pan-Indian script of Asoka's time and its regional varieties until the end of the Gupta period (sixth century C.E.). The term is also used for the scripts of central Asia that were derived from it.

We have stressed the fact that the *kharosthi* script came from Aramaic script. Concerning *brahmi*, today script historians lean toward a Phoenician origin. According to Calvet, the resemblances between the

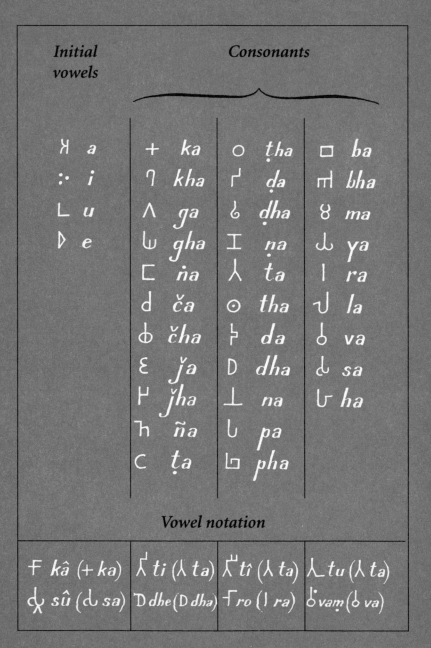

Initial vowels	Consonants		
Ⴉ a	+ ka	○ ṭha	□ ba
∴ i	٦ kha	⼧ ḍa	⊦ bha
L u	∧ ga	⺇ ḍha	8 ma
▷ e	Ⴑ gha	I ṇa	⼦ ya
	⊏ ṅa	⅄ ta	I ra
	⅃ ča	⊙ tha	⼅ la
	⏀ čha	Ⴔ da	⼑ va
	Ɛ ǰa	D dha	⼨ sa
	Ⱶ ǰha	⊥ na	⼡ ha
	ⱨ ña	∪ pa	
	C ṭa	⼫ pha	

Vowel notation

F kâ (+ka)	⅄̇ ti (⅄ ta)	⅄̂ tî (⅄ ta)	⼣ tu (⅄ ta)
⼤ sû (⼨ sa)	D dhe (D dha)	⌐ ro (I ra)	⼑̇ vaṃ (⼑ va)

Brâhmi spelling book. After Février, *op. cit.*, p. 336.

Beginning of the inscription on the pillar of Delhi-Topra (detail), northern side.
One can see spaces separating words grouped by syntax and meaning, and, more rarely, isolated
words. Facsimile. See Klaus Ludwig Janert, *Abstande und Schlussvokalverzeichnungen in
Asoka-Inschriften*, Wiesbaden, Franz Steiner Verlag (*Verzeichnis der Orientalischen
Handschriften in Deutschland*, Supplementband 10), 1972, p. 213.

two scripts are convincing. The differences in certain letters are explained
by the fact that *brahmi* script changed direction, being written from left to
right, unlike Phoenician (Calvet, *op. cit.*, p. 172).

Phoenician 11th c.	value	Brahmi 3rd c.	valuc
⪦	A	Ⅎ et ⅄	A bref et A long
🄴	B	□	B
∧	G	∧	G
△	D	D et Ⱶ	D
⊗	Ṭ	☉ et O	ṬH et ṬK
ⵚ	K	+	K
⅂	L	⌐⌐	L
∠	P	∪	P

The legend of the strange river

By discovering this relationship between Phoenician and *brahmi* script, which suggests the presence of people speaking and writing Phoenician, almost identical to the ancient Hebrew script (*ktav ivri*; see our work *Mysteries of the Alphabet*, Assouline, 1997), I remembered this legend reported in the Talmud (Sanhedrin 65b), and also by certain historians such as Pliny the Elder (24–79 C.E.) and others, a legend that tells us that the ten tribes of Israel exiled by Shalmaneser are still today beyond the river named Sambatyon (or Sanbatyon, or Sabbatyon), which has this particular trait of flowing for six days during the week and stopping from Friday evening until Saturday evening. A river that does not flow on the Sabbath! A famous traveler, Manasseh ben Israel, reports from his trip to India (1630) that he had seen the Sambatyon, a river approximately seventeen miles wide (measurement given by my source in English, *Encyclopedia Judaica*, volume 14, p. 764), stop flowing on the Sabbath. While during the week it drags away stones as big as houses, on the Sabbath it is smooth like a lake of snow or white sand.

Now, that's something to think about.

The evolution of *brahmi*

Brahmi script evolved into numerous script forms that can be classified into four large groups: the scripts of the north, those of central Asia, those of the south, and the eastern (or *pali*) scripts.

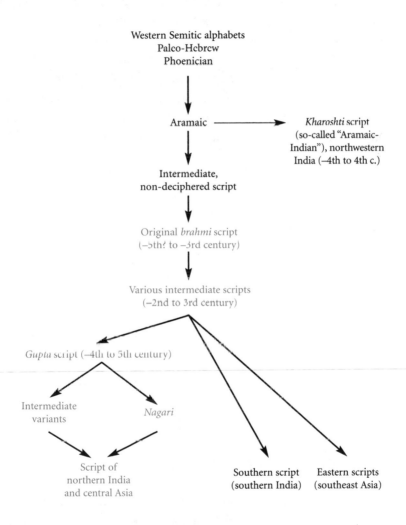

47

Chart of the evolution of Indian scripts
After Renou and Filliozat, *op. cit.*, pp. 665–702.

A privileged place for the *nagari,* or *devanagari,* script

Among all Indian scripts derived from the *brahmi* script, *devanagari,* which probably emerged in the eleventh century C.E., deserves a place apart. First of all, because of its perfection, as explained by J. Fevrier: Although the abundance of ligatures is a cause of complication, like in all Indian scripts, and multiplies the possibilities for confusion, in exchange, its phonetic notation is very precise. Since the emergence of the printing press, it has become the main script of Sanskrit, India's religious and learned language. The very name *devanagari,* "*nagari* of the gods," which seems to have been given to it by the Europeans, did not appear until the seventeenth century (Pinault, *op. cit.,* p. 100), while the Indians simply call it *nagari,* "the script of urban dwellers" (from the Sanskrit *nagara,* "city").

48

चक्रवाकः पृच्छति कथमेनतन् । राज्ञा कथयति । अहं पुरा शूद्रकस्य राज्ञः क्रोडा-
सरसि कर्पूरकेलिनाम्नो राजहंसस्य पुत्र्या कर्पूरमञ्जर्या सकलानुरागवान् अभवं । तत्र
वीरवरो नाम राजपुत्रः कुतश्चिद्देशादागत्य राजद्वारि प्रतीहारमुपगम्योवाच । अहं
वर्तनार्थी राजपुत्रः । मां राजदर्शनं कारय । ततस्तेनासौ राजदर्शनं कारितो ब्रूते ।
देव यदि मया सेवकेन प्रयोजनमस्ति तदास्मद्दर्शनं क्रियतां । शूद्रक उवाच । किं
ते वर्तनं । वीरवरोऽवदत् । प्रत्यहं ठक्कशतचतुष्टयं । राज्ञाह । का ते सामग्री ।
स आह । द्वौ बाहू तृतीयश्च खड्गः । राज्ञोवाच । नैतद्रातुं शक्यं । एतच्छ्रुत्वा
वीरवरः प्रणम्य चलितः । अथ मन्त्रिभिरुक्तं । देव दिनचतुष्टयस्य वर्तनं दत्वा
ज्ञायतामस्य स्वरूपं किमुपयुक्तो ऽयमेतावद्वर्तनं गृह्णात्यथानुपयुक्तो वा । ततस्तद्-
वचनादाकृष्य वीरवरस्य ताम्बूलं दत्वा ठक्कशतचतुष्टयं दत्तवान् । तद्विनियोगश्च राज्ञा
सुनिद्रपितः । तत्रार्धं देवेभ्यो ब्राह्मणेभ्यो दत्तं तेन । अपरार्धं च दुःखिभ्यस्तद्-

Hitopadeca. Nagari script. After *Les Caractères de l'Imprimerie nationale, op. cit.,* p. 281.

At this point, we must also consider Hindi, the great language of central India, as well as vernacular languages. Hindi's most visible characteristic is the big horizontal bar, the gallows called a *matra,* which follows the line almost without interruption—linking not only the syllables but often the words—and below which the characters are attached, with the exception of a few vowel signs that are written above. (It is remarkable that the traditional Hebrew script is also written under a guiding line, the *sirtut,* traced with a chisel.)

अ आ इ ई उ ऊ
a ā i ī u ū

ऋ ॠ ऌ ए ऐ ओ औ
ṛ ṝ ḷ e ai o au

क ख ग घ ङ
ka kha ga gha ṅa

च छ ज झ ञ
ca cha ja jha ña

ट ठ ड ढ ण
ṭa ṭha ḍa ḍha ṇa

त थ द ध न
ta tha da dha na

प फ ब भ म
pa pha ba bha ma

य र ल व श ष स ह
ya ra la va śa ṣa sa ha

Table of characteristics of the *devanagari* script, after a school manual: Judith M. Tyberg. *First Lesson in Sanskrit Grammar and Reading*, Los Angeles, East-West Cultural Center, 1964, pp. 4–5.

49

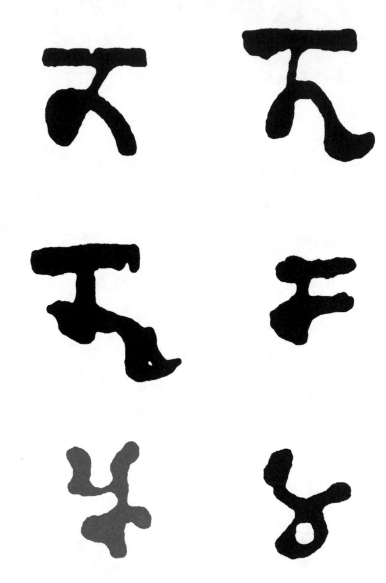

Variations of the figure 4 in various Indian scripts. After Smith, *op. cit.*, p. 74.

4

The five stages of the evolution of Indian numerals

*In vain do we push the living
into one or another of our frames.
All the frames crack.*
Henri Bergson

If we have insisted on the evolution of the Indian script, it is because the graphic form of Indian numerals, which developed into our modern numerals, experienced a parallel evolution.

The first period: from the third century B.C.E. to the first century C.E.

We mentioned earlier the edicts of King Asoka (273–323 B.C.E.), traces of the first Indian writings in *kharoshti* and *brahmi*. These, we repeat, were texts engraved on rocks and temple columns that, surprisingly, were often inside large grottoes, whether natural or dug into the mountains, in various kingdoms of his empire.

Just like with the script, we find a numeration related to the *kharoshti* script and a numeration related to the *brahmi* script. The numerical notation found in these engraved texts is incomplete.

As indicated by Geneviève Guitel (*Histoire comparée des numérations écrites*, Flammarion, 1975, p. 604), this numeration is of an additive type, which means that the values of the symbols had to be added up.

1. *Kharoshti* numeration

Concerning *kharoshti* numeration, the signs of the numerations are elementary. One line for 1, two lines for 2, and three for 3. The 4 becomes interesting, because it offers a first composition, the crossing of two lines, which forms a sign close to *x* in our contemporary Western alphabet. The 10 is also a new combination, two lines in a straight angle ˥. The 20 looks a little like our 3, and the 100 resembles a Greek lambda ⅄, or a backward *y*. It is worth noting that, just like the *kharoshti* script itself, these numerical signs did not have a succession.

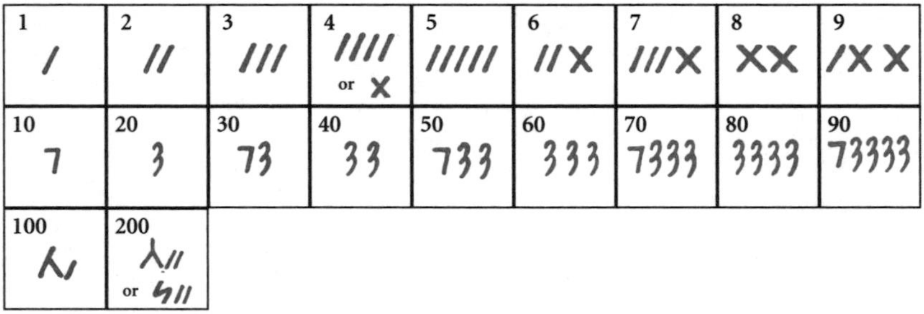
1
2
3
4
or
5
6
7
8
9
10
20
30
40
50
60
70
80
90
100
200
or

Numeration related to the *kharoshti* script.
After Renou and Filliozat, II, p. 705, reproduced by Guitel, *op. cit.*, p. 604.

2. Original *brahmi* numeration

The numeration related to the original *brahmi* script is not documented very well. The lines of the 1 and 2 are still vertical, and the 4 is still a crossed composition of two lines, but with the form of our plus sign (+). The 6 already has this loop, which will be one of its characteristics throughout its evolution.

1	2	3	4	5	6	7	8	9
ן	וו		✛		ϐ or Ɛ			

10	20	30	40	50	60	70	80	90
				ϛ or ıℲ				

100	200
	ɕ or Ħ

Numeration related to the original *brahmi* script.
After Renou and Filliozat. II, p. 705, reproduced by Guitel, *op. cit.*, p. 605.

As we indicated earlier, the *brahmi* script is written from left to right, and the numbers are also read in this order, from the largest to the smallest number. Thus, for example, the number 256 will be written according to the data in the table above:

The number 256 in old *brahmi* characters.

Note:

We must say that, even though the numbers were written from left to right, starting with the highest powers, they were pronounced starting with the numeral on the right. Thus, in our example, the reading was: 6 and 50 and 200.

3. The example of the Nana Ghat grottoes (second century B.C.E.)

In India, numerous Buddhist temples were built inside natural grottoes. The inscriptions engraved on the walls, columns, and various supports of these underground temples were particularly well preserved against the elements, humidity, temperature variations, inappropriate exposure to light, etc. In general, the subject of these inscriptions was not mathematical, but one still finds a few numbers that enabled paleographers to unveil a first evolution of the form of numerals in Indian numeration related to the *brahmi* script.

Inscriptions dating from the second century B.C.E. were found in the Nana Ghat grottoes, located about 150 kilometers from Pune (or Poona, a town located 200 kilometers southeast of Bombay, turned by the British into a spa town to escape Bombay's fierce heat).

The numerals found in this grotto show for the first time horizontal lines for the 1 and 2; the 4 evolves by acquiring a small V-shaped crown on the plus sign (see preceding table), the 6 affirms itself more clearly, but it still keeps this lower line below the loop.

1	2	3	4	5	6	7	8	9
—	=		¥		φ	?		?
10	20	30	40	50	60	70	80	90
α	O				⊣		∞	
100	200	300	400	500	600	700	800	900
ᚻ ᚼ	ᚼ		ᚼᚻ			ᚼᚻ		
1,000	2,000	3,000	4,000	5,000	6,000	7,000	8,000	9,000
T			TY		Tφ			
10,000	20,000							
Tα	To							

Numeration in the Nana Ghat grottoes.
After Renou and Filliozat. II, p. 705, reproduced by Guitel, *op. cit.*, p. 606.

The numeration of these numerals is additive. Thus, according to this table:

12 is written: α

17: α?

289: ᚼ∞?

11,000: TαT

24,400: ToTYᚼᚻ

The second stage: from the first to the third and fourth centuries

So-called "intermediary" notation: the numbers of the Nasik grottoes

Archeologists discovered other grottoes, geographically close to those we just mentioned. These are the grottoes of Nasik, a town less than 200 kilometers north of Bombay, whose tourist program still includes a visit to these grottoes. The town of Nasik, on the banks of the Godavari, is a great pilgrimage destination of Hinduism. Every twelve years, there is the Kumbh Mela; in reality, this gathering takes place every three years, but alternately in four different towns (Nasik, Ujjain, Allahabad, and Haridwar). According to the myth, the gods, fighting over the nectar of immortality, would have spilled four drops of it. These drops would have fallen on Earth at the place where these four towns were built. Kumbh Mela, with its tens of millions of pilgrims, represents the world's largest human gathering. The last Kumbh Mela in Nasik took place in 2003.

1	2	3	4	5	6	7	8	9
—	=	≡	ꓘ or ꓩ	ꓯ or ꓶ	ꓶ	?	ꓭ or ꓨ	?
10	20	30	40	50	60	70	80	90
∝	θ		⅄			Ӡ		
100	200	300	400	500	600	700	800	900
η	ꙗ			ᲈᴫ				
1,000	2,000	3,000	4,000	5,000	6,000	7,000	8,000	9,000
ꙇ	ꙩ	Ϝ	ꝗ				ꝗ	
10,000	20,000	30,000	40,000	50,000	60,000	70,000		
						ꝗ		

The numbers found in the Nasik grottoes.
After Renou and Filliozat. II, p. 705, reproduced by Guitel, *op. cit.*, p. 608.

Although in the beginning there were certain ambiguities in the reading of these numbers, they were quickly dispelled, because the inscriptions were certified by the simultaneous mention of these numbers spelled out. The inscriptions of Nana Ghat and Nasik belong to sites that are geographically near each other. It is interesting to note that, in spite of the four centuries that separate the inscription of these two places, there is a sort of design unity both in shape and in numbering, which is still additive.

1	2	3	4	5	6	7	8	9	0
—	=	☰	+	ᚺ	𝟜	ᒍ	ᔑ	ᒣ	ᒣ

Nasik numbers.
After Renou and Filliozat. *op. cit.*, p. 605, and Smith, *op. cit.*, p. 66.

We indicate, as we did for the Nana Ghat inscriptions, that at the time these Nasik inscriptions were made, the numbers were still pronounced starting with the simplest units: units, tens, hundreds, etc., even though their left-to-right writing presents the number from the largest powers to the smallest units.

Example:

8000 500 70 6

Writing of the number 8,576 according to Nasik inscriptions.
This number was pronounced: six, seventy, five hundred, eight thousand.

The third stage: from the third to the sixth centuries
Numerical notations in the *gupta* script

Between 240 and 535, we discover the Gupta dynasty, whose sovereigns reigned over the entire valley of the Ganges and its tributaries. At that time, a notation for both writing and numerals appeared. The numeration system does not include zero and does not work according to the numeration principle. This *gupta* notation, derived from the *brahmi* script, is that of northern and central India.

We can say that all the notations used in northern India and central Asia derived from this *gupta* notation.

Non-positional *gupta* numerical notation,
after the inscriptions at Parivrajaka. After Smith, *op. cit.*, p. 67.

The main difference between this numerical notation and the preceding one can already be seen for the first numbers, 1, 2, 3, which switch from relatively straight horizontal lines to curved lines that, by becoming increasingly round, will give the numerical forms of the following stages.

The fourth stage: from the seventh to the twelfth centuries
The *nagari* notation

The *gupta* script becomes more refined and round. At that time, as of the seventh century, it gives rise to the *nagari*-style script ("urban" script), later named *devanagari* or "*nagari* of the gods" because of the magnificent uniformity it later acquired.

ते वर्तनं । वीरवरोऽवदत् ।

This script became the main script of Sanskrit and of Hindi, the major language of central India today.

In parallel, *gupta*-style numerals evolved into *nagari*-style numerals in a first form named "ancient *nagari*."

1　2　3　4　5　6　7　8　9　0

१ २ ३ ४ ५ ६ ७ ८ ९ ०

Notation in ancient *nagari*.
After Smith, *op. cit.*, p. 70.

Gwalior inscriptions

Zero and position numeration in Indian notations in *nagari* script appear for the first time, according to archeological discoveries, in the inscriptions of Gwalior that date from 875 and 876 C.E., in other words. relatively late as compared to the supposed invention of zero.

Gwalior is a town northwest of Madhya Pradesh, a central region of India (as large as the entire French territory), between Maharashtra to the south and Rajasthan to the northeast (see the general map of India, p. 37).

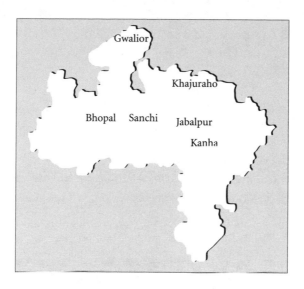

The map of Madhya Pradesh.

The town of Gwalior is well-known for its fort, which is several kilometers long. An impressive fortress that made this town one of the privileged places of the kings and the military, lovers of such places that overlook the plain and offer special control and protection.

The fort of Gwalior

Guitel indicates that these inscriptions were discovered "in a small monolithic temple located at the turn of a road leading to the fort of Gwalior" (Guitel, *op. cit.*, p. 620). There are two inscriptions. The first is written in Sanskrit verse and *nagari* script. It dates from 932 and does not give us any information about the writing of the numbers, because this date appears written out, "as it befits any versified text" (Guitel, *ibid.*). The second inscription, "which should appear in any history of numeration" (Guitel, *ibid.*), is written in prose, in *nagari* script, but in an imperfect Sanskrit. This inscription is to a certain extent "the Rosetta stone of numerals," because it includes four numbers written both in figures and in letters, thus making it possible to decipher and authenticate them. These four numbers are 933, 270, 187, and 50.

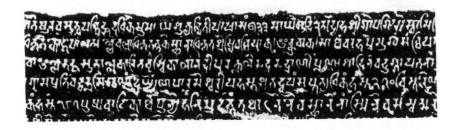

The four numbers of the second Gwalior inscription in *nagari* script.

According to the complicated calculations of historians, especially those of Sir Alexander Cunningham, the date of 933 of the Samvat era corresponds to 876 C.E. (933 less 57). (See Guitel, *op. cit.*, p. 620.)

Second Gwalior inscription (detail). The oldest document attesting the zero and position numeration. We see several numbers: on the first line, 933 (corresponding to the year 876 C.E.); on the fourth line, 270; on the fifth line, 187. Afer Menninger, *op.cit,* p. 397.

This second inscription corresponds to a long text dedicated to Vishnu and mentions a donation of the inhabitants of the city of Gwalior to the temple of Vishnu, including, in particular, a lot 270-*hasta* (a *hasta* is about 20 inches long) long and 187-*hasta* wide, slated to become a flower garden, as well as fifty garlands of the season's flowers, which the gardeners of the city of Gwalior were to contribute to the temple daily.

From this second inscription, we understand how zero and position numeration were already well rooted culturally and used customarily in the middle of the ninth century, to the point of naturally noting measurements, areas, and quantities.

Text of the second inscription of Gwalior. Guimet Museum, Paris.

The fifth stage: scripts derived from *nagari* (starting in the ninth century)

On the path to modern notation

The style of the *nagari* script continued its development and first led to the "modern *nagari*" script (also called *devanagari*).

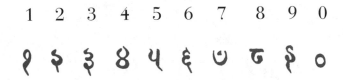

So-called "modern *nagari*" numerals (or *devanagari*)
After Peignot, *op. cit.*, p. 45.

Then, old *nagari* (Gwalior) also developed into several different branches, one of them being the Eastern Arabic numerals (called *hindi*) and the other being the Maghreb Arabic numerals (so-called *ghubar*). We will study their evolution in the second part of this first book (see further on, "Indo-Arabic numerals in the East and West," p. 80).

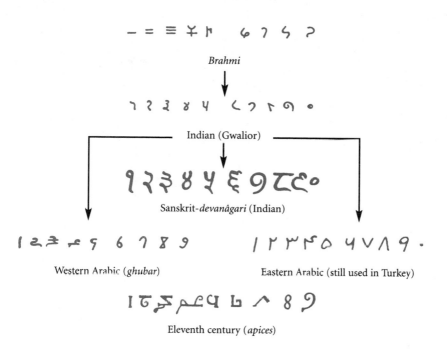

Brahmi

Indian (Gwalior)

Sanskrit-*devanâgari* (Indian)

Western Arabic (*ghubar*)

Eastern Arabic (still used in Turkey)

Eleventh century (*apices*)

Fifteenth century

Sixteenth century (Dürer)

Family of Indian numerals.
After Menninger, *op. cit.*, p. 418.

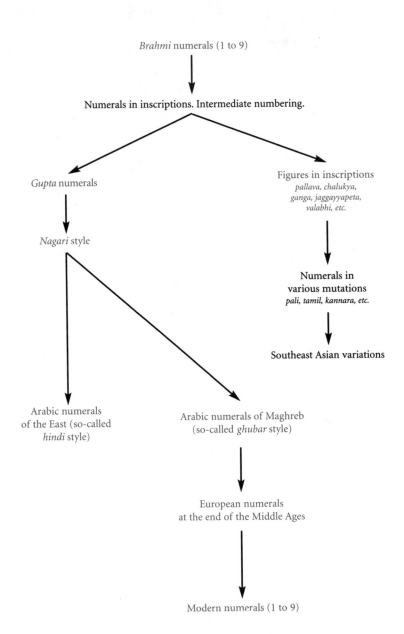

Brahmi numerals (1 to 9)

Numerals in inscriptions. Intermediate numbering.

Gupta numerals

Figures in inscriptions
*pallava, chalukya,
ganga, jaggayyapeta,
valabhi, etc.*

Nagari style

Numerals in
various mutations
pali, tamil, kannara, etc.

64

Southeast Asian variations

Arabic numerals
of the East (so-called
hindi style)

Arabic numerals of Maghreb
(so-called *ghubar* style)

European numerals
at the end of the Middle Ages

Modern numerals (1 to 9)

5

The names of Indian numerals

Rain and light are fighting
like children in the sky,
and their swords sometimes hit my window.
Christian Bobin

The names of the numerals

Before the modern notation of the numerals we have just mentioned, the numerals that constituted numbers were named orally by appellations that allowed pronouncing numbers of all possible magnitudes.

Thus, everything began by a so-called "spoken numeration" that gave each of the nine simple units a name in the language used, Sanskrit. There was also a word for 10: *dasha*; and others for 20, 30, 40…90, 100, 200… 1,000, 10,000 and more. The Indians had names for large numbers and large powers.

(We follow here Menninger's text, *op. cit.*, p. 93, and that of Tobias Dantzig, *Number: The Language of Science*, fourth edition revised, MacMillan, 1966, p. 18. There is a French edition of this book [Blanchard, 1974] but we used the first English edition of 1930. The French translation presents variations that we will indicate whenever necessary. This chapter also owes a great deal to G. Guitel's book, *op. cit.*)

Eka, ekab = one
Dvi, dva, dve = two
Tri, trayah, tisrah = three
Chatur, chatvrah, chatasrah = four
Pancha = five
Shat, shas = six
Sapta = sept
Ashta, ashtau = eight
Nava = nine

Thus, we have, for example: Dasha = 10
Sahasram = 10,000

Although they are not yet necessarily noted by signs, the numbers were spoken according to a classic additive principle.

Influences and cultural exchanges

We showed earlier that, in the beginning, the Indian script and language received Semitic influences via the Aramaic, the vernacular language of the time (we are in the few centuries that preceded the Common Era) and here, perhaps, it did so in a mythological rather than historic manner, thanks to a meeting with the ten lost tribes of Israel, whose language and script were ancient Hebrew.

Thus, we can note the phonetic similarities of:

Eka and *ehad*, which mean "one" in Hebrew;

Shat and *shit*, which mean "six" in Aramaic (*shesh* in Hebrew);

Sapta and *shabbat*, which is the "seventh" day in the Hebrew calendar

Upstream, the relationship between Sanskrit, Greek, and its Latin derivatives is even more obvious: for example, tri (Sanskrit), treis (Greek) and tres (Latin), which we can still hear in trois (French), three (English) or drei (German), and even more strikingly in ancient German, which said dri-, and without ambiguity in Breton, Welsh, and Irish, which simply continue the Sanskrit tri.

Menninger (*op. cit.*, pp. 93 and following) gives the list of all the names of numerals and numbers in the form of complete tables.

	Ireland	Wales	Cornwall	Britanny
1	oin	un	un	eun
2	da	dau	dow	diou
3	tri	tro	tri	tri
4	cethir	petwar	peswar	pevar
5	coic	pimp	pymp	pemp
6	se	chwe	whe	chouech
7	secht	seith	seyth	seiz
8	ocht	wyht	eath	eiz
9	noi	naw	naw	nao
10	deich	dec, deg	dek	dek
11	oin deec	un ar dec	ednack	unnek
12	da-	dour ar dec (deudec)	dewthek	daou-zek
13	tri-	tri ar dec	trethek	tri-
14	cethir-	petwar ar dec	puzwarthak	pevar-
15	coic-	hymthec	pymthek	pem-
16	se-	un ar bymthec	whettak	choue-
17	secht-	dou ar-	seitag	seit-
18	ocht-	deu naw	eatag	tri (ch)ouech
19	noi-	pedwar ar bym-thec	nawnzack	naou-zek
20	fiche	ugeint	ugans	ugent
30	deich ar fiche	dec ar ugeint	dek warn ugans	tregont
40	da fiche	de-ugeint	deu ugens	daou ugent
50	deich ar da fiche	dec ar de-ugeint	hanter-cans	hanter-kant
60	tri fiche	tri ugeint	try ugens	tri ugent
70	deich ar tri fiche	dec ar tri-ug.	dek warn try ugens	dek ha tri ugent
80	ceithri fiche	pedwar-ugeint	peswar ugens	pevar ugent
90	deich ar ceithri [fiche	dec ar pedwar-u.	dekwarn pesw. ug.	dek ha pevar ugent
100	cet	cant	cans	kant
1,000	mile	mil	myl	mil

Names of the numbers (Irish, Welsh, Cornish, Breton). After Menninger, *op. cit.*, p. 97.

Menninger also dedicates a whole chapter, a type of small dictionary, to the meaning of the words used to speak the numbers. He follows their evolution and offers beautiful examples of philological filiations. We give a short extract from it, with a few elements concerning *three* (*op. cit.*, p. 171, "Hidden Number Words").

The Sanskrit "three," *tri*, is found in words such as the French word *tresse*, a rope or braid of hair made with three strands.
The word *trivial* comes from the Latin *trivium*, plural *trivia*, "three roads," a term used from the Roman era to the Middle Ages to designate the three

67

basic disciplines of the curriculum: grammar, rhetoric, and dialectic. The student who had acquired this knowledge went on to the *quadrivium*, "the four roads," which consisted of arithmetic, geometry, astronomy, and music (all of them together forming the seven liberal arts). Thus, *trivial* acquired the meaning of "common thing": ordinary, banal, and uninteresting, in reference to simple, evident things that any student already knows when finishing the first part of his studies, the *trivium* (*ibid.,* p. 177).

Another example: the word *tribe*. This term derived from the Latin *tribus*, which itself comes from the Indo-European *tri-bhu-s*, from *–bhus*, (which evolved into "to be" in English). We find a form of this *be* in the *bi* of the Latin *dubitare*, which became *douter* in French and *doubt* in English, a verb that means "to be faced with two" (*du*), and therefore unable to know with certainty the impossibility of choosing.

Numerical poetry

Originally, there was no problem when the numbers were made up of numerals that were all different. Here is the example of 4,769 (see Guitel, *ibid.,* p. 609), four thousand seven hundred sixty-nine, which was spoken in growing numeration:

Nine   sixty   seven hundred   and   four thousand

9   6 x 10   7 x 100   4 x 1,000

But, in the case of numbers made up of several identical numerals, repeated several times, there was a phonetic difficulty in pronunciation and correct understanding.

Let us imagine a number such as:

4   4   4   4   4   4

It would have been pronounced:

chatur   chatur   chatur   chatur   chatur   chatur

This expression, which would have six times the word *chatur*, would be difficult to understand and memorize, and not very beautiful from the phonetic viewpoint of the number. Thus, Indian scholars started to take advantage of the richness of the Sanskrit language. Many synonyms and metaphors were invented for each numeral, drawing from philosophy, mythology, and all popular and scholarly literature. By playing on words and associations of ideas, meanings, and sounds, each numeral became the source of a multitude of synonyms, which often had great poetic force.

In our example, it would have been possible to find a symbolic and poetic expression such as:

> Cardinal points and oceans
> in the arms of Vishnu and the faces of Brahma
> positions of the human body and cosmic cycles.

Theses are six different expressions to say "four."
It would have been possible to take an example with *dvi* ("two") and its synonyms:

Yamala, yugala: terms designating twins or couples
Ashvi(n): the "knights"
Yama: the "primordial couple"
Netra: the "eyes"
Gulpha: the "ankles"
Paksha: the "wings"
Bâhu: the "arms"

(We find these lists in Louis Renou and Jean Filliozat's significant reference work *L'Inde classique. Manuel des études indiennes*, Hanoi, 1953, reprint 1985.)

G. Guitel (*ibid.*, p. 563) reports two examples, which she borrows from Woepcke (F. Woepcke, "Memoire sur la propagation des chiffres indiens," in *Journal asiatique*, first semester, Paris, 1863). The first is a verse from *Surya Siddantha*.

We read:

From the apogee of the moon: fire—emptiness—Ashvin—Vasu—snake
ocean in a yuga, in a direction contrary to the Vasu knot:
fire—couple—Ashvin—fire—Ashvin

By this method, as we indicated, the numbers are pronounced starting with the units, and following with the ascendant powers of ten. In fact, we know from Guitel that:

Emptiness = 0
Ashvin and couple = 2
Fire = 3
Ocean = 4
Vasu and snake = 8

All this enables us to translate the verse as follows:

The revolutions of the apogee of the moon in a yuga
(4,320,000 solar years) are in the number of 488,203, and
the retrograde revolutions of the knot are in the number of 232,238.

The second example is the expression used to pronounce the *yuga*, in other words the 4,320,000 solar years. We find this expression in the twenty-ninth verse of the *Surya Siddantha*. It is written: "*four nothingness—tooth—ocean.*" This surely gives the number indicated, if we know that emptiness = 0 (and so four emptinesses = 0000), the "tooth" has the value of 32, and the "ocean," as indicated earlier, the value of 4 (see F. Woepcke, *op. cit.*, pp. 113–114). We understand then that each number could become a little poem, a sort of Japanese haiku, that could be recited, memorized, understood, and commented upon literarily and philosophically. This is how the art of mathematics developed, along with the art of poetry. Certain poems that reached us demonstrate this know-how. Tobias Dantzig reproduces in his *Number, The Language of Science* (MacMillan, 1966, pp. 81–82) two extracts from *Lilavati*, a famous mathematical treatise in the form of poems.

From a bush of pure lotus,
One third, one fifth, and one sixth
were respectively offered
to Shiva,
to Vishnu,
to Surya.
One quarter was presented to Bhavani.
The rest, six flowers,
were given to the venerable teacher.
Tell me quickly what was the number of flowers…

The second extract offers the following mathematical enigma:

A necklace broke during lovemaking
One third of the beads fell to the floor
The fifth remained on the bed.
The sixth was found by the young woman
The tenth was kept by the lover.
And six beads remained attached to the thread.
Tell me how many beads were in that necklace.

Lovers embracing, eleventh-century, sandstone, Khajuraho.

In the writing of these numerical poems, the mathematicians respected the logic of the meaning, in which we never find the addition or subtraction of words that did not go together, like arrow and fire, planets and snakes, oceans and elephants.

These poems were not made only to memorize the art of calculation, but also out of a love for the play of numerals and letters. Thus, in Indian culture, speculation on numbers became a practice sought after and appreciated for its beauty and wisdom.

6

Shûnya, shûnya!
The discovery of zero

Man himself is nothing.
He is but infinite chance.
But he is infinitely responsible
for this chance.
Albert Camus

A Babylonian legend

In Babylonia, one day a king decided to build a new town and chose a place for this purpose. He asked for the advice of his country's astrologers. They consulted the planets and the stars and approved his choice of the site. However, they added a condition: In order to bring happiness to the new town, a child, brought voluntarily by his mother, had to be immured alive during the construction. Nobody came forth. Nevertheless, after three years, an old woman came, accompanied by a 10-year-old boy. When he was about to enter the wall, the child asked the king:

– "Oh king, allow me to ask your astrologers three questions. If they find the right answers, it means that they have interpreted the signs correctly; otherwise, it means they have interpreted them wrong."

The king agreed.

– "What is lightest, what is sweetest, and what is hardest in the world?" asked the child.

The astrologers thought about it for three days and said:

"The lightest is the feather, the sweetest is honey, and the hardest is stone."
Good-heartedly, the child made fun of them:
"Anybody could have given that answer. No, the lightest is the child in
his mother's arms, for to her he is never heavy; the sweetest is his mother's
milk; and the hardest in the world is for a mother to bring her child to be
immured alive."
The astrologers were confounded and admitted that they had misread
the stars.
Thus, the child's life was saved.

The reader may wonder why we wanted to tell this Babylonian legend at
the beginning of the chapter about zero. First of all, we did it to remind the
reader that, even though it was the Indians who invented and spread the
notion of zero, it was already present in a different form and according to
a different philosophy, among other sources, in Babylonian mathematical
culture (see G. Guitel, *op. cit.*, p. 668).

However, zero was not yet the philosophical sign of nothingness that it
was for the Indians, and it did not yet become a full-fledged number that
would be included in various calculations, facilitating the calculations in a
way that would revolutionize calculation and mathematics as a whole. But
this little story of ours is intended to tell us much more.
It is up to the reader to use his creativity and hermeneutical spirit—the
power of interpretation.
According to G. Guitel (*op. cit.*, p. 547), "the study of the numerations used
in India is extremely important for the history of mathematics, since it is
linked to the most perfect worldwide spreading of the written position
numerations."
As we already said in the introduction, position numeration means that
the value of the numerals is determined by their position in the writing
of the numbers. This position numeration appeared its final form by the
sixth century C.E.
It was this position numeration that gave rise to zero (first as a sign, before
it became a full-fledged number), indicating an empty space for the units,
tens, hundreds, thousands, etc.

Example:

$$0 \quad 2 \quad 3$$
$$2 \quad 0 \quad 3$$
$$2 \quad 3 \quad 0$$
$$2 \quad 0 \quad 0 \quad 3$$
$$2 \quad 0 \quad 0 \quad 0 \quad 3$$

Zero and Indian thought

In the beginning, this empty place was indicated by a simple space between the numerals, but because of the ambiguity of this reading, the Indians used a sign, a dot, or a circle.

To discover zero, it had been necessary to have a mind capable of accepting the idea of emptiness. It is noteworthy that Sanskrit had a word for it: *shûnya*, which means both "empty" and "absence."

For many centuries, this term had been the fundamental core of a religious and mystical thinking at the center of Indian life and culture.

75

Emptiness

As of the first centuries C.E., the word *shûnya* had the meaning of emptiness, sky, atmosphere, and space. As specified by Renou and Filliozat (*op. cit.*, pp. 708–709), *shûnya* also designated the non-created, the non-being, the non-existence, the non-formed, the non-thought, the non-present, the absent, nothingness, etc.

From emptiness to zero

Thus, to express the mathematical notion of absence of one of the elements of the number, unit, ten, hundred, etc., Indian scholars decided that the term *shûnya* was perfectly appropriate, from a philosophical and mathematical viewpoint. Finally, in the midst of this spoken, then written position numeration, this term became the utterly strange and practical numerical creature we now call zero.

A zero that came from heaven

Just like the other numerals, zero had many synonyms, often quite poetic.
We will cite, for example, *ananta*, the infinite, *vishnupada*, Vishnu's foot,
jaladharapatha, the voyage on water, *purna*, the completion, plenitude,
integrity, totality, etc. (See G. Guitel, *op. cit.*, p. 561 ; L. Renou and J. Filliozat, *op. cit.*,
pp. 708–709.)

The circle

The first graphic representation of zero

According to L. Renou and J. Filliozat, the ideas of sky, space, atmosphere,
and firmament, present in the first representations of the idea of emptiness
and zero, led to making drawings and signs that represented the heavens:
either a half-circle, or a circular drawing, or just simply a geometric
circle.

This is how a small circle became the graphic symbol of the concept of
zero.

The dot: a zero-dimensional object

The second graphic representation of zero

Why is it that the "dot" was also one of the first symbolical representations
of zero?

We will offer a metaphor: "The book you are reading is an object with three
dimensions, length, width, and height or thickness. Imagine that the hand
of a giant crushes it on its entire thickness. Only top dimensions remain, a
large rectangle, a plane: length-width. Imagine that the giant's hand hits
this rectangle again. An object with one dimension remains, the straight
line. And if the giant insists, only a zero-dimensional object will be left:
the dot!" (See Charles Seife, *Zero: The Biography of a Dangerous Idea*, Penguin, 2000.)

In the geometrical space with three dimensions, the successive reduction
of the dimensions leads to the conception of a zero-dimensional object:
the dot.

The four representations of zero in India

The word *shûnya* and its various synonyms were first used to orally mark the absence of the units in a certain decimal order, whether in the initial, middle, or final position.

Today, we can find four representations of and four different names for the Indian zero.

First of all, the *shûnya-kha,* meaning literally "emptiness-space." This is the name of zero as an arithmetic operator, when it was still represented, in the written or oral position numeration, by an empty space (or box) to indicate the absence of the unit, ten, hundred, etc.

Then there was *shûnya-chakra,* meaning literally "emptiness-circle." As specified by L. Renou and J. Filliozat, (*ibid.*), it is currently used in most notations in India and southeast Asia.

The third representation of zero is *shûnya-bindu,* literally the "zero-dot," which was used in the regions of Kashmir. With regard to this dot (*bindu*), "we do not have very old Indian texts concerning it, but it is attested to in Cambodia at the end of the seventh century" (G. Guitel, *op. cit.,* p. 561).

Beyond its purely geometric and mathematic aspect, *bindu* was for the Indians the original dot, endowed with creative energy, capable of giving birth to everything, archetypical; a dot symbolizing the universe in its non-manifested form before its transformation into a world of appearances (*rupadhatu*); a dot liable to give birth to all possible lines and all possible shapes (*rupa*).

The evolution of the concept of zero will make it go from a simple sign for the notation of absence to a full-fledged number designating a quantity that is null. This is the fourth representation of zero. It was then called *shûnya-samkhya* (or *sankhya*), literally: "emptiness-number."

Thus, the written position numeration, by the same token as the alphabet, became one of the fundamental elements of humankind's mental tools. Both were forged in the East, while the West was still seeking its voice. We will see in the following chapters how the West would adopt these new numerals and this revolutionary numeration and spread them the world over.

Chakra zero (the circle) and *bindu* zero (the dot).

Part Two

Indo-Arabic numerals in the East and West
(from the ninth to the twelfth centuries)

En route to Baghdad

Al-Jabr and algebra

Voyage to Arabia…

1

En route to Baghdad

One term is enough to indicate
the universe—he used to say;
But how many words do we need
to be able to half-open it?
Edmond Jabès

Baghdad, the round city

Another story that is true, or at least a true story:

(We are telling it according to a beautiful version that we owe to the exquisite storytelling talent of Denis Guedj. Read his compelling *The Parrot's Theorem*, St. Martin's Press, and you will not be disappointed.)

"It all started one day in 773, when, after an endless journey, a heavily loaded caravan traveling from India came to the gates of *Madinat al-Salam*, the city of Peace: Baghdad.

Like Alexandria, Baghdad was a new city, built in only three years. And like Alexandria, Baghdad was situated between two bodies of water, the Tigris and the Euphrates, and was built on canals. Each inhabitant—if he was wealthy—had to have a donkey in his stable and a boat on the river. Also like Alexandria, Baghdad was a cosmopolitan city. But while Alexandria was rectangular, Baghdad was called the "round city."

Baghdad's perfectly geometric fortification, as if it had been drawn with a compass, had at its center the mosque and the palace of the Caliph, from which large arteries extended in all four directions, ending at the four gates built into the surrounding wall. These gates were the only way to enter the city."

(Alexandria, created in 331 B.C.E., disappeared in 640.)

Gate of an Arab city, 1548

"It was through one of them, the Khorassan gate, that the caravan, filled with gifts for Caliph Al-Mansur (754–775), entered the round city and slowly advanced toward the palace. The crowd gathered to see it pass. Only the Caliph could ride a horse inside the palace grounds. The travelers dismounted to enter the reception hall.

The Caliph, wearing magnificent red boots and the prophet's cloak, rod, saber, and seal, in his official function of "dispenser of justice," was arbitrating a conflict between two plaintiffs. But the travelers could not see him: As custom mandated, he was hidden behind a curtain.

Because he descended directly from the prophet Mohammed (who had died in 632), the Caliph was the commander of the faithful. This was the supreme title of Islam, which gave him power over all the Muslims of the world."

Starting from a few acres of desert around the town of Medina, Islam had spread with an unheard-of rapidity. The Islamic empire would spread from the Pyrenees to the banks of the Indus. It is worth listing the countries that were conquered, or that converted, within in a few decades: the Iberian Peninsula, the Maghreb, Libya, Egypt, Arabia, Syria, Turkey, Iraq, Iran, the Caucasus, the Punjab, and soon Sicily. After Alexander's empire, after the Roman empire, the Muslim empire. Its advance lost steam only when it reached the borders of China and was stopped only twice: in Constantinople (Byzantium) in 717–718, when the Arab fleet was finally pushed back by the Byzantines, and in Poitiers in 732, when it was stopped by Charles Martel.

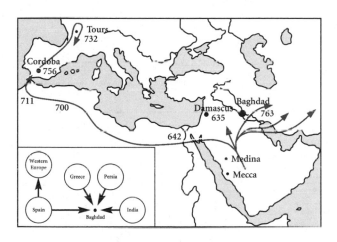

Arab conquests.
The arrows indicate the movement of the cultural influences.
After Menninger, *op. cit.*, p. 407.

The Arab civilization therefore reigned from the seventh to the fourteenth centuries over this huge geographic area. In 1236, Cordoba, capital of the Muslim West and center of the Arabic-Andalusian civilization, was taken over by Ferdinand III, king of Castile, and in 1258, Baghdad, the prestigious capital of the East, fell to the blows of the Mongols. But Arab science was still shining in the fourteenth century: on the western side and to the south, in Spain (kingdom of Granada) and North Africa; on the eastern side, in the Mamluk Empire of Egypt and, for shorter periods, around the observatories of Maraga and Samarkand.

The Fine Flower of Histories, miniature by Luqman, 1583. Map of the universe: the globe, the seven heavens, the zodiac, and the position of the twenty-eight days of the month.

Arab language and science

At that time, in 800, the populations had just converted to Islam. Religion alone was not enough to unify them. They needed a common language, the cement that would unify millions of such different people. This was the role of Arabic.

Born in the desert, spoken by a small group of people, Arabic was quite young. This is the language that would become the link and vehicle of Arab science.

The importance of translation

When we speak about Arab science, we refer to scientific works written in this language, which, during this long period, became the international language of men of letters and scholars.

In order to have reach and value recognized in the sciences, any written work had to be written in this language. Scientific effort had mobilized all the peoples conquered, from the Greeks who had immigrated to Persia after the Christian oppression, to the Andalusians and Berbers, as well as Syrians, Jews, Sabeans, Turks, the inhabitants of Central Asia, and those from the shores of the Caspian Sea.

For this language to be able to express all the new scientific notions and other things (essentially administrative) that were unknown to it, it was necessary to enrich and adapt it, to create new words, to broaden the scope of the meanings, to create new meanings.

Arabic is extremely rich; it offers a great variety of synonyms for each notion and object. Translations from Greek, Syrian, or Latin of previous scientific works raised questions of terminology and identification of the notions that increased the conceptual depth of the knowledge. Philologists and linguists participated in this effort.

The creation of a great university: the House of Wisdom

Building a language is an extraordinary adventure. This adventure is made possible by books. In Baghdad, in the Al-Karkh quarter, there was the largest book market that ever existed. The works, on papyrus or parchment, came from everywhere, from Byzantium, Alexandria, Pergamus, as well as from Syracuse, Antioch, and Jerusalem. People paid a fortune for them.

Again, the parallel between Alexandria and Baghdad becomes apparent. Alexandria had a museum and a huge library, while Baghdad acquired an institution that was a mirror image of the museum: Bayt al-Hikma, the House of Wisdom.

Low Latin translation of the *Elements* of Euclid from the Arabic, generally attributed to Adelard of Bath.

In both in Alexandria and Baghdad, an observatory had been built, as well as a library. Still, historians say that there was a difference between the two cities. In Alexandria, the museum preceded the library. In Baghdad, the library founded by Harun al-Rashid preceded the House of Wisdom, which was created by his son Al-Ma'mun.

The library in Baghdad was the authentic heir of the library in Alexandria. To be precise, the books that came to Alexandria were written mostly in Greek, while none of those that came to Baghdad in the ninth century were written in Arabic. They had to be translated.

The House of Wisdom, 1494.

Translation, translation, translation!

An extraordinary undertaking is begun

According to Denis Guedj, the group of translators of the House of Wisdom was its greatest asset. There were dozens, coming from everywhere, hard at work in front of manuscripts that also came from everywhere. The unheard-of diversity of the languages from which they translated transformed the town into a learned Babel. Greek, Sogdian, Sanskrit, Latin, Hebrew, Aramaic, Syrian, Coptic. And all these translators were scholars. It could not have been otherwise, given the nature of the works to be translated: scientific and philosophical texts. First the Greeks: Euclid, Archimedes, Apollonius, Diophantus, Aristotle. All of Aristotle! Ptolemy, the geographer; Hyppocrates and Galen, the physicians; Heron, the engineer; etc.

In vast calligraphy shops, armies of scribes labored nonstop. The works, this time written in Arabic, started to fill the shelves of the library in the House of Wisdom. The copies multiplied. The stage was set for the knowledge, which had come from the outside, to spread throughout the huge Arabic empire through these newly accessible works.

According to Denis Guedj, private libraries became increasingly numerous. The most prestigious one, belonging to the mathematician Al-Kindi, was envied by all. It was a treasure that was bitterly fought over after his death. In the end, it was acquired by the three Banu Musa brothers (Mohammed, Ahmed, and Hassan), the first Arab geometers. A true institution, the three mathematicians had their own translators sent abroad at great expense to collect the most sought-after old works.

In a period of time that was short on the scale of history, the Arab world succeeded in associating to its culture a modern knowledge of considerable size. For seven centuries, a period of time just slightly shorter than the period that lapsed between Thales and Menelaus, the sciences prospered in this region of the world.

Alexandria had had its Ptolemies; Baghdad had its Caliphs, who were lovers of the arts and sciences. A search for manuscripts quite similar to that pursued a thousand years earlier by the Ptolemies was launched by the Caliph. After Al-Mansur, who had received the gift of the Indian emissaries, there was Harun Al-Rashid, the one from *The Arabian Nights*, then his son Al-Ma'mun, a rationalist caliph.

A passionate fan of Aristotle, Al-Ma'mun did not like the assimilationists, whom he persecuted throughout his reign. He was the soul of the House of Wisdom.

This magnificent anecdote is told: When his troops defeated the Byzantine armies, Al-Ma'mun proposed an astonishing exchange to the Emperor of the Orient: prisoners for books. The deal was closed when one thousand Christian warriors, freed by the Arabs, returned to Constantinople, while, in the opposite direction, some ten extremely rare works, the jewels of Byzantine libraries, arrived in Baghdad to an exalted welcome at the House of Wisdom.

A marvelous gift

Back to our caravan...

Among the sumptuous gifts transported in those trunks from India, there was one that would have a capital importance for Arab scholars, the *Siddhantha*, which we mentioned earlier, a treatise of astronomy with its tables, written a century before by Brahmagupta.

Its pages held a real treasure: ten little drawings.

One, two, three...to nine. And we should not forget the last one, *zero*.

Of course, there are other, more scholarly, more realistic, simpler versions of this story. The most likely scenario is that the craze to translate, which we discussed earlier, led to the importation of Indian manuscripts, including those concerned with astronomy and mathematics. This trip from India to Baghdad was the first stage in the great journey of the numerals.

Truncated hollow isohedron (an Archimedean Polyhedron), also known as a triacontahedron.
(Drawing attributed to Leonardo da Vinci.)

2

Al-jabr and algebra
Portrait of Al-Khuwarizmi

Art is a wound that becomes light.
Georges Braque

Arab scholars express their gratitude to the Indian numeration system

So, around 773 or 776, the searchers of manuscripts, emissaries of the Caliph, or the Indian scholars who arrived in Baghdad in the caravan in our legend most probably brought with them, among the Sanskrit words offered to the Caliph, the *Brahmasphuta Siddhanta*, an astronomy treatise whose name means literally "Brahma's revised system," written in 628 by the Indian genius Brahmagupta when he was just 30 years of age.Caliph Al-Mansur immediately ordered that this work be translated into Arabic to help the Muslims acquire an exact knowledge of the stars and calculations. The book then took the title of *Sinhind*. He also ordered that another work be composed after this translation, to make Arab scholars familiar with the marvels of the principle of decimal position numeration, the zero, calculation methods, and the basics of Indian algebra.

Portrait of a famous mathematician: Al-Khuwarizmi

Among these scholars, there was a man by the name of Abu Jafar Muhammad ibn Musa Al-Khuwarizmi. This means the one from Kwarismia, originally from the Persian province of Khorezm, south of the Aral Sea, called "Khorasmia" by the Greeks.

Al-Khuwarizmi was one of the most famous Arab-language mathematicians of his time, and of the Arab-Islamic civilization in general. He was born in 783 in Khiva, in Khorezm, and died in Baghdad around 850.
He lived at the court of caliph Al-Ma'mun and was one of the most significant members of a group of mathematicians and astronomers who worked at the House of Wisdom, Baghdad's academy of science mentioned in the previous chapter.

Invention of the word *algebra*

Al-Khuwarizmi wrote numerous works, including a small text, published circa 820, on arithmetic. In this text, he explained the use of the new Indian figures and position numeration, which he had discovered himself in the works of Indian scholars (Menninger, *op. cit.,* p. 411).

Traditional portrait of Al-Khuwarizmi.

About this Indian numeration, he said, and repeated, that "it was the richest, quickest calculation method, the easiest to understand, and the easiest calculation method to learn," as reported (circa 900) by the astronomer Al-Hussein Ben Muhammad, better known by the name of Ibn Al-Adami.

Al-Khuwarizmi also wrote a book titled *Hisab Al-jabr w'almuqabala* ("The book of restoration and equalization"), dedicated to the fundamental methods of algebraic science.

Astronomers and scholars of the observatory in the Galata tower in Istanbul
(sixteenth-century. miniature).

Discussion of the Pythagorean theorem in an Arabic manuscript.

The solution to the equations (diophantian) implies two basic principles, the transposition of a term with change of sign:

$$A - X = B \text{ hence } A = X + B$$

and the reduction of similar terms:

$$A + X = B + X \text{ hence } A = B$$

The first process is called, in Arabic, *al-jabr* (restoration or transposition), and the second process is called *al-muqabala* (comparison or reduction). The first word gave us the word *algebra* to designate the arithmetic of these equations. But it was not the Arab mathematicians who invented the resolution of equations. They read Diophantus (refer to the glossary of proper names), and actually went further than him in the study of numerical relations, but did not yet totally invent algebra, which implies three elements: the notion of the unknown, that of equation, and especially the idea of representing numbers (known or unknown) by ad hoc symbols (for a particular use). It is this third element that was missing, just as it had been missing in Diophantus, and that would emerge only later.

Through the works of Al-Khuwarizmi, Indian numeration and Indian numerals, which became Indo-Arabic, were introduced in mathematical science (Jean Baudet, *Nouvel abrégé d'histoire des mathématiques*, Vuibert, 2002).
Two works that used the Indian system and contributed to its spreading should be cited. They were authored by Ahmad ibn Ibrahim Al-Uqlidisi: *Kitab al-fusul fi al-hisab al-hindi*, published in 953 in Damascus, and *Kitab al-hajari fi al-hisab*, published circa 960.

Notes:
From an etymological viewpoint, the word *al-jabr* designates the physician who resets the bones, the "bonesetter."
It is noteworthy that, in the biblical text, Jacob developed a limp after the famous episode known as "Jacob's fight with the angel," and that his limping was not repaired.

95

A name for posterity

Famous and held in high esteem, Al-Khuwarizmi was translated into Latin and his name became Alchoarismi; then we find it as Algorismi, then Algorismus, then Algorism, and finally Algorithm (see Menninger, *op. cit.,* p. 412). Later, the name of this scholar became synonymous with Indian-origin methods of calculation, a system consisting of the nine numerals and zero, before taking on the meaning we give it today: an algorithm is a process with various phases that must be followed scrupulously to produce a result—an action taken to resolve a problem, be it mathematical or otherwise.

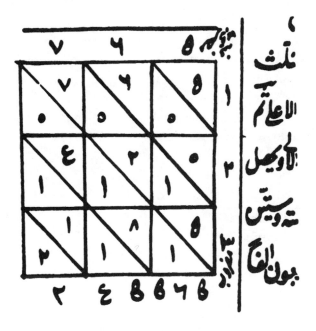

Equations in Arabic languages and operations.
Arabic manuscript from the seventeenth century, kept at the Bayrische Staatsbibliothek, Munich.
After Menninger, *op. cit.,* p. 442.

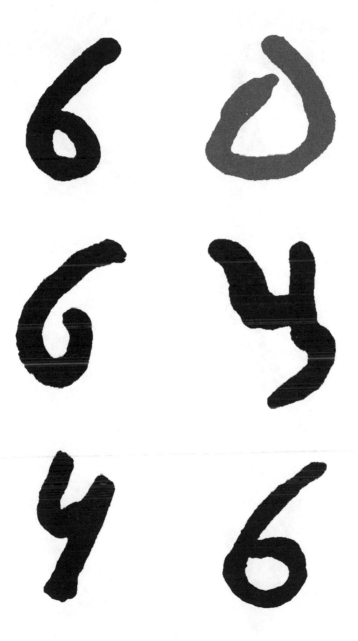

Variations of the number 6 in *ghubar* numerals. After Smith, *op. cit.*, p. 74.

Variations of the number 7 in *ghubar* numerals. After Smith, *op. cit.*, p. 74.

3

Voyage to Arabia…
From Indian numerals to
"Indo-Arabic"numerals

*What comes into the world
to disturb nothing deserves
neither consideration nor patience.*
René Char

We must go back to the graphic evolution of the writing of letters and numerals. We will show how, after being received by the Arabs, numerals took two different forms related to two variations of the Arabic script. We will discuss Eastern Indo-Arabic, or Hindi, numerals and Western Indo-Arabic, or *ghubar*, numerals. We will explain the meaning of these terms later on.

The form of Eastern Indo-Arabic numerals
Hindi numerals
As indicated by D. E. Smith and J. Ginsburg in *Numbers and Numerals*, in the beginning, the numerals inherited by the Arabs from the Indians kept, with a few variations, their original form: the nine Indian numerals in *nagari* style.

(D. E. Smith and J. Ginsburg, in *Numbers and Numerals*, N.C.T.M., 1937, p. 20. See also D. E. Smith, *Number Stories of Long Ago*, Ginn & Co., 1919, *Rara Arithmetica*, Ginn & Co.,1908, and *History of Mathematics,* Ginn & Co., 1925 [especially the first chapter in volume two]. Also of great interest is D. E. Smith and Karpinski, *The Hindu-Arabic Numerals,* Ginn & Co., 1911. See also James Fevrier, *op. cit.* [appendix II, "Les signes de numeration," pp. 578–589]. Fevrier specifies that most of the information concerning India was given to him by his colleague, Jean Filliozat. See also p. 587, the discussion on the origin of Arabic numerals, which, according to certain researchers such as baron Carra de Vaux, would actually be of Greek origin; the latter opinion was never taken into consideration by subsequent research. See also K. Menninger, *op. cit.,* p. 406, "Indian Numerals in Arab Hand.")

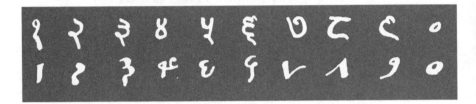

Nagari numerals and Eastern Arabic numerals, named Hindi
in the first stage after being borrowed. After Renou and Filliozat, *op. cit.*

Numerals take a 90-degree turn

Then the form of these numerals evolved, for writing technique reasons, making a 90-degree turn.

Thus, we see a turn and a graphic evolution of Indian numerals in Eastern Muslim countries, which led to the following forms:

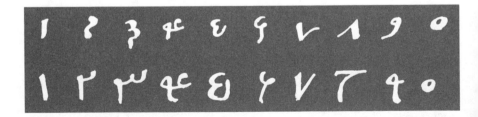

The turn is particularly characteristic for the 3.

$$3 \longrightarrow ٣$$

It is noteworthy that, in the evolution of the script, for example between Phoenician and Greek, the letters took the same turn. Thus, the letter E:

After an evolution that seems to become established and official as early as the thirteenth century, in the Arabic countries of the Near East Indian numerals appear in the following form:

$$١ ٢ ٣ ٤ ٥ ٦ ٧ ٨ ٩ ٠$$

Eastern Arabic numerals.

In this form, the nine numerals of Indian origin, which were actually called *arqamiya al-hindi* ("Indian numerals") by Arab scholars, spread to all the eastern provinces of the Arab-Muslim world. We must note, in fact (see Menninger, *op. cit.*, p. 413), that these Indo-Arabic numerals are still used today in Iran, Pakistan, Afghanistan, and even in Muslim India, as well as in all the countries of the Arab-Persian Gulf, such as Jordan and Syria, Iraq, Egypt, and Israel (where, after Hebrew, Arabic is the second official national language).

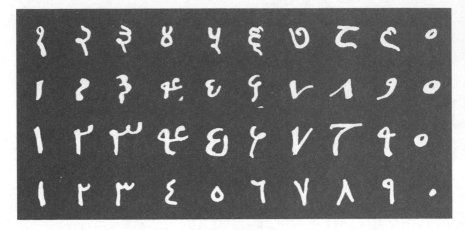

Evolution of Indian numerals toward Hindi-type Indo-Arabic numerals.
After Renou and Filliozat, *op. cit.*

Notes:

During the entire evolution of these signs, zero was still hesitating between the circle and the dot. It finally stabilizes as the dot, in a victory of *bindu* over *chakra*—something to think about. In addition, in the Eastern notational system, the little circle is used to note the 5, which is also sometimes noted by a sign in the shape of a inverted heart.

The date January 31, 1955, in Eastern Arabic numerals.
After Menninger, *op. cit.*, p. 413.

Western Indo-Arabic numerals

Ghubar or *ghubari* numerals

Along with the Eastern Indo-Arabic numerals, in the countries of the Maghreb and Muslim Spain there were Western Indo-Arabic numerals with different shapes than their Eastern cousins, which also derived directly from Indian numerals. (We must note that the word *Maghreb* means "west" in Arabic, hence "western.")

$$) \quad 2 \quad 3 \quad \varepsilon \quad 4 \quad 6 \quad 7 \quad 8 \quad 9 \quad 0 $$

Ghubar numerals, after Woepcke.

These Western Indo-Arabic numerals are named in Arabic *arquamiya alghubar* (*gubar* or *gobar*), meaning "dust numerals," in an allusion to the tablets used by the calculators who covered them with sand or dust to write and then erase to do other calculations.
(See Menninger, "The Gubar Numerals," *op. cit.*, p. 415. See also Woepcke, *op. cit.*)

From India to Maghreb, passing by…

As specified by Menninger (*ibid.*), the sciences of Indian arithmetic were transmitted to the western Muslim Arab regions through contact with Indian scholars and through the circulation of works between the eastern Arab scholars and the western Arab scholars, in addition to—and this is essential—through trade, often done by merchants who not only were initiated in the sciences of Indian calculation but also had knowledge of various languages, thus becoming the interface between different cultures, and in our case between India and the Maghreb. (See also Smith and Karpinski, *op. cit.*, pp. 101 and following; see also Woepcke, *ibid.*)

103

Eastern merchants and caravans.

Variations of 8 in *ghubar* numerals. After Smith, *op. cit.*, p. 74.

The relationship between Arabic script and the script of Indo-Arabic numerals

As we have indicated, the Hindi numerals and the *ghubar* numerals all come from the same Indian source. According to researchers in this field, the variations stem from the diversity of styles of the Arabic script itself, in connection with the different materials and the different techniques of the scribes in each region.

(Here we are referring to the old, yet still current studies of Pihan A.P., who was overseer at the Imprimerie nationale: *Exposé des signes de numération usités chez les peuples orientaux anciens et modernes,* Paris, 1860, and *Glossaire des mots français tirés de l'arabe, du persan et du turc, contenant leur étymologie,* Paris, 1847, as well as *Notices sur les divers genres d'écritures, des Arabes, des Persans et des Turcs,* Paris, 1856. See also the notes written on the characters of the Imprimerie nationale (Éditions de l'Imprimerie nationale, Paris, 1990. See also François Desroches, "L'écriture arabe," *in Histoire de l'écriture,* Flammarion, 2001, pp. 219 and following, and James Février, *op. cit.,* pp. 262 and following.)

Language, writing, and religion

As stressed by Fevrier in the introduction to his chapter on Arabic script (*op. cit.,* p. 262),"it is necessary to carefully distinguish between the Arabic language, Arabic script, and the Islamic religion." Fevrier apologizes, as he says, "for mentioning such elementary notions," but they are nevertheless important because they help avoid the worst confusions.

It is possible to illustrate this distinction by showing, for example, that "the Arabic language was sometimes noted using the Syrian alphabet or the Hebrew alphabet, that Arabic script served and still serves to write languages that not only are not Arabic but are not even Semitic, and finally, that the religion of Islam penetrated only imperfectly certain parts of the Arab world but, in exchange, extended well beyond its limits" (*ibid.*).

The oldest known inscription in the Arab language

The above remark allows us to better appreciate the fact that the oldest known inscription in Arabic language dates from 328 and was discovered near Syria in Druze country, in En-Nemara. This inscription is not yet in Arabic characters, but in Nabatean. As specified by Paul-Marie Grinevald in his notes of the Imprimerie Nationale (*op. cit.,* p. 186): "The Nabatean kingdom, first limited to the territories around the town of Petra, north of the Red Sea, gradually annexed Transjordania up to Damascus and extended to the south up to Medina. The Nabatean language was Aramaic, and its writing a transformation of the Aramaic writing that became adorned with loops, circles, and swashes."

The author of this note adds that "the importance of the Nabatean kingdom, between the Far East and southern Arabia on the one hand, and the Mediterranean world on the other, served a political power that lasted for three centuries, until 106 C.E., when the Roman province of Arabia was formed. This change did not cause the disappearance of the Nabatean writing, which survived as a popular writing, and in fact certain Arab tribes in the Syrian desert used the Nabatean script to transcribe their language" (*ibid.*). This explains the En-Nemara discovery. This inscription shows how "Arabic writing originated from Nabatean types, whose general form it preserved, along with the rules for the links of the letters."

Evolution of Arabic writing

Like Hebrew, Arabic script is written from right to left, with letters, many of which are linked together. In its most complete form, it has twenty-eight letters, twenty-five consonants, and three semivowels.

The vowels, like the absence of vocalization and the doubling of some letters, are indicated by accents placed above and under consonants. These accents are always noted in the Koran and the scholarly and teaching texts, but are not in current usage. There are also diacritics to distinguish the letters with identical shapes.

It is noteworthy that, in Hebrew, one is not allowed to punctuate the holy text, the Torah. Certainly, this difference causes significant hermeneutical behavior, such as the freedom of reading the same word with other vowels, for example, or the possibility of a game of permutations and anagrams, which are the basis for the interpretation of the Midrach, Talmud, and Kabbalah.

Text

Transcription

```
TY NPŠ MR᾽LQYŠ BR ᶜMRW MLK ᾽L᾽RB KLH DW ᾽SR ᾽LTG
WMLK ᾽L᾽ŠDYN W NZRW WMLWKHM WHRB MḤGW ᶜKDY WG᾽
BZGY FY ḤBG NGRN MDYNT ŠMR WMLK MᶜDW WBNN BNYH
᾽LŠᶜWB WWKLHN PRŠW LRWM PLM ᾽YBLᶜ MLK MBLᶜH
ᶜKRY HLK ŠNT 223 YWM 7 BKŠLWL BLŠᶜD DW WLDH
```

Translation

This is the tomb of Imroulquais, son of Amru, king of
all the Arabs, who has worn the crown and has reigned
over the two Asads and over Nizar and over their
kings; who has chased away Mahagg (?) with strength
(?) and has been victorious (?) at the siege of
Negran, city of Shammar, and has placed his sons
Maeadd and Bannan (?) as kings over the tribes and
has organized them as horsemen for Rome. No king has
attained that which he has attained in power (?). He
died in the year 223, the 7 of kisloul. Happy he who
sired him.

Inscription in En Nemara (328), after R. Dussaud and F. Macler, *Revue d'archéologie*, 1902.
Reproduced by Février, *op. cit.*, p. 264.

Clearly, Arabic characters did not appear in their final tracing until the sixth
century. As of the emergence of Islam (Hegira or the Islamic era started in
622), the script evolved toward various different styles, the most important
and widespread being Kufi, *naskhi*, and *maghribi*.

1) Kufi is a script that originated with the scribes of the town of Kufa (or
Cufa, a town founded in 638) on the Euphrates. This script was sacred and

Detail of a gate. with epigraphic decoration, from the Ince Minarelli mosque,
thirteenth century, Konya, Turkey.

religious, qualities it has kept to our days, because it was used during the first centuries of the history of Islam for liturgy, for writing religious and legal texts, for tomb inscriptions, and for inscriptions in and on mosques. The Kufi script was either sculpted with a burin on stone buildings or etched in wood or copper, hence its angular, rigid form.

Almost all the Korans dating from the first centuries of the Hegira that have reached us are written in Kufi. Over time, this script became complicated with strange arabesques, ligatures, and tangles, ornaments that made the words almost impossible to read. These are the woven Kufi, in which the ascenders or descenders are weaved together, and the flowery or "karmatic" Kufi. Very quickly, Kufi became pure ornamentation, a sort of dropped-initial style reserved for headings and to embellish the contours of texts or monuments. In fact, Fevrier reports that B. Moritz gave this Kufi script the name of monumental or hieratic (sacred) script (Février, *ibid.*).

Its characteristic is that it gives a visual impression of rising upward, suggesting the image of a town with the roofs of its houses and mosques. The large majority of the letters are above what seems to be, overall, a lower guiding line.

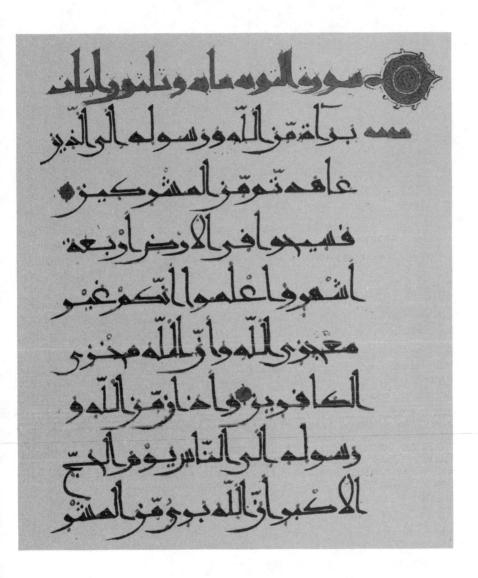

Eastern Kufi, sixth to twelfth centuries, Persia.
Manuscript kept at the Chester Beatty Library, Dublin.

أَشْهَدْ بِأَنَّنَا مُسْلِمُونَ ۞ وَإِذْ قَالَ الْحَوَارِيُّونَ يَا عِيسَى ابْنَ
مَرْيَمَ هَلْ يَسْتَطِيعُ رَبُّكَ أَنْ يُنَزِّلَ عَلَيْنَا مَائِدَةً مِنَ السَّمَاءِ
قَالَ اتَّقُوا اللَّهَ إِنْ كُنْتُمْ مُؤْمِنِينَ ۞ قَالُوا نُرِيدُ أَنْ نَأْكُلَ مِنْهَا
وَتَطْمَئِنَّ قُلُوبُنَا وَنَعْلَمَ أَنْ قَدْ صَدَقْتَنَا وَنَكُونَ عَلَيْهَا مِنَ
الشَّاهِدِينَ ۞ قَالَ عِيسَى ابْنُ مَرْيَمَ اللَّهُمَّ رَبَّنَا أَنْزِلْ
عَلَيْنَا مَائِدَةً مِنَ السَّمَاءِ تَكُونُ لَنَا عِيدًا لِأَوَّلِنَا وَآخِرِنَا وَ
آيَةً مِنْكَ وَارْزُقْنَا وَأَنْتَ خَيْرُ الرَّازِقِينَ ۞ قَالَ اللَّهُ إِنِّي
مُنَزِّلُهَا عَلَيْكُمْ فَمَنْ يَكْفُرْ بَعْدُ مِنْكُمْ فَإِنِّي أُعَذِّبُهُ عَذَابًا
لَا أُعَذِّبُهُ أَحَدًا مِنَ الْعَالَمِينَ ۞ وَإِذْ قَالَ اللَّهُ يَا عِيسَى ابْنَ مَرْيَمَ
أَأَنْتَ قُلْتَ لِلنَّاسِ اتَّخِذُونِي وَأُمِّيَ إِلَٰهَيْنِ مِنْ دُونِ اللَّهِ
قَالَ سُبْحَانَكَ مَا يَكُونُ لِي أَنْ أَقُولَ مَا لَيْسَ لِي بِحَقٍّ إِنْ كُنْتُ
قُلْتُهُ فَقَدْ عَلِمْتَهُ تَعْلَمُ مَا فِي نَفْسِي وَلَا أَعْلَمُ مَا فِي نَفْسِكَ

Naskhi, calligraphy by Ahmad Nayrizi, 1126–1714, Persia.
Manuscript kept at the Mashhad Shrine Library in Mashhad, Iran.

2) Along with this Kufi script, another one, the *naskhi* or *naskh* script ("script of the copyists") is attested early, as of the year 22 of the Hegira. More cursive, more rounded, certainly easier to use (it is written on a papyrus with a reed pen, or "calamus," and thick ink), it is still used today in the entire Arabic cultural world, especially in its eastern part. Although much more rounded than Kufi, this script is still borne by a virtual guiding line at the bottom, and the letters overall rise upward above this line.

3) After these two scripts, a third developed, which was used as the script in various regions of medieval Spain. It became and is still today the favorite script in the Maghreb (western North Africa) and especially in Morocco, where it received the name *maghribi*, or maghrebi Arabic script, or African. According to Grinevald (*op. cit.*, p. 194), "its very archaic appearance gives it the status of cursive neo-Kufi, with diacritics." In addition, "the rising letters are rounded to the left (Persian, to the contrary, rises to the right), and often the stem of certain letters is elegantly extended above the words."

From Arabic letters to Indo-Arabic numerals

We are now able to explain the relationship between Arabic letters and the so-called "Arabic," or more precisely "Indo-Arabic," numerals. Mathematical, historic, and paleographic research, comparing the shape of the letters and numerals of each region, has reached the following conclusions: Eastern or Hindi Arabic numerals follow the rules of cursive *naskhi*. Inversely, *ghubar* numerals are close in style, shape, and tracing to the curves, stems, and angles of the Arab letters of the Kufi script.

(See, among other works, Woepcke, *Mémoire, op. cit.*, pp. 62 and following; Aly Mahazéri, *Les Origines persanes de l'arithmétique: problèmes d'histoire interculturelle*, Kushiyar Abu Al-Hasan Al-Gili, 971–1029, text established, translated, and commented by Aly Mazahéri, Nice (Institut d'études et de recherches inter-ethniques et interculturelles, 1975, "Études préliminaires IDERIC" collection, number 8, translation of the work *Maqalatan fi-ocul hisab al-hind*, after the manuscript in Saint Sophia in Istanbul.)

Maghribi, with the first line in western ornamental Kufi, 975–1568.
Manuscript kept at the British Library, London.

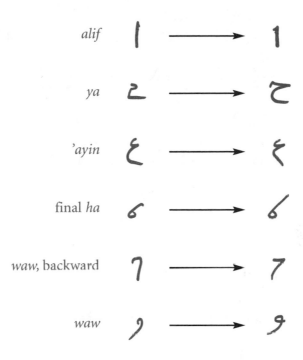

alif	ا	1
ya	ے	ح
'ayin	ع	ع
final *ha*	ه	ه
waw, backward	٧	7
waw	ٯ	9

Correspondence between *maghribi* letters and *ghubar* numerals.

From *ghubar* to the Western numerals of the Christian world

We are reaching the last leg of this long voyage of numerals. It was in their *ghubar* form that the numerals arrived in the Christian West, through the interface played by Spain between the Muslim and the Christian worlds. This is the stage to which the following chapters are dedicated.

Part Three

How Indo-Arabic numerals reached the Christian West

Gerbert of Aurillac, the mathematician pope

The importance of the Crusades

Fibonacci and the *Liber Abaci*

Numerals and the printing press

Portrait of Gerbert of Aurillac (938–1003).

1

Gerbert of Aurillac, the mathematician pope

The poets are stronger than the executioner.
Erri de Luca

The amazing Middle Ages

We are now getting to the Middle Ages. During this period, scientific knowledge was quite rudimentary.

At the time, instruction was reserved for an elite, and consisted first of learning to read and write. First, there was the *trivium*, which consisted of the study of the three basic disciplines: grammar, rhetoric, and dialectic. Then, those who continued their studies graduated to the *quadrivium*: arithmetic, geometry, astronomy, and music. These seven sciences were the so-called "seven liberal arts" (see Menninger, *op. cit.*, p. 177). The word *mathematics* is certainly quite pretentious, because what the students learned was to count and do some operations following the old Roman numeration, with pebbles or disks on the abacus, or "counting board," inherited by the West from the Romans. (See Menninger, "The Counting Board in the Early Middle Ages," *op. cit.*, pp. 319 and following.)

This arithmetic also included the technique of digital counting (on and with one's fingers), perfected by the Venerable Bede, who died in 735 (see Menninger, "The Venerable Bede and his finger counting," *ibid.*, p. 201).

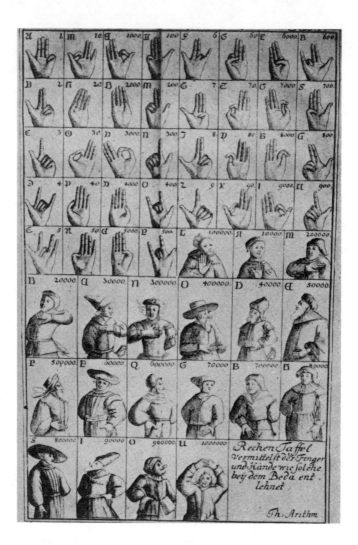

Jacob Leupold, *Theatrum Arithmetico-Geometricum,* 1727.
Reproduced by Menninger, *op. cit.,* p. 207.

In short, arithmetic knowledge and calculation and counting techniques were poor and at an extremely low level. Thus, arithmetic did not flourish until the revolution introduced by Gerbert of Aurillac, who became pope Sylvester II. And this occurred by the adoption of Indian position numeration and the first nine numerals: 1, 2, 3, 4, 5, 6, 7, 8, 9.

A new pope was appointed:
Gerbert of Aurillac

"The fate of this genius was quite unusual," wrote Lucien Gerardin, who tells us this beautiful story: "The young shepherd from Auvergne's exceptional intelligence caught the attention of a monk from Aurillac. Born circa 938, Gerbert of Aurillac was first a novice at the monastery of Saint Geraud. He learned everything they could teach him. His superior then sent him to monastery of Vic in Catalonia.

"Hatton, the bishop of this Spanish diocese, cultivated the arts of mathematics and astronomy. He appreciated the talents and intelligence of the young Gerbert and made him his secretary. He taught him to use the numeration system, as well as the Indian calculation methods that he had surely learned himself during one or several stays in Muslim Spain."

(Another version of the story says that, for his initiation in Indo-Arabic calculation, Gerbert of Aurillac traveled by himself to Seville, Fez, and Cordoba, and entered the Arab universities disguised as a Muslim scholar. See also C. Gillispie, *Dictionary of Scientific Biography*, 16 volumes, New York, 1970–1980. For Gerbert's biography, see also D. E. Smith, "The Occident from 1000 to 1500," *History of Mathematics*, volume II, p. 194, Dover, reprinted in 1958.)

The bishop took him to Rome in 965.

Gerbert became not only a good mathematician but also a fine political strategist. He made powerful friends in the capital of Christendom, and supported the ascension of Hugh Capet to the throne. "One favor is worth another," adds Gerardin: "The monarch turned the former shepherd into the archbishop of Reims."

He knew Reims well, because, between 972 and 987, he managed its diocese school. He was also the head of the abbey of Bobbio, in Italy, and became the adviser to Pope Gregory V. His ascent continued, but certainly thanks to his own merit and intelligence rather than by the power of his acquaintances, and after becoming the archbishop of Ravenna, he was elected pope on April 2, 999, right before the year 1000; he died on May 12 in the year 1003, at the age of 63.

(See Lucien Gérardin, *Le Mystère des nombres, arithmétique et géométrie sacrée*, Dangles, 1985, p. 144; see also Menninger, *op. cit.*, p. 322.)

Be it in Reims, Bobbio, or Ravenna, his teaching had an essential influence on the schools of his time and brought about the renewal of the mathematics in the Occident.

This is an essential fact: It was he, Gerbert of Aurillac, who first introduced Indo-Arabic numerals in the Christian Occident.
But, amazingly, he did not adopt the existence of zero, or the existence of what would have enabled him to use the Indian position numeration.
One can hesitate as to the meaning of this absence of zero and Indian numeration. Was this Gerbert's deliberate choice or the result of the pressure of his time, which was too deeply rooted in the classical calculation methods inherited from the Romans?

According to historians, the time was not ready to accept such revolutionary changes. In spite of his will to bring fresh blood to mathematics, and especially to arithmetic, Gerbert was hindered by the heaviness of a reactionary society made up of professional calculators, who were afraid of losing their privileges because of the facilitation and democratization of the calculations.

The abacus

Gerbert knew that his revolution had to be smooth and subtle. He could not impose, but he could propose a new direction of thought and new calculation tools. He invented a new model of abacus for which he used the nine Indo-Arabic numerals inscribed on wood or horn, called *apices* (pronounced "apiceses"), which simplified the classic Roman abacus.

It is interesting to shed a little light on the word *abacus*, which is at the core of this history of numerals and mathematics. In its original form, the abacus was a tablet covered with sand or fine dust. The numerals were traced with a stylus and erased with the fingers when needed for calculations. This sand tablet was replaced by a board on which disks were placed, arranged in lines to note the numerals and allow calculating. This abacus was in use until the beginning of the seventeenth century, and persisted in certain regions until much later.

There is a third type of abacus in which lines were engraved, allowing for balls or disks to be rolled on it.

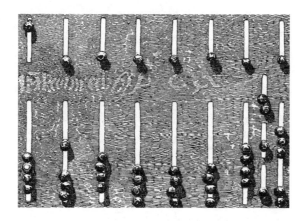

Ancient bronze abacus, today at the British Museum.
Reproduced by Smith, *op. cit.*, II, p. 167.

Concerning the etymology of the word, it is quite controversial. Several tracks have been proposed. In Latin, the term *abacus* comes from the Greek *abax*, itself probably derived from the Hebrew *avaq*, meaning "dust" (see, for example, Genesis, chapter 32, the episode of Jacob's fight with the angle). Smith (*op. cit.*, p. 156) reports other etymologies. *Abacus* could come from the Greek *abasis* (*a* + *basis*) meaning "without base" to designate a board without a foot. Another possibility is that the word derives from *a, b, ax*, meaning 1, 2, *ax*, i.e. "that which indicates the value of 1 and of 2," etc. In this case, the word *abacus* would be the equivalent for numerals what the word *alphabet* is for letters.

The *apices*
The Trojan horse of modern numerals

In the beginning of the Middle Ages, European calculators, heirs of the Roman technique, did their operations with a very complicated system of disks. They were installed on tables, which had divisions in lines and columns, distributing the various decimal powers. In the classic model of the Roman *abacus,* one placed on the columns as many small balls or disks with the value of a simple unit (*calculi*) as there were units in the order considered.

For example, if one wanted to write 4, one placed four disks in the unit column; or, if one wanted to signify the number 30, one placed three disks in the tens column, etc.

Gerbert of Aurillac had the revolutionary idea of reducing the size of the classic abacus by simplifying the number of disks used.

(See Smith, *op. cit.,* pp. 181–182; see also Menninger, *op. cit.,* pp. 322–323.)

Disk abacus, taken from Kobel's book, *Rechenbiechlin,* Augsburg, 1514. Reproduced by Smith, *op. cit.,* p. 182.

Gerbert of Aurillac eliminated the disks with simple unit values and replaced them with a single disk made of wood or horn, which was placed in each indicated column, marked with one of the nine Indo-Arabic numerals he had learned during his stay in Spain. Consequently, this abacus operated according to Indian position numeration, but without a disk for zero, which was marked like in the first Indian numeration, by an empty column.

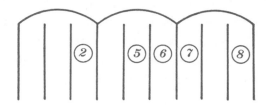

Representation of the number 2,056,708 in one of Gerbert's abaci.
This abacus is easy to recognize by the upper arcs above each column.
After Smith, *op. cit.*, p. 181.

The disks were named *apex* (in the singular) and *apices* in the plural. Each numeral was given an individual name, whose origin seems to be a mixture of Latin, Arabic, and Greek.

(Arab sounds: *arbas* for "four" and *temenias* for "eight"; Latin sounds: *quimas* for "five"; Greek sounds: *andras* for "two." See Menninger, *op. cit.*, p. 325. This author presents the existence of a zero that he calls *sipos*, derived from the Greek *psephos*, which means "small pebble or small stone." In general, other authors do not indicate a zero in *apices*. On this matter, see Smith, *op. cit.*, volume I, p. 75.)

121

Igin = 1
Andras = 2
Ormis = 3
Arbas = 4
Quimas = 5
Caltis = 6
Zenis = 7
Temenias = 8
Celentis = 9

The teaching dispensed by this totally revolutionary type of abacus allowed Gerbert of Aurillac and his students to spread the nine Indo-Arabic numerals and the new position numeration system. Gerbert's abacus was a true numerical Trojan horse that defeated the resistance of the calculators and their habits of old numeric practices.

Notes:

For a long time, the form of the numerals found on *apices* were named Boetius's *apices*, because their paternity was attributed to Anicius Mantius Severinus Boetius, a fifth century C.E. Latin mathematician. It was also claimed that they were the invention of the Pythagoreans, linked to the use of the column abacus by the ancient Greeks.

The influence of script styles

These numerals noted on *apices*, heirs of the Indo-Arabic *ghubar* numerals, took various forms according to the alphabetical script style of each region. Depending on calligraphy habits and aesthetic canons, this led to series of numerals with original graphic character. The process took place as it did in the Arab world, where scribes and copyists had adapted the same numerals to the styles of the Arabic script, as we showed in the chapter on Kufi scripts, *naskhi* and *maghribi*.

1	2	3	4
Igin	*Andras*	*Ormis*	*Arbas*

ℎ	L	v	8	6
4	L	⋀	8	9
5	6	⌄	𝛿	𝖚
4	L	⋀	8	9
𝑦	L	⋀	8	𝒥

5	6	7	8	9
Quimas	Calcus	Zenis	Temenias	Celentis

Apices. Notations according to various manuscripts.
We recognize a mixture of Indian and Arabic numerals;
all forms are already included, but not in the same series.
After *Les Mathématiciens*, Belin, 1996, p. 11.

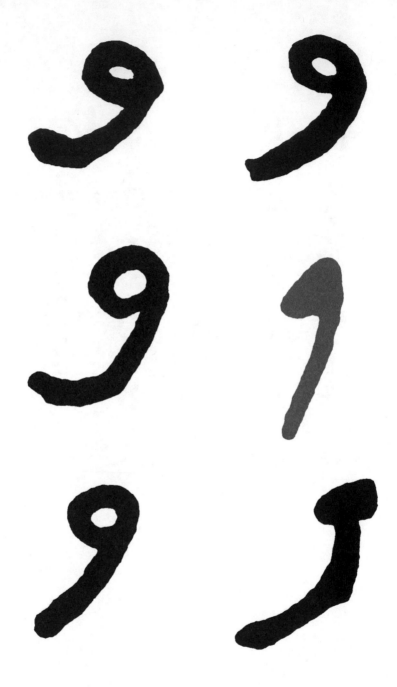

Variations of 9 in *ghubar* numerals. After Smith, *op. cit.*, p. 74.

2

The importance of the Crusades

Blessed be the same sun in other lands
that makes me a brother to all men,
since all men, for a moment
in the day, gaze at it like I do,
and in this pure moment,
full of serenity and tenderness,
they return with affliction
and with a barely audible sigh
to the true and primitive Man
who would watch the sun be born
and did not worship it yet,
because it was natural—more natural
than worshiping gold or God
and art and morality...
Fernando Pessoa

Three stages

We can consider that, historically, the introduction of the "Indo-Arabic" numerals in the European West took place in three successive stages.

The first, which we presented in the preceding chapters, is the partly successful revolution brought about by Gerbert and his numerical Trojan horse, which were his new abacus model and his notations on *apices*.

The second one coincides with a fundamental episode that some scholars consider the foundation of the history of humankind: the Crusades.

The third stage, which we will discuss later, is the phenomenon of the translations of Greek, Arabic, and Indian writings into Latin, and the work of Fibonacci.

Christ's tomb and the zero

In the two centuries that preceded the year 1000, in Spain, where the Arabic and the Western Christian cultures met and lived side by side, the Crusades provided an occasion for a second essential contact.

They facilitated an unexpected coming together, beyond war, that created a social and intellectual proximity between Christian and Arabic scholars, a cultural exchange (while certainly forced) through which Indo-Arabic numerals and position numeration (with its zero) were introduced to the Christian West.

It also seems that the Crusades marked a theological turning point of extraordinary importance, as we will explain now.

In the evolution of numerals in the Christian West, we saw a fierce opposition that historians (see Menninger and Smith) have chalked up to a strong conservatism and a will to preserve the privileges of a social class: the professional calculators. We also stress the fact that, according to certain historians (*ibid.*), Gerbert introduced only the first nine units, and not zero. We can add that the origin of the opposition to the new numeration and its Indo-Arabic numerals, based on "empty space," may have had more of a theological and philosophical nature than it seems at first glance.

Schematically, the time belonged to a Christian theology of plenitude, in which God "fills the heavens and the earth" and in which, like in the case of India, for example, there is no place for the concepts of void or nothingness.

Zero was a frightening notion. In those days, there was no way to think about the zero and accept it at the same time. The mentality was not yet ready. This gave rise to a phenomenon that few researchers saw and formulated: the epistemological importance of the Crusades concerning the issue of zero.

Tobias Dantzig offers a wonderful quote whose importance, in my opinion, has not been sufficiently measured (see T. Dantzig, *Number, The Language of Science*, MacMillan, 1930, 8th edition, 1966, pp. 83–84). He reports a thought of mathematician Carl Jacobi (1804–1851), who, in his *Treatise on*

Descartes, analyzes in a few quick traits the historic period known as the European Renaissance.

Jacobi wrote (after Dantzig, *op. cit.,* pp. 83–84):

> "History knew a midnight, which we may estimate at about the year 1000 A.D., when the human race had lost the arts and sciences even to the memory. The last twilight of paganism was gone, and yet the new day had not begun. Whatever was left of culture in the world was found only with the Saracens, and a Pope eager to learn studied in disguise at their universities, and so became the wonder of the West. At last Christendom, tired of praying to the dead bones of the martyrs, flocked to the tomb of the Saviour Himself, only to find for a second time that the grave was empty and that Christ had risen from the dead. Then mankind too rose from the dead. It returned to the activities and the business of life; there was a feverish revival in the arts and in the crafts. The cities flourished, a new citizenry was founded. Cimabue rediscovered the extinct art of painting; Dante, that of poetry. Then it was, also, that great courageous spirits like Abelard and Saint Thomas Aquinas dared to introduce into Catholicism the concepts of Aristotelean logic, and thus founded scholastic philosophy. But when the Church took the sciences under her wing, she demanded that the forms in which they moved be subjected to the same unconditioned faith in authority as were her own laws. And so it happened that scholasticism, far from freeing the human spirit, enchained it for many centuries to come, until the very possibility of free scientific research came to be doubted. At last, however, here too daylight broke, and mankind, reassured, determined to take advantage of its gifts and to create a knowledge of nature based on independent thought. The dawn of this day in history is known as the Renaissance or the Revival of Learning."

127

In this quote, we emphasize the formula "the grave was empty," articulated in a type of remarkable causal logic: "Then, mankind too rose from the dead."

Of course, because of theological texts, the faithful were used to the idea of an empty grave, but the fact of experiencing it, of making the lived history and the texts of the faith coincide, caused a revolutionary existential and theological shock. Apparently, "the empty grave" was the discovery of emptiness, the possibility of finally accepting the idea of emptiness.

Colantonio, *The Three Maries Around the Tomb and the Resurrection of Christ* (circa 1470), painting on wood (40.6 x 24.1 cm).

Emptiness existed, and this emptiness was no longer frightening, because it was articulated by the lived experience of the resurrection of Christ.
And if void was finally possible, thinkable, and acceptable, the idea of zero was too, and so was the position numeration associated with it.

After this event, Indo-Arabic numerals were accepted in the West, along with zero and the calculation methods of Indian origin. The new European calculators, who no longer worked with abaci but with pens, tracing the new numerals, also started to adopt zero to mark the missing units, thus avoiding any confusion in representations and operations. Indeed, as long as the abacus was the support for calculations, zero was not needed: The empty column indicated it by the absence of disks.

Modern numerals in the West before their definitive forms,
which emerged between the fourteenth and the sixteenth centuries. After Smith, *op. cit.*, p. 76.

The fight between the abacists and the algorists

After this period, there was a great and significant conflict between the partisans of calculation on abacus and those who had adopted the new numeration and its Indo-Arabic numerals.

The name *abacists* is given to calculators who used the first method, and the name *algorists* (by the name of Al-Khuwarizmi who used, developed, and transmitted these Indian numerals; see the chapter on this mathematician, p. 91) was given to those who used the second method.

This fight had a great impact on the cultural players of the time and appears in many iconographic representations.

The Fight Between Abacists and Algorists.
Representation of Arithmetic taken from *Margarita philosophica* (1503),
by Gregor Reisch.

Extract from a mathematical treatise from the sixteenth century. The manuscript is the work of a student of the monk Honoratus who taught in Venice. Reproduced by Peignot, *op. cit.*, p. 123.

3

Fibonacci
and the *Liber Abaci*

> *What is beauty, if not the image in which*
> *we can catch sight of the reflection of this*
> *extraordinary joy that courses through*
> *nature when a potential for life,*
> *new and fertile, has just been discovered?*
> Friedrich Nietzsche

We have presented three stages in the introduction of numerals in the European West, three strong moments that are: the work of Gerbert, the Crusades, and the translations, which we will discuss now. In this perspective, we must mention the work of Leonardo of Pisa, called Fibonacci. His work, consisting at the same time of translation, formulation, and pedagogical creation, is a decisive moment in the history of the transmission of Indo-Arabic numerals and Indian numeration.

It is also to Fibonacci that we owe the concept of zero. We will dedicate a paragraph to this subject as well.

The time of the translations
The creation of the universities (twelfth to thirteenth centuries)
The third stage in the introduction of numerals to the European West was the meeting with Arabic culture through translations.

A Lesson at the University (miniature from the fourteenth century, on parchment).
Universities were first created at the time of the introduction of the zero in the West:
the Sorbonne in 1200, Oxford in 1214, Padua in 1222,
Naples in 1224, Cambridge in 1231.

134

The first ingredient in this renaissance was the enthusiasm with which intellectuals all over Europe gathered, in order to translate into Latin, the texts of Greek antiquity translated into Arabic, and the original Arabic texts. Gerbert of Aurillac went to Muslim Spain, as we said earlier, and the philosopher Adelard of Bath converted to Islam out of his love of knowledge. It is to him that we owe the first translation of Euclid's *Elements*. He also translated the work of Al-Khuwarizmi.

Fibonacci

In the intellectual atmosphere of this European renaissance, Leonardo of Pisa, the son of Bonaccio, who was called Fibonacci, studied mathematics.

Leonardo, born around 1170, was the same age as Saint Dominick and some ten years older than Saint Francis of Assisi. We have information about the beginnings of his career in mathematics, from his uncertain beginnings to the achievement of his first work, *Liber Abaci*, in 1202.

This was at the time of the feats of Saladin and Richard the Lion Heart. In the wake of these valiant men, merchants from Pisa, Genoa, and Venice extended their area of influence to the ports of the Mediterranean and the Black Sea. (Concerning the biography and work of Fibonacci, we are following the information given by Ettore Picutti in "Leonardo of Pisa," in *Les Mathématiciens*, Belin, 1996, pp. 8 and following. See also Smith, *op. cit.*, volume I, pp. 214 and following.)

A great trade traveler

When Leonardo was a young boy, his father, who managed a customs office in Bougie, Algeria, on behalf of the order of the merchants of Pisa, called his son to him and enrolled him in the best courses on Indo-Arabic calculation methods. This is how Leonardo learned mathematics. During his many professional trips on behalf of merchants from Pisa, he met with mathematicians in Egypt, Syria, Provence, Greece, and Sicily. During "disputes," he took mathematical challenges, and studied Euclid's *Elements* in depth, since he had always considered this work a model of style and logical rigor.

This is how, during Leonardo's travels, while the ship he was on from Pisa swayed on the sea, *Liber Abaci* ("Treatise of the Abacus") was conceived, the first work gathering all medieval mathematical knowledge. The author's goal was to make all his knowledge in arithmetic and algebra available to the Latin reading world.

Liber Abaci was a new numerical Trojan horse because, in spite of its title, the work completely renewed arithmetic sciences, having nothing in common with Gerbert's school. It explained for the first time in Latin, and therefore for Western scholars, all the rules of calculation based on the nine Indo-Arabic numerals, the zero and position numeration.

A great teacher

For three centuries, until Pacioli, the teachers and students of the Tuscan school learned mathematics from the *Liber Abaci*; this book carefully keeps the balance between theory and practice. "I have rigorously demonstrated almost everything I have explained," Leonardo wrote.

It was not, and it still is not, an easy task. Leonardo of Pisa encouraged the reader to constantly do exercises. This striving for perfection made of Leonardo an exceptional mathematician, a master remembered with respect. Antonio de Mazzinghi commented in the fourteenth century: "Oh, Leonardo of Pisa, you were a great scientist, you who enlightened Italy on the practice of arithmetic."

The publication of Fibonacci's second book: the *Practica Geometriae*

"From 1202 to 1220, Leonardo of Pisa wrote nothing more. These twenty years are heavy in the history and culture of European civilization. After the fall of Constantinople in 1204, the excommunicated of the fourth Crusade founded the Eastern Roman Empire, and new manuals, this time Greek, reached Europe; other crusaders, who had gone to conquer the Albigens, devastated southern France and slaughtered its inhabitants, entrusting to God the souls of the non-heretics. In Paris, the reading of Aristotle's works was prohibited, under penalty of excommunication. The year 1212 brought the end of the dynasty of the Almohades in Spain; two years later, the British Crown lost its possessions in France, and King John, now landless, granted the Magna Carta to the noblemen. Saint Francis of Assisi was talking to the sun, the moon, and the stars, which had been included by the philosophers in Aristotle's cosmic model. The figure of Frederick of Suabia, future emperor of the West, with his court of local notaries and protonotaries and philosophers of all nationalities, was appearing on the horizon of Italian and European history" (*ibid.*).

The activity of the mathematician Leonardo of Pisa might have been limited to *Liber Abaci*, were it not for one of the philosophers at Frederick's court, Master Dominicus, who called him his friend. Dominicus behaved truly like a friend, since he incited Leonardo to write his second work, *Practica Geometriae* ("Practice of Geometry") and introduced him to the emperor a few years later. In 1220, the work was finished: It had 223 pages.

The book's contents are certainly less original and varied than that of *Liber Abaci*, but it represents a body of work of exceptional teaching value, even

for modern education. The author wanted to produce a perfect document, useful both for the lovers of *subtilitates* (subtleties) and for practitioners; this goal was achieved.

The *Practica Geometriae* was the Pisa mathematician's indirect homage to Frederick of Suabia who, at the end of the year 1220, was crowned emperor at the age of 26. Frederick II proved to be the most cultivated and the most organized of all German emperors. *Practica Geometriae* knew the same success as *Liber Abaci* and became a basic document for the teachers of the Tuscan school from Paolo dell'Abbaco to Master Benedetto and Luca Pacioli. While the *Practica Geometriae* reached maturity, a disaster befell the East and the Arab world. According to Ibn-al-Athir: "The days and the nights had never seen anything like it since the creation of the Earth." Genghis Khan invaded the sultanate of Kharezm (birthplace of the famous Al-Khuwarizmi) and Persia, and destroyed forever, in two years, centuries of culture.

A last publication: the *Liber Quadratorum* (the "Book of Squares")

Fibonacci published a third and final work: the *Liber Quadratorum* (1225). This last work shows that Leonardo was familiar with Diophantus's ideas, not for having read the work of the great Greek mathematician, which had been lost (it was not rediscovered until the Renaissance), but thanks to his knowledge of Arabic mathematicians, who had read and discussed Diophantus, and even exceeded him.

Fibonacci and the origin of the word *zero*

In his chapter on the zero, Menninger (*op. cit.,* pp. 400 and following; also p. 422, the chapter titled "The zero again") indicates the trajectory of this strange creature whose essential invention (modern form and functions) goes back to the Indians.

We have seen that the Indians called zero by the name of *shûnya*, *bindu*, or *chakra*, depending on its form (see the chapter on the zero, p. 73). By inheriting the zero at the same time as Indian numerals, the Arabs translated it using the Arabic word *sifr*, which means "void." When it reached the Christian West, *sifr* was transposed into Latin under different names:

cephirum, cifra, tzyphra, cyphra, sifra, cyfra, zyphra, zephirum, etc.

In English, explains Menninger, *cipher* meant "null" for a long time. Today, English uses the term *zero* (in German, there is the term *Ziffer*, which means a numeral and number).

Fibonacci introduced *zephirum* into Latin; the word became *zefiro* in Italian and then, by contraction, *zero*.

Menninger (*ibid.*, p. 425) reproduces this passage from the *Liber Abaci*, where Fibonacci speaks of the nine numerals in the following terms:

"The nine Indian numerals are: 9, 8, 7, 6, 5, 4, 3, 2, 1. This is why with these nine numerals, and with this sign 0, which is called "zephirum" [certain manuscripts write "cephirum"] in Arabic, we can write all the numbers we want."

Zephirum became *zefiro* in Italian, then *zefro* and *zevero*, which, shortened in Venetian dialect, gave us *zero* (just as *libra* became *livra*, then *lira*).

(See Dantzig, *op. cit.*, chapter II.)

139

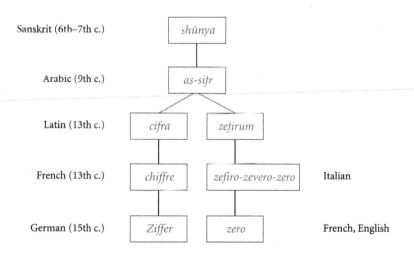

After Menninger, *op. cit.*, p. 401.

"The rabbit man"

So the man who brought zero to the West was Leonardo of Pisa. But Fibonacci will be remembered for posterity particularly because of a silly little problem he included in his book *Liber Abaci*.

Imagine that a farmer has two baby rabbits. The babies take two months to mature. They then produce another couple of rabbits at the beginning of each month. As these rabbits grow and reproduce, how many couples of rabbits will you get every month?

In the first month, you have a couple of rabbits, and since they are not mature, they cannot reproduce. The second month, you still have one couple. But at the beginning of the third month, the first couple reproduces, and you have two couples. At the beginning of the fourth month, the first couple reproduces, but the second is too young: three couples. The next month, the first couple reproduces, the second also, since they are of age, but not the third. This gives another two couples of rabbits, five in all. The number of couples of rabbits increases as follows: 1, 1, 2, 3, 5, 8, 13, 21, 34, 55...

The number of your rabbits in any given month is the sum of the rabbits you used to have in the two previous months.

Fibonacci's sequence and the golden number

Mathematicians understood right away the importance of this sequence. Take any number in this sequence and divide it by the number before it. For example, 8:5=1.6; 13:8=1.625; 21:13 =1.61538. These results are not far from an interesting number: the golden number, which is 1.61803. Further on in this book, we will return to the importance of this golden number. Although this sequence made Fibonacci famous, it was the introduction of zero that would prove the genius of his work, the nine Indo-Arabic numerals and the position numeration that makes him a fundamental figure in the history of mankind.

This is how the story of numerals ends. Or almost, because there is still one little stage left: the final stage of the evolution of numerals made official by the invention of the printing press.

4

Numerals and
the printing press

*A mathematician's sketch, like those of
the painter or the poet, has to be beautiful;
ideas, like colors or words, have to be
gathered together in a harmonious fashion.
Beauty is the first test: There is no lasting
place for ugly mathematics in the world.*

G.H. Hardy

Once numerals became popular in the European West, the printing press, and especially printers themselves and the graphic representations they were able to create, gave numerals their style; they lost the name of Indian figures or "Arabic" numerals and became modern numerals.
After *ghubar* numerals,

Extract from the oldest known Arabic manuscript (970) presenting all the numbers.
After Smith, *op. cit.*, p. 74.

and later the derivatives, namely *apices*,

Apices of the sixteenth century.
After G. F. Hill, *in Arch"ologia*, LXII (1910), reproduced by Smith, *op. cit.*, p. 76.

then with Fibonacci, modern numerals emerged, as in this beautiful English manuscript that presents for the first time these numerals in an English language text, dated circa 1300.

142

First page of the Egerton *Book of Numbers* (housed in the British Museum, London), one of the oldest English manuscripts dealing with mathematics. Reproduced by Smith, *op. cit.*, p. 79.

At the time of the quasi-official date of the invention of the printing press, 1492, the numerals had a more or less final form, as can be seen in the manuscript below.

SCYTHIE INTRA IMAVM MON TEM SITVS

CYTHIA intra Imaũ montem terminatur ab occaſu Sarmaria Aſiati ca ſcãm lineã expoſitã A ſeptentrione terra in cognita. Ab oriete Ima o monte ad arctos vergente ſcãm meridia nã ferme lineã q̃ a p̃dicto oppido vſq̃ ad terrã incognitam extenditur+ A meridie ac etiam oriente Satis quidẽ & Sugdianis & Margiana iuxta ipſorũ expoſitas lineas vſ q̃ oſtia oxe amnis in byrcanũ mare exeũtiſ ac etiã parte q̃ binc eſt vſq̃ ad Rba amnis oſtia q̃ gradus babet 87 $\frac{7}{2}$48 $\frac{7}{2}$ $\frac{2}{3}$. Ad oc caſum aũt vergitur in gradib? 8$_4$ 44 $\frac{2}{4}$

Rbymmi ſſ oſtia	91	48 $\frac{2}{4}$
Daicis ſſ oſtia	94	48 $\frac{2}{4}$
laxarti ſſ oſtia	97	48
lſtai ſſ oſtia	100	47 $\frac{3}{2}$
Polytimeti ſſ oſtia	103	44
Aſpabotis ciuitas	102	44

Manuscript of Leonard Holle, Ulm, 1482.
Reproduced by Peignot, *op. cit.*, p. 67.

Afterward, printers gave the numerals a form and beauty whose multiple styles to this day demonstrate the human creativity and intelligence awakened by these strange and fascinating creatures: numerals.

Gothic romantic numerals. After Peignot, *op. cit.*, p. 88.

Gothic romantic numerals. After Peignot, *op. cit.*, p. 88.

Numerals in roman Didot. After *Les Caractères de l'Imprimerie Nationale, op. cit.*, p. 103.

Numerals in italic Didot. After *Les Caractères de l'Imprimerie Nationale, op. cit.*, p. 102.

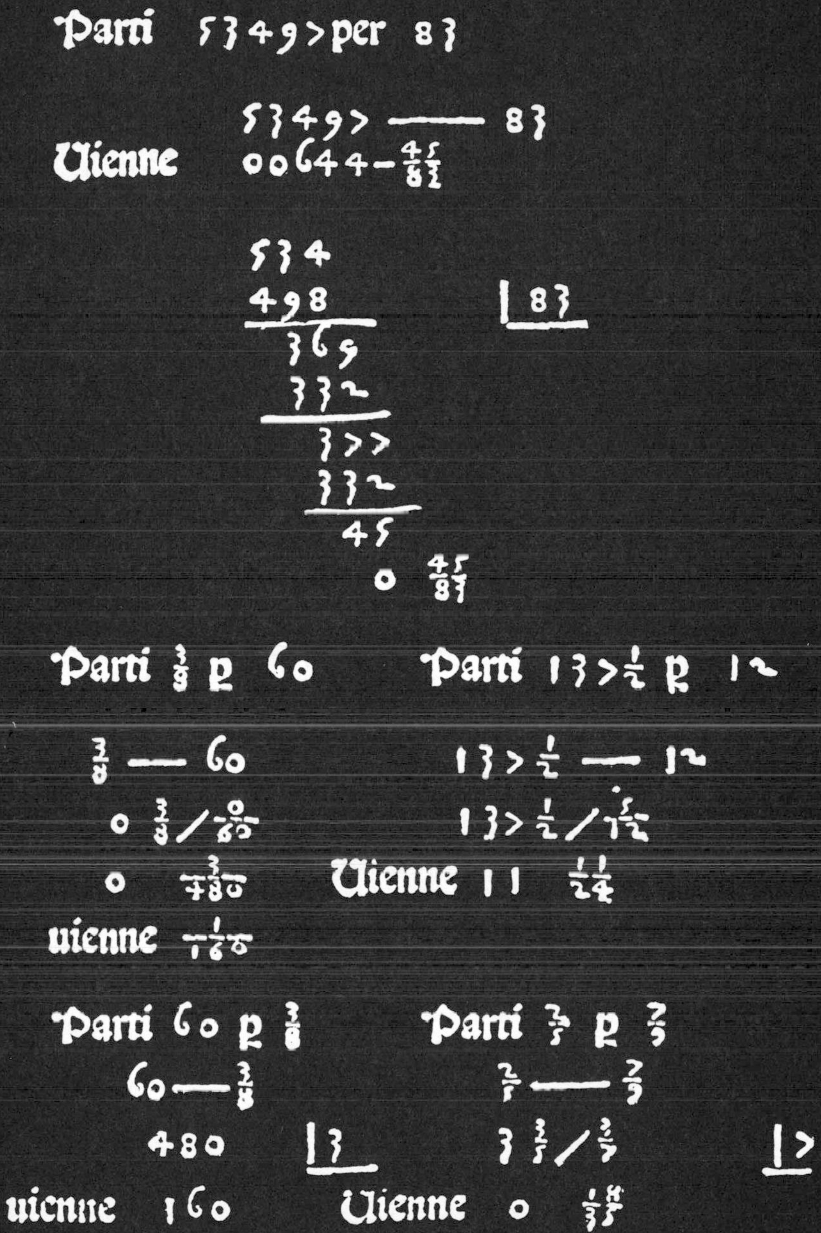

Parti 5349>per 83

Uienne
5349> ——— 83
00644-45/83

534
498 |83
365
332
3>>
332
45
    0 45/83

Parti 3/8 p 60   Parti 13>½ p 12

3/8 — 60   13>½ — 12
0 3/8 / 8/60   13>½ / 1/12
0   3/480   Uienne 11 11/24
uienne 1/160

Parti 60 p 3/8   Parti 3/7 p 2/7
60 — 3/8   3/7 — 2/7
   480 |13   3 3/7 / 3/7 |>
uienne 160   Uienne 0 18/77

53,497 divided by 83: first printed example of modern division
(in Calandri, *Arithmetica*, Florence 1491). Reproduced by Smith, *op. cit.*, p. 142.

Part Four

Kabbalah, isopsephia, and the name of Allah

Our ancestors, the…

Kabbalah, numerals, and letters

Isopsephia

1

Our ancestors, the…

As if the "true" and the "false"
were the only two
modes of intellectual existence!
Maurice Merleau-Ponty

Along with the history of modern numerals, whose great voyage we sketched in the previous chapters, there were and still are other ways to note the numbers, and therefore other numerals, to which we will briefly refer in this concluding chapter.

The Babylonians, the Egyptians, the Chinese, the Japanese, the Mayans, etc., had a rich and original numerical notation, as well as a great mathematical culture.

The magnitude and complexity of these ancient notations and numerations, some of which are still in use, do not allow us to discuss all their subtleties here. We present a few of them, as an example, with a somewhat longer paragraph on the Kabbalah, which is still a particularly intriguing subject for those who have a passion for numerals, letters, and numbers.

(If, in a single culture, there was an evolution of graphics and numeration, we will present only one stage. This chapter is more illustrative than demonstrative.)

The Babylonians

Tablet from Larsa. Archaic Babylonian cuneiform script.
The chevrons represent the tens, and the lines the units.
The first operation indicates: $40 \times 60 + 1 = 49^2$;
the second: $41 \times 60 + 40 = 50^2$;
After *Le Matin des Mathématiciens, op. cit.,* p. 11.

148

The Egyptians

| 1,000,000 | 100,000 | 10,000 | 1,000 | 100 | 10 | 1 |

Base numerals. After Peignot, *op. cit.,* p. 13.

The number 27,529 in archaic Egyptian. After Smith, *op. cit.,* p. 10.

The Mayans

1	hun	•		11	buluc	
2	ca	• •		12	lahca	
3	ox	• • •		13	ox lahun	
4	can	• • • •		14	can lahun	
5	ho	——		15	ho lahun	
6	uac	≟		16	uac lahun	
7	uuc	≟		17	uuc lahun	
8	uaxac	≟		18	uaxac lahun	
9	bolon	≣		19	bolon lahun	
10	lahun	══				

Numerals used in Mayan written numeration. After Guitel, *op. cit.*, p. 403.

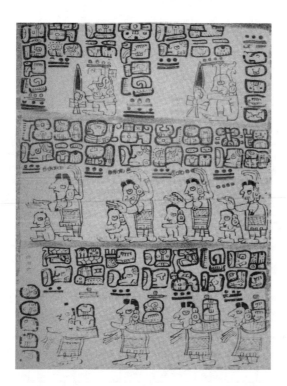

Mayan manuscript with numbers. After Peignot, *op. cit.*, p. 31.

The Chinese

Extracts from *Suanxue Keyi*, a collection of exercises on the mathematics course of Li Shanlan, published in the sixth year of the reign of Emperor Guangxu (1880). The algebraic notations use both European symbols (the "equal" sign elongated, fraction bar, parentheses, zero) and Chinese script characters. After *The Mathematicians, op. cit.*, p. 157.

1	2	3	4	5	6	7	8	9
10	20	30	40	50	60	70	80	90
100	200	300	400	500	600	700	800	900
1,000	2,000	3,000	4,000	5,000				

Numeration of the oldest Chinese coins.
After J. Needham, volume III, reproduced by Guitel, *op. cit.*, p. 483.

The Japanese

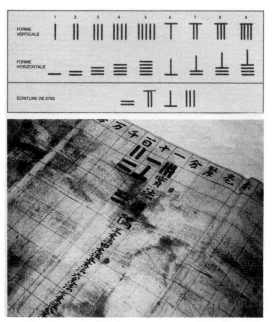

Representation of numbers with rods. In China, their use for calculation
would go back at least to the period of the fighting kingdoms (453–221 B.C.E.).
The numbers were represented according to a decimal and positional system,
and two types of rods (red and black) were used to distinguish between numbers
according to their sign. After *The Mathematicians, op. cit.*, p. 145.

Portrait of Seki Takakazu (?–1708), a dominant figure in the Japanese tradition of mathematics.
After *The Mathematicians, op. cit.*, p. 143.

The Romans

I	V	X	L	C	D	M
1	5	10	50	100	500	1,000

Inscription on a military stone from the Popilia road in Lucania (circa 130 B.C.E.).
Text of the inscription: "I have built the road from Regium to Cappua and all the bridges,
all the military stones and all the post relays. From here to Novceria there are 51 miles,
to Capua 84, to Muranum 74, to Consentia 123, to Valencia 180, to the statue
erected on the shore of the sea 231, to Regium 237, from Capua to Regium 321 miles.
As a praetor in Sicily, I chased the deserters and killed 917 men
After Menninger, *op. cit.*, p. 244.

2

The Kabbalah,
numerals, and letters

God certainly not incarnate,
but in some fashion inscribed,
living His life—or a part of His life—
in the letters: in the lines
and between the lines
and in the exchange of ideas
between readers who comment on them...
Emmanuel Lévinas

153

The word *Kabbalah* designates the mysteries of the mystical Jewish tradition. Both a theoretical and a practical philosophy close to meditation, Kabbalah is first of all a way toward spiritual elevation...
It is a tradition transmitted orally from master to disciple, then transcribed in works which are still difficult to access today, of which the book of Zohar is certainly the best known.

The word *Kabbalah*
The word *Kabbalah* comes from the Hebrew *qabbala*. It is derived from the verb *leqabbel* and the root *QBL*, which means "to receive or welcome." Thus, the word *Kabbalah* means "receipt."

To respect the Hebrew form, we should write *qabbala*. In fact, according to the authors, there are several spellings, including *qabbala*, *cabbala*, *cabala*, *kabbalah*, and *kabbala*. The tradition of the most classic transcription today is *Cabala* or *Kabbalah*.

If we start thinking about the Kabbalah with this note on transmission, it is to stress the essential link of the Kabbalah with mathematics. Indeed, at the forefront, mathematics is both "study" and "teaching," as a practice and a reflection on this event of transmission. It would not be false to say that the best translation of the word *qabbala* is "mathematics," which is more correct indeed than "mystical," for example, since the etymology of *mathematics* is a Greek verb meaning "to transmit, to learn, and to teach."

The Kabbalah: numerals and letters

As to the Kabbalah, the world was created with the letters of the alphabet. The letters are the center of any relationship in the world. Thus, to live is to know how to read, decipher, and interpret texts. The letters have a power and a role in the process of the liberation of the soul and the healing of the body. Thus, there are relationships between psychoanalysis and the Kabbalah, and between the Kabbalah and therapy in general.

The Hebrew alphabet has twenty-two consonants and a vocalization system with ten vowel signs. Only the consonants must be written, the addition of vowels being optional and serving to make reading easier. The text of the Torah is written on parchment, with ink, in hand, and it is never dotted, except in printed editions. This absence of vowels offers great flexibility in interpretation and combinations of the letters between them, giving the language movement, the paramount key to the dynamics of the living. (See our work *Mysteries of the Kabbalah,* Abbeville Press, 2001.)

But the Hebrew letters are also numerals. Consequently, the text proper is a coded document. Thus, the Kabbalah becomes "an art of making the numerals speak."

This relation between numerals and letters is gematria.

Alef	א	a	1
Bet or vet	ב	b	2
Gimel	ג	c	3
Dalet	ד	d	4
He	ה	e	5
Vav	ו	f, u, v, w	6
Zayin	ז	g, z	7
Het	ח	h	8
Tet	ט	t	9
Yod	י	i, j, y	10
Kaf	כ	k	20
Lamed	ל	l	30
Mem	מ	m	40
Nun	נ	n	50
Samek	ס	x	60
Ayin	ע	o	70
Pe or phe	פ	p	80
Tsade	צ	tse	90
Qof	ק	q	100
Resh	ר	r	200
Shin or sin	ש	s or ch	300
Tav	ת	t	400
Kaf final	ך	k	500
Mem final	ם	m	600
Nun final	ן	n	700
Fe final	ף	p	800
Tzade final	ץ	tse	900

Correspondence table of the Hebrew alphabet.

Literal or alphabetical numeration

The mathematical science of the biblical and Hebrew civilization is almost identical to that of its Egyptian and Babylonian neighbors at the time, from which it receives and with which it shares influences. We find, for example, the same geometric knowledge as attested by the knowledge of π, which, according to the biblical text, has the value 3.

Although it knows and uses base 10 and base 60, Hebrew numeration is different from the Egyptian and Babylonian ones; it is closer to that reproduced by the Greek, namely a literal numeration, in which the letters of the alphabet serve to note the numbers. In other words, the letters are also numerals.

The Hebrew alphabetical numbering has a decimal base. It consists of using the twenty-two letters of the Hebrew alphabet, plus the five final letters, associating them in this order:
– the first nine letters with the nine simple units, from 1 to 9,
– the next nine with the nine tens, from 10 to 90,
– the last four with the numbers 100, 200, 300, 400,
– the five final letters with the numbers 500, 600, 700, 800, 900.

Philosophy of the gematria

The *gematria* is not a game of numerals and letters, but a method to open, interpret, and give dynamics to thought.

It is a tool to interpret and open the texts, a way of opening oneself to something different: a pretext, a springboard, a passage. It is not enough to state equations and show equalities. The meaning is neither in the original nor in the resulting word, but in the dynamic movement between the two. It is a starting point for thought; it is not the thought.
We should note that the reader must pay less attention to the dimension of the numbers than to the words placed in relationship by numeral equivalences, whose matching is always of great philosophical importance. It is this matching that gives rise to the meaning.

Example:
The word *Adam*, "man," is written ADM (*alef, dalet, mem*) and has a gematria of $1 + 4 + 40 = 45$. The number 45 is written with the two letters *mem*
and *he*, is read *ma*, and means "*what?*" The philosophers and Kabbalists
develop, based on this play on numerals and letters, an entire thinking on
the "essence of man" question. The essence of man would be to not have
an essence, to have been programmed to be deprogrammed, and thus to
open himself to freedom.
(See our work *C'est pour cela que l'on aime les libellules*, Points Seuil, 2000.)

The passage from a "word-in-letters" to a "number-in-numerals" that then
returns to a word made up of letters, and so forth, takes us to a knowledge
that is no longer a totaling, but a process of opening and dynamics.
Gematria is not a translation but a proposition, an invitation to a foreign
road. It allows us to go "beyond the verse," according to Emmanuel
Levinas's beautiful expression.

Note:
There is a little gematria that uses the same numerical values as classic
gematria but takes into account only the units.
Thus, 10 and 100 become 1, 20 and 200 are 2, and 30 and 300 are 3, etc.
In the example of Adam (ADM), the little gematria is $1 + 4 + 4 = 9$. In the
end, it comes to the same, because $1 + 4 + 40 = 45$ becomes $4 + 5 = 9$.

Zero parallel

In gematria, by the passage from word to number, numerical equivalences
constitute a jolt of de-meaning. Through this process, the reader escapes
the heaviness of an existing meaning that risks being simply the spoken
word and no longer a speaking word.
In this jolt of de-meaning, the reader does not discover a new meaning
right away, but finds himself at the heart of a suspension of the meaning,
at a zero degree of meaning, a form of essential silence of the spirit that
then opens to a privileged form of mediation, to a "zero degree of meaning," a pre-semantic or post-semantic moment by which he can and
should wander outside the meaning.

Then man reaches the "zero parallel," as was beautifully put by Maurice Blanchot: "An imaginary line, a geographic point null but representing—precisely by its nullity—this zero degree toward which one would say that man strives, by the need to achieve an ideal landmark from which, free from himself, from his prejudices, his myths, and his gods, he would be able to go back to himself with a changed approach and a new affirmation."

וַיַּעַשׂ אֶת־הַיָּם מוּצָק עֶשֶׂר
בָּאַמָּה מִשְּׂפָתוֹ עַד־שְׂפָתוֹ עָגֹל ׀ סָבִיב וְחָמֵשׁ בָּאַמָּה
קוֹמָתוֹ וְקָוֶה שְׁלֹשִׁים בָּאַמָּה יָסֹב אֹתוֹ סָבִיב׃

The bronze basin of Solomon's temple. Its dimensions give pi a value of approximately 3. The Hebrew inscription is taken from the First Book of Kings (7:23).

3

Isopsephia

With 32 marvelous ways of wisdom
God outlined and created the world
through the three senses of the root SFR:
The written book, the number and the story.
32 marvelous ways of wisdom:
The ten Sefirot and the
22 letters of the alphabet
32 marvelous ways, the 22 letters
of the alphabet and the 10 vowels.
Sefer Yetsira

159

The Greeks knew of and used a process identical to gematria. This process is named *isopsephia*: from *iso*, meaning "same," and *psephos*, "account." The isopsephia process consists of using, as in the Hebrew gematria, the numerical value of the letters of a word or a group of letters, and transposing this number to bring it close to another word, according to the numerical value obtained. (On this issue, see G. Guitel, *Histoire comparée des numérations écrites*, Flammarion, 1975, pp. 239 and following.)

A	1	H	7	N	13	Τ	19
B	2	Θ	8	Ξ	14	Υ	20
Γ	3	I	9	O	15	Φ	21
Δ	4	K	10	Π	16	X	22
E	5	Λ	11	P	17	Ψ	23
Z	6	M	12	Σ	18	Ω	24

Ancient Greek numeration. After Guitel, *op. cit.*, p. 241.

1	α		alpha
2	β		beta
3	γ		gamma
4	δ		delta
5	ε		epsilon
6	ϛ		[digamma]
7	ζ		zeta
8	η		eta
9	θ		theta
10	ι		iota
20	κ		kappa
30	λ		lambda
40	μ		mu
50	ν		nu
60	ξ		xi
70	ο		o micron
80	π		pi
900	ϡ		[sade]
90	ϙ		[koppa]
100	ρ		rho
200	σ		sigma
300	τ		tau
400	υ		upsilon
500	φ		phi
600	χ		khi
700	ψ		psi
800	ω	———	oméga

Classic Greek alphabet.
After Guitel, *op. cit.*, p. 243.

1	ا	'	'alif
2	ب	b	ba
3	ج	ğ	gim
4	د	d	dal
5	ه	h	ha
6	و	w	waw
7	ز	z	za
8	ح	ḥ	ha
9	ط	ṭ	ta'
10	ي	y	ya'
20	ك	k	kaf
30	ل	l	lam
40	م	m	mim
50	ن	n	nun
60	س	s	sin
70	ع	ʿ	'ayn
80	ف	f	fa'
90	ص	ṣ	sad
100	ق	q	qaf
200	ر	r	ra'
300	ش	š	sin
400	ت	t	sin
500	ث	t̲	ta'
600	خ	ḥ	ha'
700	ذ	d̲	dal
800	ض	ḍ	dad
900	ظ	ẓ	za'
1,000	غ	ġ	gayn

Arabic alphabet.
After Guitel, *op. cit.*, p. 277.

160

Name of Allah, in calligraphy (numerical value: 66).

Book Two

2

Numbers

The Great Family

Part One

Crazy about numbers and crazy numbers

Memoirs of a mathematician

Numbers and number theory

164 Pythagoras and the harmony of numbers

1

Memoirs of a mathematician

Don't linger at the edge of results.
René Char

"I was barely 5 when, looking at the tables of multiples of integers shown on the covers of my schoolboy's copybooks, I noticed that the population of numbers had a certain regularity. The revelation started with the number 5. All its multiples ended alternatively in either 5 or 0. The story was more complicated with 2: Its multiples all ended in even numbers. [...]

5 7 2 3

Later, in high school in Melun, the meeting of the intersection points of the heights, medians, bisectors, and mid-perpendiculars of the triangle taught me how mathematics extended from arithmetic to geometry. For months and years, I paid attention only to integers, playing with them in thousands of combinations. I tried, for example, to raise each number to a power in which the exponent was equal to itself, and so forth.

Other numbers came to join the integers of my childhood, prime numbers and, for example, those you find in mathematical games.

Rational numbers, which at the time I called fractions, came to join integers, but I wasn't interested.

I found more pleasure in irrational numbers, such as √2 or π. But in high school they did not teach me the difference between algebraic numbers and transcendent numbers.

$$\sum_{i=0}^{\infty} \frac{1}{16^i(8i+k)} = \sqrt{2}^k \sum_{i=0}^{\infty} \left[\frac{x^{k+8i}}{8i+k}\right]_0^{1/\sqrt{2}}$$

$$= \sqrt{2}^k \sum_{i=0}^{\infty} \int_0^{1/\sqrt{2}} x^{k-1+8i}\, dx$$

$$= \sqrt{2}^k \int_0^{1/\sqrt{2}} \frac{x^{k-1}}{1-x^8}\, dx$$

Beginning of the demonstration of Simon Plouffe's formula concerning the decimals of π.

I started to write down in a notebook all the numbers I found that seemed worthy of attention. The list grew longer and more refined after I graduated from the university. Soon it had more than a hundred elements. Before World War II, my collection had taken the form of a file in which, for certain numbers, the same card held several different properties.

$$\sqrt{2}$$

Soon I discovered that the great majority of my interesting numbers consisted of integers that could be placed in order. Several of the non-whole 'real' numbers, almost all of them algebraic or transcendent numbers, could be added in the correct order.
In April 1944, there was no way to take my file to the Fresne prison or to the Dora deportation camp, where I was transferred. But my memory was intact, and my beloved numbers visited me every day, together with other solace-bringing friends, such as music, poetry, history, and sciences.
When I came back in May of 1945, my file had vanished. I made up a new one, changing my terminology, and I baptized the pieces of my herbarium *Remarkable Numbers*. This made me redefine my subjective criteria of 'remarkability.' I gave this character to numbers that had made a difference in the history of mathematical thought."

The memories of the great French mathematician Francois Le Lionnais offer us this beautiful expression, "remarkable numbers," which we will use in our personal herbarium. We will also give this feature of "remarkability" to certain numbers, obviously not all of them, that made a difference in the history of mathematical thought, but especially to those that counted, and still count, in our own encounter with the universe of mathematics, philosophy, and the Kabbalah.

We will also give a few details about the classic numbers whose exact definition we sometimes forget because we see them too often.

Since Pythagoras was one of the greatest pioneers of the theory of numbers, we will dedicate a special chapter to him, and will talk about his biography and his passion for this world in which "everything is a number."

Canon by Johann Sebastian Bach (1685–1750),
whose compositions often use special links between numbers.

2

Numbers
and number theory

We find pebbles and trees,
but three pebbles and two trees? Never.
To see them, an operation
would be necessary.
Jean-Toussaint Desanti

169

The etymology of the word *number*

The word *number* comes from the Latin *numerus*. In Greek, *number* is *arithmos*, which gave rise to the word *arithmetike*, then in Latin *arithmetica* and in English *arithmetic*, meaning the science of numbers.

Arithmos also refers to "measure," "rhythm," "crowd," and "quantity." In this word, the prefix *a-* is not depriving. Although this term is phonetically close to *rhythm*, the roots are different, even though bridges were established between the two terms over time, especially through the word *rhyme*, which we find in poetry.

The difficulty of defining a number

It is hard to define what a number is. This difficulty is ancient; all mathematicians have struggled with it, and so far nobody can say exactly what the nature of the number is.

Several conceptions of "number" have been proposed: religious, magical, physical, metaphysical, logical, formalist, relational conceptions.

Georg Cantor and his wife in 1880. Cantor (1845–1918) is both the father of relational theory and the creator of transfinite numbers.

In the beginning, numbers were used in a very concrete way to count groups of objects, animals, and people. At the dawn of humankind, the number first had the status of *number of*. Only later did the *number of* become *number*, with the birth of the idea of abstraction.

The theory of numbers

As far back as we can go in time, we find two types of arithmetic. The first is pragmatic, utilitarian, and is one with the art of calculating, of counting: managing the assets of individuals and societies, assuring their subsistence, enabling exchanges, evaluating work, etc., hence the establishment of systems of weights and measures, tariffs for merchandise, codification of exchanges. It is a quantitative mathematics, that of trade and assets management.

The other arithmetic no longer has to do with things, objects one owns. It is no longer management arithmetic, but an activity of the spirit, a scholarly activity, speculative, at first pervaded by the religious spirit, later and today purely abstract. Some of its problems stemmed from music and astronomy, but most of them came from the pure pleasure of seeking relations between numbers. It is no longer just a tool, a technique of numbers, but a true game, a true science of numbers, which today we call the "theory of numbers."

Note:
When speaking about this technique of numbers and science or the theory of numbers, the Greeks gave it two different names: *logistic* for the former and *arithmetic* for the latter. (This distinction is attributed to Plato in the fourth century B.C.E.)

The Babylonians had two different numeration systems for the two types of arithmetic, with base 10 for the first and 60 for the second. We can briefly summarize the types of problems that arose from the elemental study of the theory of numbers by dividing them into two categories:

171

– those that consider each number as an individual, examine its form and properties, and then try to classify it;

–those that try to establish relations between two, three, or several numbers.

The theory of numbers has the peculiarity that, for almost twenty centuries, it created a reservoir of exciting subjects for mathematicians, with the feature, found in many problems, that a statement formulated in a very simple way has as its counterpart a problem that is extremely difficult to solve.

Sumerian property tablet: count of goats and sheep.
Baked clay, length: 7.8 cm; width 7.8 cm; thickness: 2.4 cm. Tello (Mesopotamia),
time of the archaic dynasties: year 5 of Urukagina, king of Lagash (2351–2342 B.C.E.).

The anecdote of the taxicab

A well-known anecdote shows how, for Srinivasa Ramanujan (1887–1920), a company of numbers was similar to the company of people—he *knew* them, with their qualities and their defects. The mathematician G.H. Hardy reports: "I remember that once I went to see him, when he was living in Putney. I took a taxicab with the license plate 1729 and I noticed that somehow this number seemed malicious, and I hoped it was not a bad omen.

– 'No, he answered, it is a very interesting number: It is the smallest number that can be decomposed in two different manners into the sum of two cubes.'

Naturally, I asked him whether he knew the answer to the problem for the fourth powers. He answered, after thinking a little, that he could not find an example, and he thought that the first number in this category had to be very big."

Indeed, 1,729 is the smallest integer decomposable into the sum of two cubes, in two ways:

$$1{,}729 = 12^3 + 1^3$$
$$= 10^3 + 9^3$$

Portrait of Srinivasa Ramanujan, born in India in 1887. He succeeded in reconstructing, almost by himself, the edifice of the theory of numbers, and proposed original formulas and theorems.

174

As to the smallest number decomposable in two ways into the sum of two fourth powers, it is 635,318,657, and it was discovered by Leonhard Euler:

$$635,318,657$$
$$= 158^4 + 59^4$$
$$= 133^4 + 134^4$$

3

Pythagoras and the harmony of numbers

The new claim in the field of knowledge is a mathematical one. The following phrase, often quoted but still little understood, comes from Kant:
"I affirm that in each particular theory of nature, science as such is found only insofar as Mathematics is present."
Martin Heidegger

175

Understanding the secrets of the universe

Giving a numerical basis to the knowledge of nature was the project of the Pythagoreans. Pythagoras and the Pythagoreans were seeking the order and harmony that unite all things. To find them, they needed to study the numbers themselves. This was the foundation of arithmetic, the science of numbers, which they insisted on distinguishing from logistics, the art of pure calculation. By this separation, they raised arithmetic above the needs of merchants.

Thus, it is to Pythagoras and his pupils that we owe the foundations of the theory of numbers, the first attempts to establish a classification and a relation between mathematical creatures.

Fantasy portrait of Pythagoras.

Pythagoras, the Pythagoreans, and harmony

Although Pythagoras lived in the sixth century B.C.E., the Pythagorean school blossomed in the fifth century B.C.E. with his disciples, who were Philolaus of Croton, the Eleatic School (from Elea, a town in southern Italy), Parmenides and Zenon, Democritus the atomist, Hippasus of Metapontum, Hippocrates of Chios, and the Sophist Hippias of Elis, a geometer.

Pythagoras the traveler

Pythagoras of Samos was the student of Thales for a few years. He acquired his mathematical knowledge during his voyages. It is believed that he went as far as India and Brittany, but it is more likely that he gathered several of his mathematical techniques and tools from the Egyptians and the Babylonians.

The latter had exceeded the limits of elementary arithmetic and were able to do complex operations that had enabled them to elaborate advanced accounting systems and erect outstanding architectural constructions.

177

Reconstruction of the ziggurat in Babylon called *Etemenanki,*
"Temple of the creation of Heaven and Earth," the famous biblical "Tower of Babel."

Of course, the Babylonians and the Egyptians considered mathematics to be a simple instrument, useful to solve practical problems; thus, while seeking certain elementary rules of geometry, their goal was to reestablish the boundaries of the fields covered during the annual swell of the Nile.

The first disciple

After twenty years of traveling, Pythagoras had assimilated all the mathematical rules of the known world. He then started out for his native island of Samos, in the Aegean Sea, with the intention of founding a school dedicated to philosophy, and especially to the mathematical rules he had discovered. He hoped to find many recruits with an open spirit, who would help him develop radical new philosophies. But, in his absence, the tyrant Polycrates had changed the island: Formerly liberal, it had become intolerant and conservative. Polycrates invited Pythagoras to his court, but the philosopher understood that this was a maneuver to keep him silent and declined the honor. He left the city and went to live in an isolated cave, where he could meditate without being bothered.

178

Feeling lonely, in the end Pythagoras offered money to a boy to become his student. This student's name was also Pythagoras. Pythagoras the master paid Pythagoras the pupil three obols for each lesson. After a few weeks, he realized that the boy's initial reluctance to learning had turned into enthusiasm. To measure his success, Pythagoras pretended that he could no longer pay the student and that the lessons had to end; the boy offered to pay for his education rather than cutting it short. The student had become a disciple.

The Pythagorean school had been born. It lasted almost 150 years and had hundreds of disciples.

The flight to Italy

Because of his teaching, which was considered inadmissible due to social reforms, Pythagoras was forced to flee the island, together with his mother and his only disciple. He sailed to southern Italy, which was then part of Magna Graecia, or Great Greece, and settled in Croton. There, he was lucky

Emmanuel Levinas (1904–1996).
A student of Edmund Husserl (1859–1938) and Martin Heidegger (1889–1976), he was one of the
most outstanding philosophers of the twentieth century. He invited us to think about philosophy
not only as the "love of wisdom" but also as "the wisdom of love."

enough to find the ideal protector—Milo, the richest man in the city and one of the strongest men in history.

Milo, the supporter of the arts, and the creation of the Pythagorean Brotherhood

Pythagoras's fame as "the wise man of Samos" was already spreading in Greece, but Milo's reputation was even greater. This Herculean character had been crowned twelve times at the Olympic and Pythic games, which was a record. But besides being an athlete, Milo cultivated and studied philosophy and mathematics. He arranged his house so as to offer Pythagoras enough room to have a school there. This is how the most creative spirit and the most powerful body got together.

In the safety of his new abode, Pythagoras founded the Pythagorean Brotherhood, a group of 600 disciples who not only were capable of understanding his teachings but also of enriching them with new ideas and proofs.

The word *philosophy*

Soon after founding the Brotherhood, Pythagoras invented the word *philosophy* and thus expressed the purpose of his school: Philosophy seeks to discover the secrets of nature.

Today, the word *philosophy* has two meanings. The Greek word is made up of the root *philein*, "to love," and *sophia*, which means "wisdom." In general, the word *philosophy* is translated by the expression "love of wisdom," but we can reverse the terms and propose, with Levinas, the translation "wisdom of love."

How could one become a disciple?

It was not easy to be accepted as a disciple. Pythagoras started by noticing whether the candidate was able to "hold his tongue," as he said. Could he not speak and keep for himself what he had heard during the lessons? In the first stage, the disciple's silence interested him more than his words.

The classroom was divided in two by a curtain. Pythagoras was on one side, the candidates on the other; they did not have access to teaching other than by hearing it. They heard him but did not see him. The test lasted for five years. The curtain was extremely important in the life of the Pythagorean school: Crossing it meant that one passed the tests successfully. The members of the school were divided into two categories depending on which side of the curtain they were on. Outside the space where Pythagoras sat were the exoterics. Inside, and for the rest of their lives, were the esoterics. Only they could see Pythagoras.

Plato and his Disciples,
engraving by O. Knille, nineteenth century.

The transmission of secrets

In this vein, the texts of the Pythagoreans were also kept secret. Written in a language with double meaning, they played on two levels of interpretation: One level could be understood by everybody; the other was reserved for only the inner circle. The Pythagoreans spoke of symbols and enigmas. Most of the knowledge was transmitted from person to person. This type of transmission gave rise to a second way of classifying the disciples. There were the acusmatics, who were told the results, but not given the demonstrations, and the mathematicians, who were told the results and given the demonstrations.

Thus, the *acusmata* were words transmitted only orally, for which no written trace existed.

Consequently, all the members of the school had to use their memory. In the morning, a Pythagorean never got up without reviewing in his mind the events he had lived the previous day. He tried to remember precisely what he had seen, what he had said, the people he had met.

The ear, music, and harmony

It seems that the way Pythagoras taught was not a simple obstacle course for the disciples, but the consequence of fundamental thoughts on teaching and the meanings used in this primordial relationship between master and disciple—this relation that is the very essence of mathematics.

The fact of never seeing the master establishes a relationship through the ears that replaces the sense of sight. This situation makes the disciple more attentive to the words that are said and to all musical sounds. It educates and refines his ear, preparing him for harmony. It is noteworthy that in Hebrew, ear, *ozen*, also means "balance" (we know today that, from an anatomical viewpoint, the inner ear is the organ of balance). In fact, we understand why the various legends about Pythagoras always return to the same anecdote concerning the discovery of the scale—in other words, a certain harmony in music.

A place for women

On joining the Brotherhood, every disciple had to donate all his possessions to a common fund. If a disciple left the group, he received double what he had brought when he arrived, and a stela was erected in his memory. The Brotherhood was an egalitarian institution and included numerous sisters. Pythagoras's favorite student was Milo's own daughter, the beautiful Theano. In spite of their age difference, in the end they were married.

The dangers of initiation

Hatred and vengeance

There were many candidates for initiation into the brotherhood, but only the most brilliant students were accepted. One of those rejected was named Cylon. He felt insulted and would take revenge for his humiliation twenty years later In the meantime, during the sixty-seventh Olympic Games, in

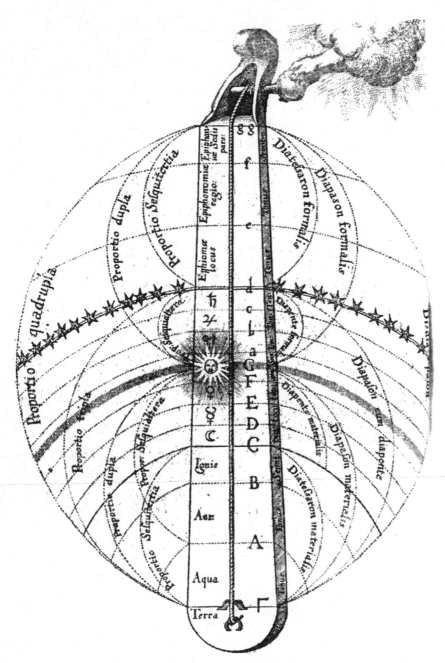

Mystical monochord: the harmony of the monochord of philosophy
and the harmony of the universe.

510 B.C.E., a mutiny broke out in the neighboring city of Sybaris. Telys, the leader and hero of the mutiny, savagely persecuted the partisans of the previous government and forced many of them to take refuge in Croton. Telys demanded that the traitors be expelled to Sybaris to face their punishment, but Milo and Pythagoras convinced the citizens of Croton to resist the tyrant and protect the refugees. Furious, Telys gathered an army of 300,000 men and marched on Croton, which Milo decided to defend with 100,000 armed citizens. After seventy days of war, general Milo won and, in vengeance, flooded Sybaris by diverting the course of the river Crathis.

The death of Pythagoras

The war had ended, but Croton was divided regarding the distribution of the loot. Fearing that the lands would be given to the Pythagorean elite, the people of Croton grew defiant. The masses already felt increasing resentment against the Brotherhood, which stubbornly kept its discoveries secret, but things got worse when Cylon emerged as the voice of the people. Kindling the fear and envy of the crowds, he led the throngs to the assault of the most brilliant school of mathematics the world had ever seen. Milo's house and the contiguous school were surrounded, the exits were blocked so that no one could flee, and the buildings were set on fire. Milo was able to escape from the fire, but Pythagoras and many of his disciples died.

Milo of Croton (540–516 B.C.E.).
Sepia ink drawing by Salvatore Rosa (1615–1673).

Part Two

The classics

The wisdom of the irrational

Yearning for infinity

Odd and even

Prime numbers

1

The wisdom of the irrational
Whole, rational, irrational, and transcendent

Big people love numbers.
When you tell them about a new friend
they never ask you the essential things.
They never say:
"What is the tone of his voice?
What games does he like?
Does he collect butterflies?"
They ask you:
"How old is he?
Does he have any brothers?
How much does he weigh?
How much does his father make?"
Only then do they think they know him.
Antoine de Saint-Exupéry

Before embarking on the exploration of certain remarkable numbers, perhaps we should briefly meet a few important members of the great family of numbers. This meeting will familiarize us with or make us remember the main types of numbers used in mathematics.

Decimals, a classification criterion
The various classes of numbers are divided, first of all, by whether or not a number has decimals, and then, if they do, based on the properties of these decimals.

Numbers without points
1. Natural whole numbers
The simplest numbers are the whole numbers. For example:

$$1 \qquad 2$$

$$25 \qquad\qquad 4589$$

$$\text{or}$$

$$45376859094632$$

The simplest numbers have two characteristics:
– They have no decimal, meaning that they have no numeral after the point, and therefore no point. This is why they are called whole numbers.
– They have no sign. They are called natural whole numbers. The adjective *natural* indicates that they can represent quantities of objects in nature— for example, apples or sheep. When one counts sheep, one does it with natural whole numbers.
All these numbers have the property that they are unchanged by addition or multiplication. Indeed, if we add or multiply two natural whole numbers, we always get a natural whole number. Although they are very simple, natural whole numbers play a fundamental role in mathematics. They are the foundation on which the other numbers are built.

2. Relative whole numbers

These are whole numbers that have a sign, for example:

$$-253 \quad -48 \quad +39 \quad +15$$

When we consider the numbers that have a sign, we need to take into consideration 0, which has no sign and separates the positive numbers from the negative numbers. The sign is an important quality, because it specifies the position of the numbers relative to 0. Negative means smaller than 0, positive means bigger. Hence, the adjective *relative* is used to qualify these numbers.

Since natural whole numbers are numbers without sign, they cannot be positive. But, by convention, a whole number written without sign can be interpreted as a natural whole number or a relative positive whole number, depending on the context. Inversely, to write a relative negative whole number, we have to write the sign "−"; otherwise, the number in question could be confused with a positive whole number.

Identified thus, the set of natural whole numbers is contained in that of the relative whole numbers.

Numbers with a decimal point

There is a huge diversity of these numbers. Indeed, a number with a point can have any finite or infinite quantity of decimals.

Examples with a finite number of decimals:

2.9673
042058
337456
236214
495

Examples with an infinite number of decimals:

$$1/3 = 0.3$$
$$3333333$$
$$3333333$$
$$333333...$$

The dots indicate that the decimal 3 is repeated infinitely.

There are three categories of numbers with a decimal point:

1. Rational numbers

If we take a natural whole number and divide it by another natural whole number, the result will have either a finite number of decimals, or decimals in an infinite quantity.

The latter, in turn, are divided into two categories. In the first, the decimals are repeated periodically after a certain numeral, after the point (these are the rational numbers); and in the second, the decimals are not repeated periodically, and therefore are unforeseeable before the calculation. Examples with a finite number of decimals:

$$2/1 = 2$$
$$3/2 = 1.5$$
$$5/16 = 0.3125$$
$$173/64 = 2.703125$$

These four numbers have a definite quantity of decimals:

$$0, 1, 4, \text{ and } 6$$

Examples with an infinite periodical number of decimals (in these examples, the periodic group starts right after the point):

$$1/11 =$$
$$0.0909090909...$$

$$55/111 =$$
$$0.495495495495...$$

Example of any decimals, here 39, before the appearance of the periodic group, here 285714.

$$11/28 =$$
$$0.39$$
$$285714$$
$$285714$$
$$285714...$$

Notes:

We can state this property in a more concise manner. Indeed, the numbers with a finite quantity of decimals can be considered to have an infinite number of decimals when we add 0 to the infinite.

For example:

$$3.478 =$$
$$3.478000000000000000$$
$$0000000000\ldots$$

If we take this note into consideration, the preceding property is stated more concisely:

The decimals of the division of one natural whole number by another are periodic starting from a certain rank.

The division of relative whole numbers is like that of natural whole numbers. The only difference is that the result is a number with a sign. This sign depends on the sign of the whole numbers involved in the division. Since the periodicity of the decimals is independent of the sign, it is also valid for the result of the division of one relative whole number by another.

Definition

The numbers with periodic decimals after a certain rank are called rational numbers. The group of numerals (142857) returns periodically, which enables us to foresee the sequence of the decimals. It is this possibility of foreseeing a periodic development that makes these numbers rational.

$$1/7 =$$
$$0.142857$$
$$142857$$
$$\ldots$$
$$142857, \text{etc.}$$

Rather than trying to note the decimal writing of a rational number, even if it has a remarkable property, for convenience purposes we note these numbers by fractions. In the preceding example:

$$1/7$$

In the same way in which we absorbed the natural whole numbers into the relative whole numbers by making the positive whole numbers identical to the natural whole numbers, we can include the relative whole numbers in the rational ones. To do so, we make the relative whole number p identical to the rational p/l. For example:

$$3 = 3/1$$
$$\text{or}$$
$$-4 = -4/1$$

By their definition, and as their fractional notation suggests, rationals are well suited for division.

The division of two rationals (if the number by which we divide is not 0) is always a rational number.

The sum, difference, or product of rational numbers is always a rational number. Consequently, all rationals are unchanged in the four operations. However, we cannot divide a natural whole number by just any other natural whole number. I have 25 cows and 3 children, I want to give the same number of cows (alive!) to each child. It is not possible.

The reverse concerning the property of the decimals obtained by division is true.

If the decimal writing of a number is finite, or periodical, starting from a certain rank, then the number is rational.

In other words, rational numbers are the only numbers that have a periodical decimal writing. So, the periodicity characterizes the rationals.

A number is rational
if and only if its decimal development
(or in any base)
is periodical starting from a certain numeral.

$$135/11$$
$$=$$
$$12.\ 27\ 27$$
$$27\ 27\ 27$$
$$27\ 27\ 27$$
$$27\ 27\ 27$$
$$27\ 27\ 27$$
$$27$$

2. Irrational numbers

They can be constructed geometrically (example: $\sqrt{2}$ diagonal of a square of side 1) but cannot be expressed by a fractional value, no matter how complicated. In addition, unlike with rational numbers, no law allows for defining the periodic return of the numerals or group of numerals, even if certain periodicities exist.

The most famous irrational number is $\sqrt{2}$. Its decimal writing offers an infinity of unforeseeable decimals.

$$\sqrt{2} =$$
$$1.41421356237309504$$
$$88016887242097\ldots$$

Example :

If we want to place an increasing quantity of zeros between two consecutive 1s, we write 1, then a 0, then 1, then two 0s, then 1, then three 0s, then 1, then four 0s, etc. Consequently, the decimal 1 cannot be repeated at regular intervals.

$$0.10$$
$$100\ 1000\ 10000\ 100000$$
$$1\ldots$$

Another example:

$$0\ .\ 1\ \ 2\ \ 3\ \ 4\ \ 5\ \ 6\ \ 7\ \ 8$$
$$9$$
$$10\ \ \ 11\ \ \ 12\ \ \ 13$$
$$14\ \ \ 15\ \ldots$$

where the decimals are natural whole numbers one after the other. This writing is not periodical, because the decimal 1 is not.

Notes:

One of the properties of irrationals is their power of being the solution to an algebraic equation of a degree higher than 1. Consequently, these are algebraic numbers.

For example, the solution to the algebraic equation $x^2-2=0$ is $+\sqrt{2}$ and $-\sqrt{2}$. Consequently, $\sqrt{2}$ is an algebraic number.

3. Transcendent numbers

Irrational numbers are not algebraic.

π is the best known of all. It is irrational because its decimals are infinite and unforeseeable, and it is not the solution to any equation of a degree greater than 1. There are other transcendent numbers, such as e (=2.718), Euler's constant (=0.577215), e^{π}, and perhaps π^e.

The irrational root of 3 governs the octahedron
(drawing attributed to Leonardo da Vinci).

2

Yearning for infinity

The fascinating number π

*My entire being screams
in contradiction against itself.
Existence is undoubtedly a choice...*
Søren Kierkegaard

A transcendent number is an irrational number whose decimals are not periodical, and that is not the solution to any algebraic equation. π is the best known example. π is surely the most famous number in mathematics. Whole books have been written about its history and the works it has inspired—and still inspires. What has always fascinated mathematicians is that a number defined on the basis of a geometric shape as simple as the circle bears so many mysteries and is rich with such complexity.

π is defined not as a number but as a ratio of magnitudes, between the area of a circle and the square built on its radius.

It was Archimedes who, in the third century B.C.E., proved that this ratio was independent of the radius of the circle considered, and equal to the ratio between the length of a circle and its diameter. Without being able to demonstrate it, the Greeks knew that this was a ratio of incommensurable magnitudes.

In the seventeenth century, when the ratios of magnitudes acquired the status of numbers, π became a number thought to be irrational, although nobody knew how to prove it.

ΑΡΧΙΜΗΔΟΥΣ ΚΥΚΛΟΥ ΜΕΤΡΗΣΙΣ.

Πᾶς κύκλος ἴσος ἐστὶ τριγώνῳ ὀρθογωνίῳ, οὗ ἡ μὲν ἐκ τοῦ κέντρου ἴση μιᾷ τῶν περὶ τὴν ὀρθήν, ἡ δὲ περίμετρος τῇ βάσει.

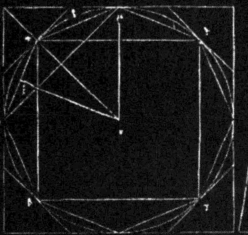

Quadrature of the circle by Archimedes (Greek manuscript).

Portrait of Archimedes (278–212 B.C.E.).

The notation π appeared for the first time in 1632, in a book by the English mathematician William Oughtred (1574–1660). It represents the first letter of the Greek word *periphereia* ("circumference").

The irrationality of π was proven in 1761 by the Swiss Johann Lambert, thanks to a demonstration that used the so-called "continuous fractions."

π is irrational and transcendent

Especially since the beginning of the twentieth century, we have been interested in the statistical distribution of the decimals of π, in other words, the way in which the numerals from 0 to 9 appear in the decimal sequence. We know that since π is irrational, its decimal development is not periodical. But can we discover certain particularities by studying its decimals?

Starting from a certain rank, it is possible that a numeral can no longer be found, that we have only one type of sequence of numerals, or...

Such a particularity would disclose a deep property that we could try to interpret from a theoretical viewpoint.

But, in spite of all the statistical tests done, so far nothing has been found. It is amazing, if we think that π has a very special definition. This makes us wonder whether there is a difference between the decimals of π and a sequence of numerals taken at random. But what are the properties of a sequence of numerals taken at random? And how would we characterize such a sequence? This type of question, which forces us to wonder about the concept of randomness, leads to some important theories.

The calculation of π

The calculation of π, or rather of its approximate value, goes back to the most ancient times.

The first estimate of π of which there is a record comes from the Babylonian civilization. On a tablet dating from approximately 4000 B.C.E., we can read thoughts about the ratio between the length of a circle and the perimeter of the hexagon inscribed (equal to three times the diameter), which means estimating π at $3 + 1/8$, i.e.

$$3.125$$

On a Babylonian tablet written in cuneiform characters, the approximation
$\pi = 3 + 1/8$. The Babylonians supposedly obtained it by comparing the perimeter of the circle
to the perimeter of the hexagon inscribed, equal to three times the diameter.

This is quite a remarkable result, since we know today that the beginning
of the decimal writing of

π is 3.14159

We find another estimate of π in the famous Rhind papyrus, dating from
1650 B.C.E. The Egyptian scribe Ahmes indicates in it that the
area of a circle is equal to that of a square with a side equal to 8/9 of the
diameter, i.e. 16/9 of the radius, This means that $(16/9)^2$ is taken as the
value of π, i.e. approximately 3.16.

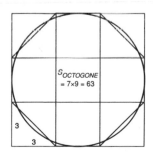

The rule of the reduction of the ninth, used in problem 48 in the Rhind papyrus
(at the right in hieratic writing), leads to the value $\pi = (16/9)^2$. It would originate
from the approximation of the surface of a disk by that of an octagon (left).

Ahmes does not say how this result was obtained, but we think it comes from the estimate of the area of a circle by that of an octagon, a figure found in the tiles of the time.

These old estimates had a practical purpose. For example, they helped calculate the area of a circular lot of land or the volume contained in a cylindrical grain silo. But the Babylonians and the Egyptians did not care about clearly defining π.

The Greeks brought a desire for mathematical rigor. By using complex geometric methods that estimated the perimeter of regular polygons with ninety-six sides, Archimedes obtained the frame of π:

$$3.1410369 < \pi < 3.1427201$$

This is a remarkable frame, since its amplitude is lower than two thousandths. The upper member of the frame, 22/7, a very simple fraction, would serve for a long time as a practical estimate of π; it is enough to solve many concrete problems. It was only after the sixteenth century and the emergence of decimal numbers that it would be replaced by the practical estimate:

$$3.14 \text{ or } 3.1416$$

After Archimedes, mathematicians in all countries looked for estimates of π. The methods remained geometric for a long time, using regular polygons, as Archimedes had done. In the second century C.E., the Chinese gave the estimate 142/45, i.e.

$$3.155$$

In 1498, the Indian Aryabhata gives an estimate of 62,832/20,000, i.e.

$$3.1416$$

We again find this value with the Arabs in the ninth century. In the West, the German Ludolph Van Ceulen succeeded in the sixteenth century in calculating the first thirty-five decimals of π, using regular polygons with 262 sides, i.e. about 4 quadrillion sides. This titanic calculation, to which Van Ceulen dedicated his life brought glory to its author, but put an end to the calculation of the decimals of π by Archimedean methods. No one will go farther than Van Ceulen using these techniques, because of the emergence of analytical methods, which brought new definitions of π and did away with the geometrical methods.

In 1719, the Frenchman Thomas De Lagny calculated 127 decimals. This record was broken only in 1794 by the Austrian Georg von Vega, who calculated 140. Johann Dahse came up with 205 in 1844. Then there were 248 in 1847 (Clausen); 440 in 1853 (Rutheford); 530, also in 1853 (Shanks); and 707 in 1873 (again Shanks). These 707 decimals calculated by William Shanks were for a long time the record number of decimals of π calculated. Shanks's 707 decimals appear on the ceiling of the room dedicated to π in the Palais de la Decouverte in Paris. The performance was improved only in 1947, when D.F. Ferguson calculated 710 decimals with an office calculator.

For the sake of anecdote, it was noticed at that time that Shanks's decimals were false starting from the 528th, because, it was supposed, of one term he had forgotten; this forced the management of the Palais de la Decouverte to partially redo their ceiling.

The computer age

In 1948, with John Wrench, Ferguson further improved the number of known decimals of π, calculating 808 of them, again with an office calculator. This calculation of 808 decimals by Ferguson and Wrench marks the end of the era of "handmade" calculation of the decimals of π. With the introduction of computers, the number of decimals of π that could be calculated increased very quickly. In 1949, in Philadelphia, a computer programmed by George Reitwiesner calculated 2,037 decimals in seventy hours. In 1954, also in the United States, a computer programmed by Nicholson and Jeenel calculated 3,092 decimals in ten minutes.

ENIAC, the first electronic computer, beat the record in the calculation of the decimals of π in 1949.
Mission accomplished with 2,037 decimals, almost double the previous record,
obtained the same year with a mechanical calculator.

In 1958, in Paris, a computer programmed by François Genuys calculated 10,000 decimals in one hundred minutes, The mark of the 100,000 decimals was crossed in 1961, in Washington, by Shanks and Wrench, and that of 1million decimals in 1973, in Paris, by Jean Guilloud and Martine Boyer. In 1976, Brent and Salamin invented a new, very rapid algorithm. This was the beginning of a new period, in which the number of the known decimals of π increased spectacularly because of the appearance of ever more efficient algorithms. Today, we are up to more than 200 billion decimals of π.

Analytical machine invented by Charles Babbage (1791–1871),
used to evaluate multiples starting from a given value of π.

19951	41908	16682	24900	74207	11186	48815	47728	91718	65359	67765
19952	39579	93350	33427	28214	60541	69649	60098	47069	79585	59264
19953	30428	70363	66471	30713	14782	33061	15764	19913	22242	06460
19954	99898	83076	26858	36055	52740	99047	84676	10760	42417	84215
19955	06285	17557	35299	96478	62552	95428	36742	98706	64579	43375
19956	80101	40740	21161	86144	84329	76574	42634	28528	70477	85563
19957	08309	63143	52787	83041	94501	97029	46575	77773	28167	46858
19958	08745	39316	03937	25331	58992	80579	43463	14087	35860	86177
19959	88263	34927	74615	11849	11655	13068	18467	13677	34882	33410
19960	85136	40394	79392	08876	88633	63394	61382	35834	47940	81569
19961	61091	42938	77347	13893	42377	36191	09646	05642	44474	77908
19962	20760	49660	27135	61689	54106	44483	21365	98082	93890	97296
19963	18912	11834	29149	06163	89638	61069	37520	89534	68839	83344
19964	46710	98212	43478	07238	74074	57697	55450	74368	46747	13502
19965	48588	18399	66556	81963	44528	81194	18331	72636	82505	06118
19966	64900	39412	55205	74571	20360	35578	02514	19043	52671	83721
19967	92138	48299	05803	22469	58424	32315	89844	32510	39654	43535
19968	05354	32292	16747	04077	86146	84859	76255	74461	53511	88003
19969	14305	69954	92784	71674	54497	26976	12839	33251	83819	72223
19970	28360	70752	27812	92813	01065	69412	62948	73063	42688	37338
19971	18174	21706	08647	54827	63942	42391	40275	32180	42951	90341
19972	16351	70469	80742	33515	56057	05756	24509	99253	20178	74996
19973	36640	47347	70389	85587	30650	76038	70997	73184	31281	09897
19974	89882	08543	55955	09432	53902	37189	52168	20233	44245	57257
19975	53078	79263	39855	09016	45594	23733	96625	22335	16487	50589
19976	55694	21729	72448	95998	82508	92321	12034	79589	41546	54603
19977	03787	86175	91571	66139	88693	26873	74968	47305	49653	29378
19978	21475	64810	57938	08285	30053	24470	80506	56929	42234	00109
19979	59348	29461	45390	78890	66162	64021	50130	73533	00331	92074
19980	56372	63770	77099	93999	22886	21224	32488	02062	63485	08885
19981	30360	10723	43689	01360	64275	81425	28398	78594	91799	79611
19982	21963	79757	65192	45218	67096	08809	21371	11977	50008	78159
19983	30430	72934	48839	30957	57415	92413	75285	97779	72918	93453
19984	85050	80383	19867	74590	02518	65791	72370	80857	41642	97153
19985	80788	40607	13068	68036	19824	19715	77476	38950	72534	68404
19986	56919	27595	31937	22370	22290	15580	06560	76047	38547	35990
19987	44779	96748	74996	97694	27137	66869	55331	95125	33776	40985
19988	07096	60306	32639	26164	94560	86841	40374	56842	07194	05950
19989	70174	30354	69182	15090	04664	93998	55174	13893	85197	57312
19990	15682	61622	86223	10010	96729	74760	60130	28331	19371	61140
19991	87472	70676	25585	67775	11995	66674	86151	96491	29701	93318
19992	08499	41096	18139	29649	27893	60902	12535	44332	73750	64260
19993	62429	94120	32736	25582	44174	98345	09873	09453	43661	59072
19994	84163	19368	30757	19798	06823	15357	37155	57181	61221	56787
19995	93642	50138	87117	02327	55557	79302	26678	58031	99930	81083
19996	05763	07652	33205	07400	13939	09580	79016	37717	62925	92837
19997	64874	79017	72741	25678	19055	55621	80504	87674	69911	40839
19998	97791	93765	42320	62337	47173	24703	36976	33579	25891	51526
19999	03156	14033	32127	28491	94418	43715	06965	52087	54245	05989
20000	56787	96130	33116	46283	99634	64604	22090	10610	57794	58151

Last page of the book *1,000,000 décimales de* π, by Jean Guilloud and Martine Boyer, sometimes called "the most boring book in the world."
The 2,500 decimals on this page go from the 997,501st to the 1 millionth.

A yearning for the infinite

"But, one may wonder, what is the reason for this chase after the decimals of π? This calculation may have a theoretical motivation, namely to bring out, in the sequence of decimals, particularities that would reveal something profound about the nature of π. Specifically, any progress in the number of the known decimals lets us refine the study of the statistical distribution of the decimals. On the other hand, this hunt for decimals is quite exciting in itself.

The complexity of π makes the search for its decimals an excellent engine to push mathematics forward. It forces mathematicians to reflect on the various concepts related to the nature of numbers and mathematics itself; it requires rapid algorithms that need to be discovered and can then be adapted for various functions, possibly proving to be of great mathematical interest; finally, performing the actual calculations represents an excellent test for the power of computers."

Jean Pézennec, *Promenades au pays des nombres.*

Still, it seems that the motives of the hunters of decimals often have nothing to do with reason.

Isn't this one of the expressions of man's humanity, his yearning for the infinite?

3

Odd and even

The dialectic of chaos and the cosmos

That night, there will be room for everyone
At the table of the Father.
Someone from among those
working with the vines all day
will give grace for each and all
by breaking the bread.
Pierre Emmanuel

According to the Pythagoreans, harmony pervaded the entire universe. The order of the heavens themselves was expressed on a musical scale—the music of the spheres. But a word was needed to say it, and Pythagoras invented it: *cosmos*. Order and beauty. And the world's history was symbolized by the cosmos's fight against chaos.

This notion of order and cosmos guided one of the mathematicians' main endeavors: classification. Pythagoras started by establishing a first classification of numbers. Today, we find it so natural that it looks like it has been there forever. But in fact it was a great novelty. He distributed whole numbers into two categories, even and odd, namely those that are divisible by two and those that are not.

2 is the first *even number* and the only *prime* even number
3 is the first *odd number*.

Thus, he established the rules of calculation for even numbers:
For addition:

$$Even + even = even$$
$$Odd + odd = odd$$
$$Even + odd = odd$$

And for multiplication:

$$Even \times even = even$$
$$Odd \times odd = odd$$
$$Even \times odd = even$$

The Tetractys

At the heart of Pythagoras's doctrine we find the Tetractys, which means "quaternity," four consecutive elements.

The first line of the Pythagorean oath reveals how important it was for his followers:

"Nay, I swear it by him that gave our soul the Tetractys,
Which contains the fount and root of ever-flowing nature."

The numbers 1, 2, 3, 4 and their consecutive sum ($1+2+3+4=10$) are at the basis of the way the Pythagoreans conceived the universe, by analogy:

1 = the Creator
2 and 3 = the Matter
4, 5, and 6 = the Spirit
7, 8, 9, and 10 = the Visible Manifestations

The number 10: the *decad*

The *decad*, the sum of the Tetractys, has a sacred role as well. In truth, as Pythagoras taught, the number 10 is the most beautiful because it contains:
– as many even numbers as odd ones:

1, 3, 5, 7, 9 are odd
2, 4, 6, 8, 10 are even

– as many prime numbers as compound ones:

1, 2, 3, 5, 7 are prime
4, 6, 8, 9, 10 are compound

Tetractys and space

One of the key teachings of the Pythagorean school was that everything is number—and that nothing can be understood or known without resorting to numbers. The Tetractys represents the number of points needed to create the dimensions of the universe:

1 is the point, its dimension is zero (zero-dimensional object), and it generates other dimensions:
2 points define a straight line, with dimension 1;
3 points form a triangle, with dimension 2;
4 points linked between them form a tetrahedron, with dimension 3.

The Pythagoreans made the Tetractys their symbol. They pushed the mystique of numbers to the extreme, by building a universe in which the numbers were given a philosophical and mystical function.

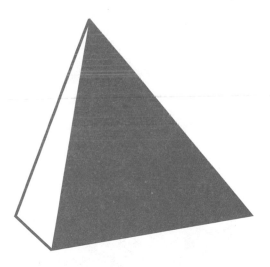

Tetrahedron, the geometrical figure of Tetractys.

Double Tetractys

In *Of Isis and Osiris*, Plutarch mentions Tetractys (paragraph 76):

"In turn, the Pythagoreans graced the numbers and the geometrical figures with the names of gods [...]

As to the number called Tetractys, namely 36, as everybody says, it is their most sacred oath; they call it Universe. It is made of the first four even numbers and the first four odd numbers added together."

According to the Greeks, the equality

$$(1 + 3 + 5 + 7) + (2 + 4 + 6 + 8) = 36$$

was considered symbolically. Since they saw in the opposition of odd and even numbers the polarity of male and female, this "double Tetractys" contained a male Tetractys and a female Tetractys, in the way of the four gods and the four goddesses, in an act of universal creation; they saw the universe emerge from it under the numerical cloak of 36.

4

Prime numbers

Between earth and heaven, a ladder.
Silence is at the apex of the ladder.
The word or writing,
persuasive as they might be,
are but intermediate stages.
It is enough to set foot lightly
without insisting. To speak, is sooner
or later to be cunning. To write,
is sooner or later to be cunning.
One moment or another.
Inevitably. Irresistibly.
Only silence is without malice.
Silence is first and last.
Silence is love—and when it isn't,
it is more miserable than noise.

Christian Bobin

213

Definition of prime numbers and compound numbers

There are two types of positive integers: prime numbers and compound numbers.

– A positive number is said to be prime when it has only two divisors, itself and one.

For example, 7 can be divided only by 7 and by 1.

$$7 \div 1 = 7$$

$$7 \div 7 = 1$$

– A number is said to be non-prime or compound when it can have more than two divisors.

Example:

$$24 \text{ is divisible by } 1 \ (= 24)$$
$$24 \text{ is divisible by } 24 \ (= 1)$$

But a number can have divisors other than itself and one.
Thus, 24 can also be divided by
2, 3, 4, 6, 8, and 12.

Notes on the number 1:

We must note that the unit does not belong to either one of these two types and, in most cases, it cannot be considered a prime number, because the properties of prime numbers do not always apply to 1.

Prime twins

For centuries, mathematicians have tried to discover the underlying reasons for prime numbers. Perhaps there is no arrangement. Some prime numbers come in pairs, two numbers apart; we call them prime twins.

Two prime numbers are twins
if they are as close to each other as they can be,
meaning, if the difference between them is equal to 2.

Here are a few pairs of prime twins:

$$(3,5), \ (5,7), \ (11,13), \ (17,19), \ (29,31)$$

A long-standing mathematical conjecture indicates that there is an infinity of prime twins. So far, the conjecture has not been proven or refuted.

We must note that prime twins are only two numbers apart, which is as close as possible for two prime numbers. If the difference between them were 1, one of the numbers would necessarily be even and therefore divisible by 2.

Goldbach's conjecture

Christian Goldbach affirmed in a letter to Euler written in 1742:

> All even integers are
> the sum of two prime numbers.

For example:

$$34 = 29 + 5$$
$$48 = 31 + 17$$
$$18 = 7 + 11$$
$$20 = 17 + 3$$
$$30 = 17 + 13$$

Two and a half centuries later, after being checked with a computer on more than 100 million even integers, this affirmation has not yet been demonstrated, and it remains a problem that troubles contemporary mathematicians.

It is interesting to note from the beginning that this conjecture also works for odd numbers above 5. But here, we must have *three* prime numbers.

> All odd numbers are
> the sum of three prime numbers.

Example:

$$55 = 31 + 19 + 5$$

It's a beautiful conjecture: It always works, even though no one is able to say why.

Sequence of prime numbers

How many prime numbers are there? This is the first question that arises about prime numbers, since they constitute the basic material for all natural numbers (see Goldbach's conjecture p. 215) and these natural numbers grow indefinitely. Is it possible to list them all, or do they also constitute an unlimited sequence?

Prime numbers below 100:

$$
\begin{array}{cccc}
2 & 3 & 5 & 7 \\
11 & 13 & 17 & 19 \\
23 & 29 & 31 & 37 \\
& 41 & 43 & 47 \\
& 53 & 59 & \\
& 61 & 67 & \\
71 & 73 & 79 & \\
& 83 & 89 & \\
& 97 &
\end{array}
$$

The sequence of prime numbers is unlimited.

We owe this important theorem to Euclid. Note that the differences between successive primes are variable: For example, in this list, the differences are worth $1, 2, 2, 4, 2, 4, 2, 4, 6, 2, 6, 4, 2, 4, 6, 6...$ The Greek mathematician Euclid proved that there is an infinity of prime numbers. However, these numbers do not appear regularly, and there is no formula to devise them. Consequently, the discovery of the large prime numbers implies producing and testing millions of numbers.

For example:

$170,141,183,460,469,231,731,687,303,715,884,105,727$

This number with 39 numerals has long been considered the greatest known prime number. It is the equivalent of $[(2\text{ power }127)-1]$, meaning that it represents the number of grains that should have been given to the inventor of the game of chess, had this game had 127 squares (see the anecdote starting on page 21).

The sieve of Erathostenes (276–194 B.C.E.)

It is not difficult to recognize the prime numbers lower than 100, by eliminating all those that are multiples of 2 (in other words, the even numbers), then eliminating the multiples of 3 (in other words, one number out of three), the multiples of 5 (ending in 5 or 0), then the multiples of 7.

This method, which consists of letting pass only prime numbers and which has been known since antiquity, is called the "sieve of Erathostenes." Erathostenes was a Greek mathematician (third century B.C.E.), a friend of Archimedes.

Note:

Prime numbers (except 2) can be separated into two groups:

– the first group ($5, 13, 17, 29...$) consists of numbers that, when divided by 4, give a remainder of 1 (which can be written $4k+1$);
– the second group ($3, 7, 11, 19, 23...$) consists of numbers that, when divided by 4, give a remainder of 3 (which can be written $4k+3$).

Thus:

– all the numbers in the first group can be expressed as the sum of two squares, and can be so only in one way;
– none of the numbers in the second group can be expressed that way.

Part Three

Special numbers

Perfect numbers

The mysteries of 6 and 28

"Friendly" numbers

1

"Friendly" numbers

Let us stay by the lamp and talk a bit;
All that one may say is not worth
the avowal of the silence lived;
It is like the hollow of a divine hand.
Rainer Maria Rilke

Pythagoras and the Pythagoreans were particularly interested in the study of arithmetic numbers (1, 2, 3...) and their fractions. Arithmetic numbers are also called whole numbers, and technically, fractions are called rational numbers, meaning proportional ratios between whole numbers. In the infinity of numbers, Pythagoras's Brotherhood sought those that had a particular meaning, and sometimes the most special ones were called *perfect* numbers. According to Pythagoras, numerical perfection depended on the divisors of a number, because certain numbers divide perfectly into an original number.

Excessive or abundant numbers

Pythagoras pointed out three categories of numbers: perfect numbers, excessive numbers, and imperfect numbers.

When the sum of the divisors of a number is greater than the number itself, the number is called *excessive* or *abundant*.

For example, the number 12:

12 is an excessive number, because the sum of its divisors is 16 (greater than 12; the divisors of 12 being 1, 2, 3, 4, and 6).

$$1 + 2 + 3 + 4 + 6 = 16$$

and

$$16 > 12$$

The first abundant number is 12.

Imperfect or deficient numbers

On the other hand, when the sum of the divisors of a number is less than the number itself, the number is called *imperfect* or *deficient*.

For example, 10:

10 is an imperfect number, because the sum of its divisors is 8 (less than 10; the divisors of 10 being 1, 2, and 5).

$$1 + 2 + 5 = 8$$

and

$$8 < 10$$

Perfect numbers

The most significant and the most uncommon numbers are those in which the sum of the divisors corresponds to the number itself: These are the perfect numbers. 6 is the first of all perfect numbers.

For example, 6:

6 is perfect, because the sum of its divisors is equal to it (the divisors of 6 are 1, 2, and 3).

$$1 + 2 + 3 = 6$$

$$6 = 6$$

Note:

Originally, the adjective *perfect* was reserved for the first triangular numbers known in the Tetractys:

$$1 + 2 = 3$$

$$1 + 2 + 3 = 6$$

$$1 + 2 + 3 + 4 = 10$$

Addition, multiplication, squares, and cubes of 6

Sometimes 6 is said to be doubly perfect, because the addition and multiplication of its divisors actually gives a number equal to it.

$$1 + 2 + 3 = 6$$

$$1 \times 2 \times 3 = 6$$

There is a particularly interesting link between 6 and its divisors:

$$1^3 + 2^3 + 3^3 = 6^2 = 36$$

$$1^2 \times 2^2 \times 3^2 = 6^2 = 36$$

6 and the Pythagorean theorem

The Pythagorean triplet 3, 4, 5, which is the basis of the construction of the Pythagorean triangle, also has an essential link with the number 6 and its divisors.

$$3^3 + 4^3 + 5^3 = 6^3 = 216$$

$$1^3 \times 2^3 \times 3^3 = 6^3 = 216$$

Perfect numbers are rare

Between 0 and 1000, there are only three perfect numbers, namely 6, 28 and 496. 28 is perfect because the sum of its divisors (1, 2, 4, 7, 14) is equal to it.

$$1 + 2 + 4 + 7 + 14 = 28$$

The fourth perfect number is $8,128$, the fifth is $33,550,336$ and the sixth is $8,589,869,056$.

An ancient method to build a perfect number

Euclid gave, in these terms, the way of generating perfect numbers: "Starting from the unit, we build a sequence of numbers that are each other's double. When the sum of all these numbers is a prime number, it is enough to multiply the sum by its last term to obtain a perfect number." According to this formula, we prepare the successive sums:

$$1 + 2 = 3$$
$$1 + 2 + 4 = 7$$
$$1 + 2 + 4 + 8 = 15$$
$$1 + 2 + 4 + 8 + 16 = 31 \text{, etc.}$$

Omitting 15, which is not prime, we then form the successive perfect numbers. Indeed, according to Euclid's method, $3, 7, 31$ are indeed prime numbers. The last terms are indeed, respectively: $2, 4, 16$; which when we multiply the sum by its last term, gives:

$$3 \times 2 = 6$$
$$7 \times 4 = 28$$
$$31 \times 16 = 496$$

Notes:

Euclid's method is such that the perfect numbers found are always even because we multiply by a power of 2.

We do not know whether there is an infinity of such perfect even numbers. We also do not know whether or not there are perfect odd numbers; these questions have been asked for more than 2 million years.

Perfect numbers and the balance of the personality

The ancient Greeks called a perfect number *arithmos teleios*, which means "that which is equal to its own parts." With this in mind, we feel inclined to make a comparison with human events, and seeing perfect numbers, we think of homogeneous, balanced personalities, while most people are comparable with numbers that, in the end, contain less than what they appear to at first glance. The third type of numbers, more uncommon, symbolically reminds us of those personalities whose interior wealth is not obvious right away.

As indicated by the following fact, such comparisons were made in ancient times. In ancient Greece, mathematicians figured out couples of numbers paired off so that the "shortage" of one was counterbalanced by the "surplus" of the other. This particularity is embodied in the numbers 220 and 284, which we will discuss in more detail further on. As can be easily established by what we said earlier, the sum of the divisors, or the "content," of 220 is 284, while the sum of the divisors, or "content," of 284 is 220. What is missing in content from one of the numbers (284) exists in surplus in the other number (220).

Significantly, such couples of numbers were named *philoi arithmoi*, "friend" (or "friendly") numbers; their name came directly from the realm of human moral relationships, We see this idea everywhere, whether we want or not, and when we look at numbers from the viewpoint of the subdivision of the unit, we go way beyond it. In other words, in these thoughts, we switch from the physics of numbers to their metaphysics.

Hollow icosidodecahedron (Archimedean polyhedron), also called truncated dodecahedron or triacontadohedron (drawing attributed to Leonardo da Vinci).

2

The mysteries
of 6 and 28

*The snow speaks to whiteness
a language that rice does not know.*
Edmond Jabès

225

The perfect numbers pointed out by Pythagoras and his school also appear in other traditions, especially in the texts of the Bible and the Kabbalah. There is indeed no doubt that the Kabbalah tradition not only knew but also used perfect numbers since the remotest antiquity. Biblical patriarchs used them, and the way the biblical text is set up is the most obvious proof.

The perfection of 6

The eleventh chapter of the *Tikuney Zohar* (one of the main books of the Kabbalah) teaches: "What is the meaning of the word *bereshith*, the first word of the book of Genesis? The literal translation is 'in the beginning,' but the Kabbalah tradition decomposes the word *bereshith* into two words and reads *bara shith*, meaning 'He created six.'"

For the Kabbalists, the beginning, the genesis of the universe, started with the creation of "six."

The very structure of the text emphasizes this idea: Indeed, the first word in the Bible, *bereshith*, meaning "He created six," has six letters.

First word of the Bible in Hebrew: *bereshith.*

Thus, we may understand why the entire structure of Hebrew time is based on the existence of the number 6.

The world was created in 6 days. Then came the Sabbath.

The slave works for 6 years. He is freed on the seventh.

One can work the land for 6 years. On the seventh, the earth rests; it is the *shemita.*

The world is created for 6,000 years; the seventh millennium will be Messiah's time; etc.

The perfection of these numbers did not go unnoticed by Christian commentators and theologians. The proof is in the remarks of Saint Augustine, who said in *The City of God:*

"God, even though he could have created the world in an instant, decided to dedicate to it six days in order to reflect on the perfection of the universe."

In addition, Saint Augustine indicated that six was not a perfect number because God had chosen it, but rather because the perfection was inherent in the nature of the universe: "Six is a perfect number by itself and not because God created all things in six days; rather, the opposite is true: God created all things in six days because the number is perfect. And it would still be perfect even if the work of the six days had not happened."

The wisdom of the number 28

Hebrew commentators note that the first verse of Genesis has precisely twenty-eight letters, 28 being the second perfect number. The *Book of Zohar* always insists on this structure of the first verse by the expression "the twenty-eight letters of the creation of the beginning" (*kaf-het atvan de maasey bereshith*).

בְּ רֵאשִׁית בָּרָא אֱלֹהִים אֵת הַשָּׁמַיִם וְאֵת הָאָרֶץ:

The first verse of the Bible in Hebrew.

In other texts, the number 28 is discussed at length. We can note that in Hebrew this number is written *kaf-het,* two letters that mean "strength."
The word *hokhma,* "wisdom," is read like *koah-ma,* an expression that may mean the strength of *what?,* i.e. the "strength of questioning" or "What is it with 28?" as if the interrogation on this number 28 would be a special kind of wisdom by itself.
The great commentator Rachi was not wrong to dedicate his first comment on Genesis to an evocation of this "strength 28." He cites verse 6 of Psalm 111, which reads *Koah maasav higuid leamo:* "He hath showed his people the power (*koah,* 28) of his works."
The Kabbalists note that the number of phalanges of the hand is 14. This figure is written in Hebrew: 10 + 4, i.e. *yud-daleth,* which is precisely the word *yad,* "hand."
Thus, the word *hand* would be the link between the body, the numerals, and the letters. The anatomic structure of the organ (14 phalanges) states a numeral (14), which becomes letters and words (*yud-dalet* = *yad*).
Rabbi Nahman of Braslav, Hasidic master of the nineteenth century, explains, based on these remarks, the importance of clapping one's hands during prayer. Indeed, the two hands put together produce the sum of 14 + 14 = 28.

We must note that the word *ahava,* "love," when read according to "dynamic *gematria*" (see the third book on *gematria*) is also equal to 28.
Indeed, in Hebrew, *ahava* is written with the letters *aleph-he-bet-he.*
In dynamic cumulative *gematria,* this becomes:

aleph	1
aleph - he	1 + 5 = 6
aleph - he - vet	1 + 5 + 2 = 8
aleph - he - vet - he	1 + 5 + 2 + 5 = 13
	Total = 28

227

The 28 times of the world

There is another text, besides the first verse of the Torah, which gives us an indication about the importance of the number 28. It is a group of famous verses from the Ecclesiastes (*Kohelet*). At the beginning of chapter III, we read:

A time to be born	and a time to die.
A time to plant	and a time to pull what is planted.
A time to kill	and a time to heal.
A time to break down	and a time to build up.
A time to weep	and a time to laugh.
A time to mourn	and a time to dance.
A time to cast stones	and a time to gather them together.
A time to embrace	and a time to refrain from embracing.
A time to seek	and a time to lose.
A time to keep	and a time to cast away.
A time to tear	and a time to sew.
A time to whisper	and a time to speak.
A time to love	and a time to hate.
A time for war	and a time for peace.

Human existence is presented in eight verses and twenty-eight hemistiches, twenty-eight fundamental times that cut life down to its very essence. The Hebrew version of this text strongly emphasizes this structure of 28, by showing it according to a pattern called *shira*, or "song," extremely rare in the entire Bible.

3

"Friendly" numbers
Talismans of love

Every word is a doubt,
Every silence, another.
Yet,
The fusion of the two
Allows us to breath.

Every sleep is a sinking
Every waking is another.
Yet,
The fusion of the two
Allows us to awaken anew.

Every life is a form of evanescence.
Every death is another.
Yet,
The fusion of the two
Allows us to be a sign in the vacuum.
Roberto Juarroz

Imperfect-perfect numbers

We are now going to consider a type of number pair for which this character of pair is especially important, namely the *friend*, or *friendly*, or *amicable* numbers.

The Greeks called a number "perfect" when it was equal to the sum of its divisors, as we just saw. Then they tended to transfer this notion of perfection from an isolated number to a pair of numbers. The idea was to find two numbers, each of them imperfect by itself, while the two of them together would become perfect, both of them having the same sum of divisors.

Example:

16 and 33 are imperfect-perfect numbers. Indeed, the divisors of 16 are 1, 2, 4, and 8, whose sum is 15; the divisors of 33 are 1, 3, and 11, with the same sum of the divisors, 15.

What makes 16 and 33 a pair is their common "content," 15. However, the "parity" can go even further and can be structured even more intensely. 16 and 33 become a pair only because of something that is outside of them, namely the number 15.

The "parity" would be even closer if the common ground of the two numbers forming a pair did not need to be obtained by adding a third number that represents their common content. This requirement would be met if we could find pairs of numbers in which the sum of the divisors of one of the two numbers would be the other number; consequently, staying with our example, the sum of the divisors of 16 is 33, and the sum of the divisors of 33 is 16. Of course, this is not true for these two numbers.

Amicable numbers

But there are numbers that meet this criterion. These are the *amicable* numbers.

The so-called "amicable" numbers are close relatives of the perfect numbers that fascinated Pythagoras.

They consist of pairs in which each is the sum of the other's divisors. The Pythagoreans made the extraordinary discovery that 220 and 284 are amicable numbers.

Indeed, the divisors of 220 are:

$$1, 2, 4, 5, 10, 11, 20, 22, 44, 55, \text{ and } 110,$$

whose sum is 284.

On the other hand, the divisors of 284 are:

$$1, 2, 4, 71, \text{ and } 142,$$

whose sum is 220.

Hebrew love talisman (constant 34).

Thus, the pair 220 and 284 is considered to symbolize friendship. In his book *Mathematics, magic, and mystery*, Martin Gardner mentions medieval talismans engraved with these numbers and worn by those who sought love.

An Arab numerologist describes the practice of cutting the number 220 into a fruit and 284 into another, eating the first one and presenting the second one to his beloved as a mathematical aphrodisiac.

Al-Farisi (1260–1320) discovered the pair:

$$17{,}296 \text{ and } 18{,}416$$

This coupling was known under the name of "Fermat's pair," because Fermat rediscovered it several centuries later, in 1636. Around 1500, Al-Yazdi discovered the couple:

$$9{,}363{,}584 \text{ and } 9{,}437{,}056$$

This was known as "Descartes's pair," because Descartes rediscovered it one century later.

Leonhard Euler inventoried up to sixty-two pairs of amicable numbers. Strangely, none of them mentioned the much smaller numbers: Indeed, in 1866, at the age of 16, Niccolo Paganini discovered the pair:

$$1{,}184 \text{ and } 1{,}210$$

Sociable numbers

In the twentieth century, mathematicians took the idea one step further, searching for so-called "sociable" numbers. These are numbers that go by threes or more and form sets. For example, in the set made up of the five numbers 12,496; 14,288; 15,472; 14,536; and 14,264, the sum of the divisors of the first forms the second, the sum of the divisors of the second forms the third..., and the sum of the divisors of the fifth forms the first number.

The greatest known social series has 28 numbers, the first being 14,316.

The production of amicable numbers

The pair 220 and 284, and others, can be found by a complicated yet interesting method, because it is based on the dynamics of the first prime numbers.

Indeed, if we take the numbers 1, 2, and 3 as a series, added up (1 + 2 + 3), we get the first perfect number: 6.

Then we use as the next material for the series of doubles built on 6:

$$6, 12, 24, 48, 96, 192\ldots$$

and we keep extracting from them two consecutive numbers; this leads to the binaries 6, 12; 12, 24; 24, 48; 48, 96; 96, 192; etc.

Then we add a third number to each binary of numbers. In this third number, each of the two numbers must be contained. In other words, it is their product; this gives us the following numerical triads:

6	12	12	24	24	48	48	96
	72		288		1,152		4,608

Then we transform each of the triads into a new triad, reducing each number in the triad by 1; we thus obtain the triples:

5	11	11	23	23	47	47	95
	71		287		1,151		4,607

Based on this, we now take only the triads in which the three numbers are all prime numbers. So, in our example we are left with these triads:

$$5 \quad 11 \qquad\qquad 23 \quad 47$$
$$71 \qquad\qquad\qquad 1{,}151$$

Then we multiply the two upper numbers:

$$55 \qquad\qquad 1{,}081$$
$$71 \qquad\qquad 1{,}151$$

Then we enter below all the triads the series of doubles built on the number 4:

$$4 \quad 8 \quad 16 \quad 32 \quad 64$$

and we multiply the preceding numbers by the multiple of 4 corresponding to them (in our case, 4 and 16):

$$220 \qquad\qquad 17{,}296$$
$$284 \qquad\qquad 18{,}416$$

An expression of peace and friendship

Let us go back to the pair 220 and 284. It is considered a symbol of friendship.

The biblical text mentions one of these numbers in a context where it obviously functions as such a symbol.

"When the patriarch Jacob is pursued by his brother Esau, who wants to kill him, he decides to welcome him and try to reconcile with him. But he still prepares for war, in case Esau will not accept the reconciliation. In addition, he starts to pray and sends him lavish gifts to put him in a good mood. These gifts consist of successive flocks of animals. The first two flocks he sends are precisely 220 heads."(See Genesis 32:14.)

233

When the verses do not contain numbers, commentaries create them, using plays on numerals and letters. When the numbers are explicitly mentioned in the text, they say *darshenu*, "interpret us."

What do these numbers, 200 and 284, mean? How were they chosen? What secrets do they hide? The only plausible answer is that Jacob knew about the tradition of the pair of amicable numbers 220 and 284.

"The map of love"
Declaring one's love

220 and 284 seem to come from a tradition already known to the patriarchs. But what is their meaning beyond their purely numerical aspect? In Hebrew, 220 is written *resh-kaf*, which is pronounced "*rakh*" and means "tender."

284 is written *resh-pe-dalet* and is pronounced "*rapad*," which is a Hebrew root meaning "preparing a mattress," or "preparing a bed of love."

We find this root in the Song of Songs (2:5):

"Stay me for I am faint,

Make me a bed in the apple orchard for I am sick with love"

Thus, sending the message "220/tender" invites the answer "284/the love bed has been prepared."

Sometimes there are real dangers in the "map of love."

Anthropomorphic numbers, nineteenth-century engraving.

Part Four

Love triangles

Triangular numbers

The Pythagorean triangle

The triangle of Isis

Pythagoras, Fermat, and Wiles

Pascal's triangle

The golden number

1

Triangular numbers

Geometry cannot define
movement, numbers, space;
yet these three things are those
that it considers particularly.
Blaise Pascal

The Greeks became renowned thanks to a quite remarkable idea: to use space to represent numbers. The geometric idea consists of projecting various mathematical realities into space. If, instead of writing the numbers using a numeration system, we represent them by groups of points, we discover remarkable arithmetic properties.

We can imagine a number—the same as any abstract principle—as a tangible reality; if we cannot materialize it, at least we can visualize it.

The Pythagoreans represented simple numbers in the form of patterns of points in space, no doubt by analogy with the patterns of the stars. This arithmetic-geometry allowed them to distinguish several families, in addition to the unique point number ".," which belongs to all the groups and is their common ancestor.

Linear numbers

• • •

(number 3)

• • • • •

(number 5)

Triangular numbers: "T"

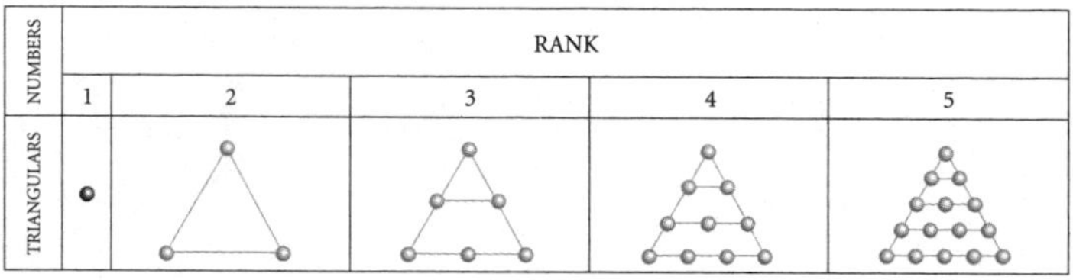

		RANK			
NUMBERS	1	2	3	4	5
TRIANGULARS	○				

The principle of this triangle pattern—also called *theosophical* addition—allows us to determine, for example in numerology, the secret value of a number; in other words, the total of what it contains, both apparent and hidden.

For example, the number 4 contains: 1, 2, and 3 hidden, and 4 apparent.
These triangular numbers are called *sacred numbers.*

In general, we can calculate the secret value of a number according to the following rule: If n is the natural base number, its triangular number T answers to the formula:

$$T = \frac{n\ (n+1)}{2}$$

Example:
for n = 3

$$T = \frac{3\ (3+1)}{2} = \frac{12}{2} = 6$$

The square numbers: "K"

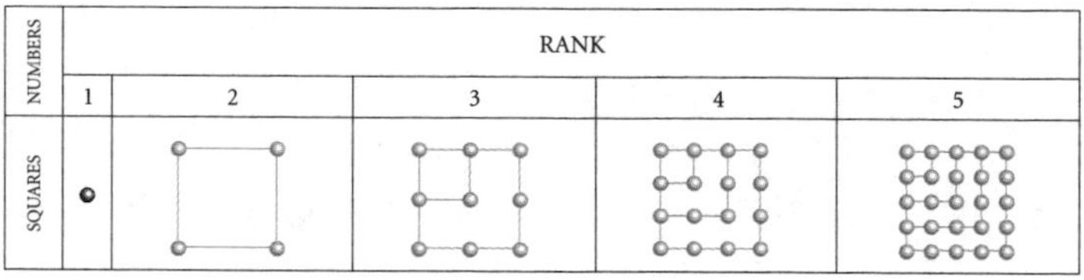

		RANK			
NUMBERS	1	2	3	4	5
SQUARES	○				

A strange geometric property allows us to obtain a square number by adding an odd number to another square "at a straight angle."

Thus, the successive square numbers are built by fitting series of squares inside each other, in a way the Pythagoreans called *gnomons* or *measures*.

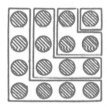

239

It is important and interesting to note that a square number decomposes into two different and successive triangular numbers, while a rectangle number (or *heteromerous*, meaning "with a different length") contains two identical triangular numbers.

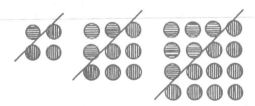

If we note as K the square number (some note it as C),
we have the following formula:

$$K1 = 1^2 = T1$$
$$K2 = 2^2 = T1 + T2$$
$$K3 = 3^2 = T2 + T3$$

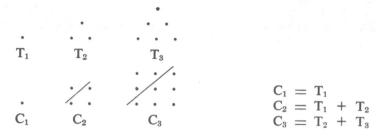

$$C_1 = T_1$$
$$C_2 = T_1 + T_2$$
$$C_3 = T_2 + T_3$$

Polygonal numbers

The triangular and square or rectangular numbers we have just seen draw basic geometric figures that are polygons when they are beyond the point named, a rank 1 figure. Thus, in the figure of the triangle, triangular numbers are constructed, and in the square, square numbers; continuing in this vein, we will have pentagonal (5), hexagonal (6), heptagonal (7) numbers, etc.

The following table describes the first polygonal numbers (written in numerals):

NUMBERS	RANK				
	1	2	3	4	5
TRIANGULARS					
SQUARES					
PENTAGONALS					
HEXAGONALS					
HEPTAGONALS					

Rank	1	2	3	4	5	6	7	8	9	10
Triangular	1	3	6	10	15	21	28	36	45	55
Square	1	4	9	16	25	36	49	64	81	100
Pentagonal	1	5	12	12	35	51	70	92	117	145
Hexagonal	1	6	15	15	45	66	91	120	153	190

There are mathematical formulas for each polygonal number. We indicated earlier the formula for triangular numbers; here, for example, is the formula for pentagonal numbers:

If n is the basic natural number,
its pentagonal number P answers to the formula:

$$p = \frac{n(3n-1)}{2}$$ Example: if $n = 3$, $p = \frac{3(9-1)}{2} = 12$

A few properties of triangular numbers

The sum of the n first cubes is the square of the nth triangular number. For example, the sum of the first four cubes is equal to the square of the fourth triangular number: $1 + 8 + 27 + 64 = 100 = 10^2$.

The additions of triangular numbers reveal many interesting motifs:

$$T1 + T2 + T3 = T4$$
$$T5 + T6 + T7 + T8 = T9 + T10$$
$$T11 + T12 + T13 + T14 + T15 = T16 + T17 + T18$$

15 and 21

15 and 21 are the smallest pair of triangular numbers whose sum and difference (6 and 36) are also triangular.
About 15 and 21, we can say that they are the respective numerical values of two names of God:

Yah (yod-he) and EHYeH (aleph-he-yod-he)

$$10 + 5 = 15 \text{ and } 1 + 5 + 10 + 5 = 21$$

Gauss's discovery

Any number can be expressed as the sum of a maximum of three triangular numbers.

Karl Friedrich Gauss, a German mathematician and philosopher at heart, kept a diary all his life. His most famous phrase, dated July 10, 1796, is certainly this isolated line:

$$\text{Eureka} = \Delta + \Delta + \Delta$$

which means that he had discovered that any number is expressed as the sum of three triangular numbers.

Palindromes

We find some exceptional triangular numbers, such as triangular palindromes, which read the same way from left to right and from right to left:

$$666 \text{ and } 3003$$

Another example is the 2,662nd triangular number, which is $3,544,453$, where the number and its index are both palindromes.

Mathematician Charles Trigg found that also for $T1111$ and $T111111$, the numbers and their indexes are palindromes:

One note about the relationship between square and triangular numbers:

$$617,716 \text{ and } 6,172,882,716$$

We can easily see that the square of an even number is even and that of an odd number is odd.

Thus:

$2^2 = 4$	even number
$3^2 = 9$	odd number
$4^2 = 16$	even number
$5^2 = 25$	odd number
$6^2 = 36$	even number
$13^2 = 169$	odd number

It was Diophantes, a Pythagorean who lived 200 years after Pythagoras, who pointed out the following law:

Any odd square number is equal to the sum
of eight triangles plus the unit.

$$K = 8T + 1$$

This law can be verified for $9, 25$, and 169, for example. If we look at the table of triangular numbers, we see that the first number is 1.
9 is the square of 3. It is equal to (we must remember that $T_1 = 1$):

$$9 = 8T_1 + 1$$
$$9 = (8 \times 1) + 1$$

25 is the square of 5. It is equal to (we must remember that $T_2 = 3$):

$$25 = 8T_2 + 1$$
$$25 = (8 \times 3) + 1$$

169 is the square of 13. It is equal to (we must remember that $T_6 = 21$):

$$169 = 8T_6 + 1$$
$$169 = (8 \times 21) + 1$$

Hence the following diagram. It has 169 small squares. This represents the number K = 169 which is an odd square ($13^2 = 13 \times 13$). A small black square is placed in the center of the figure and the other 168 are grouped in 8 rectangle "triangles." One of these triangles is hashed.

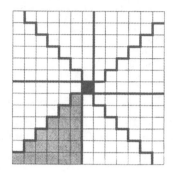

Polyhedral numbers

Triangular or square numbers are numbers that exist and are visualized on a plane. There are also numbers whose geometric existence has three dimensions: polyhedral numbers.

There are five regular polyhedrons:

Symbols	Names	Number of faces F	Number of edges A	Number of summits S	Nature of the faces
T	TETRAHEDRON	4	6	4	P_3 = equilateral triangle
C	CUBE	6	12	8	P_4 = square
O	OCTAHEDRON	8	12	6	P_3 = equilateral triangle
D	DODECAHEDRON	12	30	20	P_5 = pentagon
I	ICOSAHEDRON	20	30	12	P_3 = equilateral triangle

The best known polyhedral number is the cube.

2

The Pythagorean triangle

Infinity itself
has a front and a reverse.
The gods are always on the front side,
though they sometimes remember
there's a reverse.
Man is always on the reverse side
and cannot remember elsewhere.

But infinity itself
can twirl in the air
like a coin
flipped by we know not who
with its sarcastic shimmerings.

Thus sometimes roles are traded,
but not, without a doubt, memories.
Man is the reverse side of infinity,
even though chance places him
for an instant
on the other side.
Roberto Juarroz

Of all the links between numbers and nature studied by the Pythagorean Brotherhood, the most important is the one that bears the founder's name: the Pythagorean theorem.

It offers an equation that applies to all right triangles and therefore defines the right angle itself. From here, the right angle defines perpendicularity, i.e. the link between the vertical and the horizontal and, in the end, the relationships between the three dimensions of our familiar universe.

Thanks to the right angle, mathematics defines the very structure of the space in which we live.

The knot string

It was certainly during one of his voyages that Pythagoras became familiar with the knot string.

We should remember that, historically, the first instruments of measurement identified appeared along with geometry in Babylonia and Egypt, the best known being the twelve-knot string used by the builders of the pyramids. Its total length was just over six meters, and it was divided into twelve equal segments, each measuring one cubit, the distance from the

elbow to the tip of the longest finger of a man, and representing about twenty inches. The number 12 comes from a base 12 used in Babylonia. Enclosed in a triangle whose sides correspond respectively to 3, 4, and 5 segments (an Egyptian triangle), it allows us to determine the right angle because the triangle so formed is a right triangle. This remark is important because it explains the interest shown to this shape and these measurements.

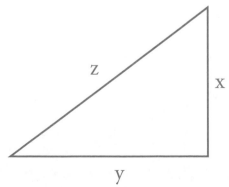

A simple formula

All right triangles are governed by the Pythagorean theorem.

We measure the longest side of a right triangle, z, called the hypotenuse, and we calculate the square of its value. The most remarkable result of this operation is that z^2 will always be equal to the number obtained by the sum of the squares of the other two sides, x and y.

In a right triangle, the square of the hypotenuse is equal to the sum of the squares of the two sides of the right angle.

In other words (or rather, in different symbols):

$$x^2 + y^2 = z^2$$

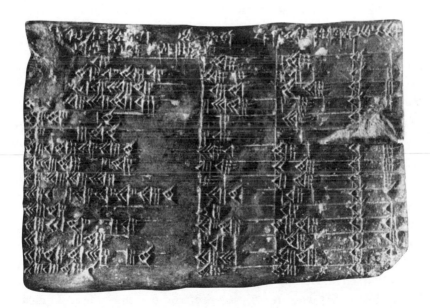

In the ruins of Nippur, a Mesopotamian city located south of Baghdad, a tablet was discovered, the "Plimpton 322," approximately 4,000 years old (c. 1900 B.C.E.). On it, there are some fifteen triple numbers, proving the famous Pythagorean ratio.

What new thing?
The notion of mathematical proof
The Pythagorean theorem does not belong to Pythagoras. Long before him, the Egyptians, and particularly the Babylonians, had discovered a certain relationship between the triples of whole numbers, which is precisely that of the famous theorem.

On a Babylonian tablet, the "Plimpton 322," named after the British archeologist who discovered it, a scribe printed some fifteen whole number triples in which the sum of the square of two of them was equal to the square of the third. The table was engraved more than 1,000 years before Pythagoras was born.

What is new then in the Pythagorean theorem, and why is it such an extraordinary event for mathematics and civilization in general? In fact, what is remarkable is that the Pythagorean theorem is true for all imaginable right triangles. It is a universal mathematical law. (Inversely, if a triangle is consistent with the Pythagorean theorem, it is a right triangle.)

What is new with Pythagoras is the proof he offered of the universality of these properties of the right triangle.
Pythagoras's predecessors used certain properties of right triangles, but they did not know that these properties were valid for all right triangles. Certainly they applied to the triangles these scholars studied, but they did not have any demonstration for the others.

The reason that Pythagoras could claim this theorem is that he demonstrated its universal validity. And the reason for his certitude stems from the concept of mathematical proof.

The idea of the classic mathematical proof is rooted in a series of axioms, propositions that we can suppose are true or self-evident. Logical reasoning then allows us to reach a conclusion, step by step. If the axioms and the logic are correct, the conclusion will be irrefutable. This conclusion is the theorem.

Mathematical proofs are based on this logical process, and once they are established, they remain valid until the end of time. Although the philosopher Thales had already offered certain elementary geometric proofs, Pythagoras pushed the idea much further and was able to express far more ingenious mathematical propositions.

The demonstration of the proof of the Pythagorean theorem was so sensational that one hundred oxen were sacrificed in token of gratitude to the gods. It marked a great stage in the history of mathematics and one of the most memorable breakthroughs in the history of civilization. Its meaning was twofold.

– First, it developed the concept of proof. A mathematical result had a deeper truth than any other, because it stemmed from deductive logic.
– In addition, the Pythagorean theorem linked abstract mathematical method to a concrete object. Pythagoras showed that mathematical truth could apply to the scientific world and give it a logical foundation.

The birth of triplets

We indicated earlier that the Pythagorean theorem had been known for a very long time.

For any given triple, an infinity of others can be immediately deduced by multiplying each number of the triple by the sequence of natural whole numbers. Some of the Babylonian triples come from this immediate generalization of the standard triple $(3, 4, 5)$, by which $9 + 16 = 25$ $(3^2 + 4^2 = 5^2)$. Thus, we can obtain very simply the following triples: $(6, 8, 10)$, $(12, 16, 20)$, $(24, 32, 40)$, etc.

Not to mention the "banal" solution: $(1, 0, 1)$.

Other triples are less easy to obtain. Some are obtained by the formula:

$$a^2 + (a + 1)^2 = b^2$$

For example, the triples $(119, 120, 169)$ and $(20, 21, 29)$.

Truncated hollow isohedron (an Archimedean polyhedron),
also known as a triacontahedron. (Drawing attributed to Leonardo da Vinci.)

3

The triangle of Isis

Given a wall
what happens on the other side?
Jean Tardieu

The *nuptial number,* or *the number*

The numbers 3, 4, 5 were quite popular in antiquity, especially with the Sumerians and the Babylonians.

The great Babylonian unity, the *sar* (the "circle"), obtained by squaring the base 60, i.e. 3,600, and which originally represented for the scribes the great number, i.e. the infinity (the same as 20,000 for the Hindus), later led to the great *sar:* 60³, i.e. 216,000 (which in turn led to the *sar* of *sar:* 60⁴, i.e. 12,960,000)—in other words, *the number* or *nuptial number,* in its arithmetic form of $3^2 \times 4^2 \times 5^2$.

The nuptial number and the sacred triangle of Isis

Consequently, the nuptial number is related to the sacred triangle 3, 4, 5, which in fact is a variation of another, older, Egyptian sacred triangle, called the "triangle of Isis," as reported by Plutarch in chapter 56 of his book *On Isis and Osiris*:

> "It seems likely that the Egyptians considered this right triangle the most beautiful of triangles, and it was especially to this figure that they compared the nature of the universe. In fact, Plato also seems to have used it to represent marriage in geometrical form in *The Republic*.

Indeed, in this right triangle, the number 3 represents one of the sides of the right angle, the number 4 is the base, the number 5 is the hypotenuse, and its square is equal to the sum of the squares of the sides that contain the right angle. So, we must see the side of the right angle as representing the male, the base of the triangle as representing the female, and the hypotenuse as the product of the two. We must consider Osiris as the prime principle, Isis as the substance that receives his influences, and Horus as the effect resulting from the union of the two."

(Cited by Jouven, *Les Nombres cachés: esotérisme arithmologique*, Dervy)

Thus, we can stress once again that the right triangle with equal or proportional sides at 3, 4, 5 was always known (this figure is already mentioned by the Sumerians), but it was indeed in Egypt that it was the most popular.Called the "triangle of Isis," it served materially to trace right angles, and metaphysically to evoke the Egyptian trinity of Osiris, Isis, and their son Horus. The Pythagoreans named the hypotenuse of this triangle

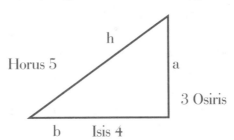

"the invincible one" or "the dominant one." The numbers 3, 4, 5, which express its sides, are related to the perfect number 6 by the cubic perfection relation $3^3 + 4^3 + 5^3 = 6^3$. The Egyptians knew about this relationship. The Jewish Pythagorean Pilon of Alexandria (second half of the first century C.E.) reports in his *De Vita contemplativa* that the Therapists, monastic members of a Judeo-Pythagorean sect, held meetings every seven and fifty days, because 7 is the virgin number and 50 is the sum of the squares built on the sacred triangle $(3^2 + 4^2 + 5^2 = 50)$, as well as the product of the pentad (5) by the decad (10)—in other words, the product of the microcosm by the macrocosm.

As to the trinity of Isis, Osiris, and Horus, its written legend is as vast as its iconography. The cult of Isis, "the beautiful goddess" with a forehead adorned with cow horns symbolizing the crescents of the moon, was the most popular and enduring of all Egyptian cults. It gradually gained followers throughout the Mediterranean, spreading first in Greece, where Isis was assimilated to Ceres-Juno-Proserpine, then in Rome, then in Gaul, undergoing numerous changes. Certain Alexandrine sects of the Late Period even assimilated Isis to the Virgin Mary, mother of Christ, and the Egyptian cult of Isis, accompanied by her husband Osiris and her son Horus was sometimes compared (all proportions kept) to the Christian Trinity. (On the relationship between Moses and the triangle of Ises, see p. 341.)

Plutarch also speaks of the cult of the goddess:
"Moreover, at the time of the winter solstice, they lead the cow seven times around the temple.
There are some who declare that Isis is none other than the Moon, and their proof is that, in the statues of Iris, the horns she wears are the imitations of the crescent moon.
For this reason, they call upon the Moon in love affairs, and Eudoxus [Eudoxus of Cnidus, 408–355 B.C.E. a Greek astronomer and mathematician] asserts that Isis is a deity who presides over love affairs.
Isis is the female principle of Nature and is receptive to every form of generation. Plato calls her the gentle nurse and the all-receptive. She has an innate love for the first and most dominant of all things, which is identical with goodness, and this she yearns for and pursues...
She offers herself to it gladly, so that fertility, which flows in her breasts, imparts her likeness to it. She feels a sweet joy, the thrill of life, while she senses within her certain proof of a happy fertility. For creation is the image of being in matter, and the thing created is a picture of reality."
(Plutarch, *ibid.*, 52, 53.)

253

Pierre de Fermat (1601–1665)

4

Pythagoras, Fermat, and Wiles

In one of the stories from
The Arabian Nights, *the narrator
tells God that he is a horse
that is faster than the gaze,
so fast in fact
that he precedes destiny.*
Pascal Quignard

255

Fermat

Pierre de Fermat is the founder of number theory, a branch of mathematics that deals with the properties of integers. Born in 1601 near Toulouse, Fermat lived in the South of France, far from the great European intellectual centers. He was not a professional mathematician, but a magistrate whose mathematical works were not published during his lifetime. He participated in the mathematical life of his time only through private correspondence with other scholars. Fermat stated a large number of interesting theorems, which were not demonstrated until a long time after his death.

Fermat was one of the most brilliant and astonishing mathematicians in history. He could not have verified all the numbers, but his certainty that the equation $x^n + y^n = z^n$ if $n > 2$ was based on a proof, the same as Pythagoras who had not verified all the triangles to demonstrate the validity of his theorem. A note in Latin confirms this fact, since he wrote in the margins of the Latin version of the *Arithmetica* by Diophantus of Alexandria (who lived around 250 B.C.E.): "I have a beautiful proof for the theorem, but the margin could not contain it." This conjecture is called "Fermat's Last Theorem." This theorem is one of the most famous problems in modern mathematics. And the most powerful spirits of all centuries and all nations tried to resolve this equation. Leonhard Euler, the eighteenth-century genius, had to admit his failure. In the nineteenth century, Sophie Germain took the identity of a man to pursue studies that were until then forbidden to women. Evariste Galois, on the eve of his death, scrawled on a few pages a theory (see Glossary of proper names) that revolutionized science. Yutaka Taniyama was so disappointed that he killed himself, while Paul Wolfskehl found in this enigma a reason for living.

Andrew Wiles

Finally, in 1993, "a young British Princeton professor, Andrew Wiles, succeeded in solving, after seven years of solitary research and a few months of doubt, the fate of this fantastic problem before the amazed scientific community." (Simon Singh, *Fermat's Last Theorem*, Fourth Estate, 1998.)

According to his biographers, Fermat's Last Theorem had captivated the imagination of young Andrew Wiles, who had discovered this enigma in the mathematics book *The Last Problem*, by E. T. Bell (Simon & Schuster, 1961)

> "Sitting in the reading room of the Milton Road Library, a 10-year-old boy struggled with the worst mathematical problem. Usually, half the difficulty was understanding the question, but here it was simple: 'Prove that there is no integer solution to the equation $x^n + y^n = z^n$ when n is greater than 2.' Unmoved by the fact that geniuses had failed to resolve it, Wiles got to work immediately, using all the techniques in his schoolbooks to try to reconstitute the demonstration. Perhaps he would be able to find a trick that everybody but Fermat had neglected. He dreamed that he would astonish the world.
>
> Thirty years later, Wiles was ready. In the auditorium of the Isaac Newton Institute, after several hours of demonstration, he scribbled another equation on the blackboard and, trying to repress a

triumphant expression, he faced the audience. The conference was coming to a glorious end, and the public knew it. One or two people had surreptitiously brought cameras into the hall, and flashes accompanied Wiles's conclusion.

With the chalk in his hand, he turned once more toward the blackboard. A few logical lines completed the demonstration. For the first time in more than three centuries, Fermat's challenge had been taken. More flashes went off, fixing this historic moment. Wiles wrote Fermat's Last Theorem, turned to the audience, and modestly said, 'I think I will stop here.'

Two hundred mathematicians applauded and shouted their approval. Even those who expected the outcome were smiling in awe. After three decades, Andrew Wiles had realized his dream." (S. Singh, *op. cit.*, *ibid.*)

Andrew Wiles, a happy genius!

Blaise Pascal (1623–1662), French physicist, philosopher, and mathematician-genius.
But did you know that he invented the eight-seat carriage? It was the first public
transportation in Paris (the fare was 5 sols), in 1662.

5

Pascal's triangle

*The world, for us, has become infinite
again, in the sense that we cannot refuse
it the possibility of lending itself
to an infinite number of interpretations.*
Friedrich Nietzsche

While the sacred triangle and the Pythagorean theorem caught the attention of mathematicians and metaphysicians, there is another triangle that is just as important, and that has an infinity of properties, discovered and discussed by the theory of numbers. It is Pascal's triangle.

The first seven lines of Pascal's triangle are represented as follows:

```
1                          1
1 1              or       1 1
1 2 1                    1 2 1
1 3 3 1                 1 3 3 1
1 4 6 4 1             1 4 6 4 1
1 5 10 10 5 1       1 5 10 10 5 1
1 6 15 20 15 6 1   1 6 15 20 15 6 1
```

In 1653, Blaise Pascal was the first in the West to write a treatise on this progression of numbers.

Let's have a look at the triangle on the bottom right of the preceding page. We see that each entry other than 1 is the sum of the two numbers above it. For example, to obtain the 2 in the third line, we add the two 1s in the second line. To obtain the 6 on the last line, we add the 5 and the 1 in the sixth line. This operation is repeated indefinitely.

There are many fascinating arrangements in this triangle. For example, if we start with any 1 on the left side, and consider the ascending diagonal, we find that the sum is one of Fibonacci's numbers (Fibonacci's sequence 1, 1, 2, 3, 5, 8, 13..., in which every number is the sum of the two previous ones).

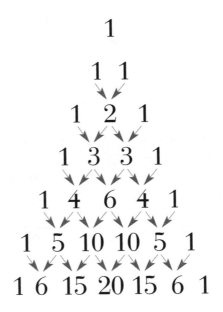

$1 = 1$

$1 + \text{nothing} = 1$

$1 + 1 = 2$

$1 + 2 = 3$

$1 + 3 + 1 = 5$

$1 + 4 + 3 = 8$

$1 + 5 + 6 + 1 = 13$

Note:

Every other diagonal ends with 1, the other with the sequence of numbers 1, 2, 3, 4, 5…

Many researchers discovered fascinating geometric shapes in the diagonals, in addition to the existence of perfect squares with many hexagonal properties. They expanded the triangle to negative integers and greater dimensions.

Computer-generated graphs are a good method to show the remarkable internal shapes of Pascal's triangle.

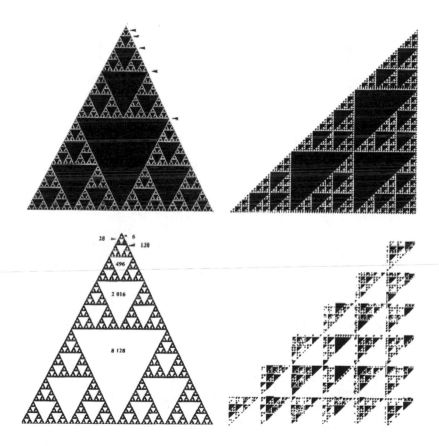

Remarkable internal shapes of Pascal's triangle, obtained by using a computer.
After Pickover, *Wonders of Numbers,* Oxford University Press, 2003.

It is noteworthy that the Arabs knew about this famous triangle (Omar Khayam mentions the arrangement around the year 1100); the Chinese also knew about it, as proven by the triangle of the Chinese mathematician and scholar Chu Shih-Chieh, who in 1303 published a work showing the following diagram:

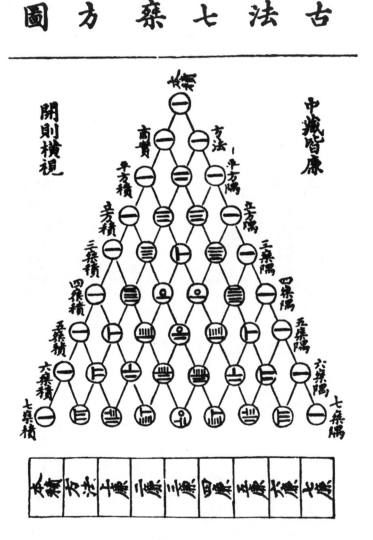

Page taken from the work titled *Su yuan yu zhian*, published in 1303 by the Chinese mathematician Chu Shih-Chieh. After Needham, *op. cit.*, reproduced by Jouven, *Les Nombres cachés*, p. 107.

6

The golden number

The marvelous consolation of finding
the whole world in one soul,
my entire species
in the dear creature that I embrace.
Friedrich Hölderlin

The golden number from generation to generation

The golden number serves for harmonious, balanced constructions found in nature and in many mathematical or geometrical arrangements.

The Egyptians had used the golden number, giving it the value of 1.614. Among other places, we find it in the pyramid of Cheops and in the temple of Luxor.

The triangle 1, 2, √5

There is a very simple right triangle, very easy to build: Its short side is 1, and its longer side is 2. In this case, the hypotenuse measures √5 (square root of 5). The hypotenuse is not an integer as it is in Pythagoras's triangle.

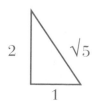

2   √5

1

Indeed, in Pythagoras's triangle, the sides are 3 and 4 and the hypotenuse is 5.

Based on our metric system and current calculation methods, we get:

Short side:	1
Longer side:	2
Hypotenuse:	$\sqrt{5} = 2.236$
Total:	5.236

The royal cubit

We note here that the dimension of the Egyptian "royal cubit" is 0.5236 meters.

Note:

Ancient measurements were generally based on the measurements of an important person: a king or an emperor. This is why, in France, the foot was the measure of Charlemagne's large foot, i.e. 0.324 meters, called the "king's foot."

The length of the cubit, depending on the time period and the country, varied broadly, ranging from 0.442 to 0.720 meters.

The Egyptians used two different cubits: The royal cubit, which we just mentioned, was divided into 7 palms, and the small cubit, which had only 6 palms, measured 0.450 meters.

The royal cubit and the golden number

Half the royal cubit is one foot: 0.2618. We discover that:

2.618 less 1 (short side) = 1.618

2.618 less 2 (longer side) = 0.618

But 1.618 is the famous golden number, Phi, and 0.618 is its reverse: 1/Phi.

The Greeks

In Egypt, the golden number was among the secret knowledge of the priests. Euclid discovered its geometric demonstration.

The Greeks, who used it for the Parthenon, attributed the discovery of the golden number to Pythagoras.

In 1225, Fibonacci stated the value of the golden number (1.618); this is the measurement that is usually considered.

This golden number often plays a key role in the balance of a painting or a construction. Renaissance painters, like Titian and Michelangelo, made use of it, the royal gate of Chartres cathedral is a good example.

265

Detail of the main portal in Chartres cathedral.

Rogier van der Weyden (1400–1464), *Descent from the cross*, 1435.
This painting is precisely organized around the golden number.

From the companions to Le Corbusier

In the Middle Ages, brotherhoods, companionships, guilds, and the freemasons shared this notion for the construction of cathedrals. While many architects, such as Le Corbusier, deliberately used the properties of the golden number, artists surely used it not with calculation, but due to their instinct for harmony.

For a human body with harmonious proportions, the distance from the navel to the ground multiplied by 1.618 gives the height.

We find the Phi module in the measurements of the egg and of the regular pentagon (see below).

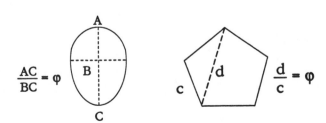

Certain theoreticians found the golden number in the human skeleton, even in blood, and declared that our body was built according to the golden number. Plato went further when he claimed that human thought, when calculating the golden number, had reached one of the canons used by God when he decided to order the universe.

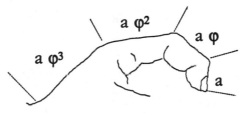

The golden number is everywhere

This golden number was a favorite of nature and artists alike, which supported Pythagoras's theory that music, beauty, architecture, nature, and the cosmos were all connected and inseparable. According to Pythagoras's idea, the golden number reigned over the universe, and what was true for the Pythagoreans quickly became true for the entire Western world: The supernatural link between aesthetics, proportions, and the universe was for a long time one of the main dogmas of Western civilization.

At the time of Shakespeare, scientists were still talking about the revolution of spheres of various sizes. Discussions about the celestial music spread throughout the cosmos.

In art

Phi is present in geometry, as well as in the arts.

There are numerous antique statues whose proportions, when studied, appear to be directly copied from the golden number or from one of Fibonacci's sequences. Leonardo da Vinci's sketches are full of such references. The same is true for less important and spectacular objects than statues, but these objects, such as ancient vases and certain cult accessories, are just as artistic A very large number of paintings by master artists, especially from the Renaissance, are pervaded by the presence of the golden number on several levels.

Albrecht Dürer, *Melancholia*, engraving, 1514.

First of all, their authors truly perfected—in value—an ideal canon of human beauty, especially in women, which owes nothing to chance, but respects on all points a vertical scale based on the golden number.

In addition, the proportions of the paintings themselves were carefully calculated. The rectangles chosen—especially for tall paintings designed to be hung vertically—were most often close to Phi, which made it much easier to harmoniously decompose them into Phi.

Music consists of the relationships between notes, measures, and rhythms according to how they fit together—in other words, numbers organized in a knowledgeable way. In ancient Greece, music, which certain people viewed as similar to the harmony of the spheres, was actually considered an integral part of the theory of mathematics, while the latter was itself born of the harmony of the cosmos. These harmonic relationships are closely related to the golden number.

Furthermore, many string instrument makers, when creating their violins, were concerned with the aesthetic of their proportions. Many of these craftsman, taking inspiration from the remote ideas of antiquity, used certain theories on the beauty of shapes and the means of reproducing them, especially with the golden number.

Thus, applying the rules that had sometimes fallen into oblivion—at least apparently—the master string instrument makers of the Renaissance established a few laws, which we have already mentioned when we divide a segment of a straight line into two parts, so that the ratio between the whole and the largest part is equal to the ratio between the large and the small part. If the length of the whole is equal to 1, the division point in question is at 0.618 from one of the ends. Under the circumstances, we can imagine a shape in which all dimensions are linked by the golden number.

Fibonacci and the golden number

Fibonacci, whom we cited in Book One of this work, presents a sequence rightly named Fibonacci's sequence, in which each term is equal to the sum of the two immediately preceding terms. Thus:

1, 1, 2, 3, 5, 8, 13, 21, 34, 55, 89, 144, 233, 377, 610, 987, 1,597, 2,584, 4,181, 6,765...

When we divide each number by the previous number, we obtain values that are more or less equal to Phi.

$$55 \div 34 = 1.617$$

$$89 \div 55 = 1.618$$

$$610 \div 377 = 1.618037$$

A troubling example

In most plants, the number of petals is 3, 5, 8, 13, 21, 34, 55, or 89.

The numbers we find in plants—concerning not only the petals but also other elements—present mathematical regularities. They correspond to the beginning of Fibonacci's sequence.

If you look at a giant sunflower, you will see that its head has a series of tiny flowers—which become seeds—arranged in a motif (the floret). This arrangement consists of two families of intersecting spirals, one turning clockwise and the other counterclockwise. In certain species, the number of clockwise spirals is 34, and the counterclockwise one is 55. These are consecutive Fibonacci's numbers. The precise number depends on the species concerned, but frequently it is 34 or 55, or 55 and 89, or even 89 and 144—also consecutively numbered in the same sequence. Equally, pineapples have 8 rows of scales turning in a spiral to the left—diamond-shaped scales—and 13 turning in a spiral to the right. Again, these are two of Fibonacci's numbers. (See Ian Stewart, *Nature's Numbers*, Basic Books, 1997.)

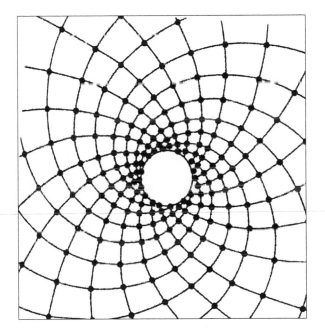

Head of a giant sunflower in which the florets
are arranged in spirals according to the golden number.

Part Five

Is God a mathematical hypothesis?

Numerical values of divine names

The transcendence of π

Fermat and the Kabbalah

1

Numerical values
of divine names

To invent a tale. A story.
It will not be written for a child,
nor for an adult.
Written for no one.
The story of no one.
It will start no matter where,
no matter how.
With this word: God.
The rest will follow, by itself…
Christian Bobin

273

The various names of God are various manifestations of his essence

One of the essential questions of the Kabbalah is: Who is God?

Here, this question is written in English. It could also be asked in other languages, and then one would replace the word *God* by *Dieu*, *Got*, *Zeus*, etc. But these terms will never express the specific way Judaism has for speaking about God. Indeed, it has many ways of indicating the divine, and they are not equivalent.

The study of these various names of God is mainly the object of the Kabbalah of the divine names, which studies the shape of the letters, the numerical values of each name, and the particular forces these names contain.

The ten names of God

Kabbalah tradition reveals ten names of God. Some are used more and are better known than others. Each of them corresponds to a particular *sefira*.

Yhvh is not pronounced. It is the ineffable name, or *shem hameforach*, also called *shem havaya*. This name is also used in connection with *midat ha'hessed* or *midat ha'rahamim* (generosity and compassion). It will appear in a context where God manifests himself in his attribute of generosity or compassion.
Numerical value: 26.

Adni is pronounced "adonai." This is the sound form of the previous name. It is said *shem adnut* or *shem adni*. It is forbidden to take it in vain.
Numerical value: 65.

Yah is a name derived from the tetragrammaton. We find it in the very famous formula *hallelujah*, which literally means "praise the Lord." Made up of two letters, one masculine (*yod*) and the other feminine (*he*), it represents the force of unity within the couple, within the high worlds and the netherworlds, within the heavens and the earth.
Numerical value: 15.

It is interesting to compare this numerical value to the constant of the so-called "Saturn" magic square.

El is a name that means "God" but also "toward." It is often used in connection with another divine name or an adjective or compliment: "the house of God" (*Beth-El*), "God Almighty," etc.
Numerical value: 31.

Eloah is a name derived from the previous one. It is built on the form *el*, plus the last two letters of the tetragrammaton *vav-he*.
Numerical value: 42

Elohim is the God of the Creation. It is one of the most commonly used names in biblical literature. It expresses the forces of nature. It is also derived from the name *el*, but it includes the two other letters of the tetragrammaton *yod-he*, plus the letter *mem*, which makes it look like a plural.
Numerical value: 86.

Ehieh is the name of God who appeared for the first time to Moses in the episode of the burning bush. It means "I will be."
Numerical value: 21.

Shaddai is an important name that governs the balance of the forces of nature between disorder and organization.
Numerical value: 314.

El Shaddai is a name derived from the previous one.
Numerical value: 345.
We must note the importance of this name in connection with the Pythagorean holy triangle, whose sides are respectively 3, 4, 5. It also has the same numerical value as MoShHe, Moses' name.
The fact that Moses was an Egyptian prince is extremely important. Indeed, the name Moshe would come from the secret transmission of Pythagoras's theorem, whose presence is attested in Egypt several millennia before the Greeks. Also to be noted is the fact that the constant of 345 is found in the architecture of certain pyramids.

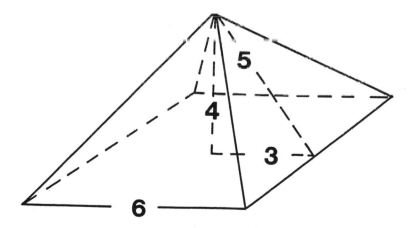

Layout of a pyramid built according to the values 3, 4, and 5 of the Pythagorean triangle.

Tzevaoth: "God of the armies." *Tzavah* means "army." This translation is confusing, because it suggests a military God. In fact, in the language of Kabbalah scholars, it is the army of angels of the celestial spheres, organized in various hosts and legions. Thus, *Tzevaoth* can be translated as "army of letters" (*ot*). It would therefore be the name of the manifestation of the divine in the text.

Numerical value: 499.

2

The transcendence of π

The tree can become a burning flame
the man a speaking flame.
Friedrich Novalis

Tzimtzum, or "retreat"

The *tzimtzum* theory represents one of the most surprising and daring conceptions in the history of the Kabbalah. Originally, *tzimtzum* meant "contraction" or "withdrawal."

Rabbi Isaac Luria, one of the greatest Kabbalists of all time, asked himself the following questions:

– How can there be a world if God is everywhere?

– If God is "everything in everything," how can there be things that are not God?

– How can God create the world *ex nihilo*, if there is no nothingness?

Rabbi Isaac Luria answered by formulating the theory of *tzimtzum*, according to which the first act of the Creator was not to reveal himself to the outside. Far from being a movement outward or an exit from his hidden identity, the first stage was a withdrawal, a retreat. God "withdrew from himself into himself" and, by this act, gave void a place within him, thus creating a space for the future world.

God was able to manifest himself only because he previously withdrew. God left a void, a space called *hallal ha'panui*.

The Kabbalists stress this astonishing fact: The space of the world is a space void of God, an atheistic, atheological space.

For the Kabbalah, the universe was born not because the Creator created the being, something from nothing, but because God, who is infinite, left a place, a void, in which the creation became possible.

In the beginning, there was the void. This remark is fundamental when placed in perspective with the issue of zero.

The forces that make the existence of the universe possible

The question posed to the Kabbalists after they established the original void was that of the possibility of maintaining this void. What forces at work in Creation make the retracted infinite stay at the periphery of the empty space and not refill this space? In other words, what forces maintain the void and allow the world to hold and survive, as void?

To answer these questions, Rabbi Isaac Luria imagined a force coming from the void itself, as if in the cosmic void there was a voice repeating infinitely, "Enough. Do not come back!"

The mystery of the circle and the straight line

From a mathematical viewpoint, the void of the circle, its inner space (the possibility of a surface of the circle) consists of a certain relationship between the straight line and the circle.

If we turn a straight line from one of its ends, it draws a circle, in which it is the radius. By turning, the radius maintains the circle. The circle exists only because of the straight line that constitutes a force represented by the radius. Greek mathematicians, especially Archimedes, tried to formulate mathematically the relationship between the circle and the radius that maintains the void around its center. They found a number that, many years later, in the West, was named π, the initial of the word *perimeter*. (It is noteworthy that, although π is a Greek letter, this name came much later).

The perimeter or circumference of the circle is then obtained by the following formula (where R represents the length of the radius):

$$2\pi R$$

and the surface of the circle is obtained by the formula:

$$\pi R^2$$

So the "mystery" of the circle is the ratio between the straight line and the circle.

This ratio is defined by π, a transcendent number whose exact value can never be reached, that escapes any attempt to a definition and to being locked in frozen measurements, whose proximate value is 3.14 and whose rational value is 22/7 (22 sevenths).

The number π is a window to infinity and, because of this, it is has a deep link with theological thinking.

3.141591653589793238461643383279502
88419716939937510581097494459130781 6
40618610899861803482534211706798214 80
865132723066470938446

π and its first decimals.

The number π and the name *shadai*

As we have seen, the space of the world was created by a withdrawal of the infinite and by a force that kept the light of the infinite at the periphery. In Hebrew, this "no return" force is named *shadai*, a word that means "enough, sufficient," as an abbreviation of the expression "he who said to the world, 'Enough,'" *she-dai*.

Shadai is the name of God, the self-limiting. This is the name of the limitation (in kabbalistic Hebrew, this limitation is called *din*), whose purpose is to make the Creation possible and therefore to balance entropy and the expansion of the world (in Hebrew, *hessed*).

Here, the metaphysical speculations of the masters of the Kabbalah meet the calculations of the Greek mathematicians. One of them, Rabbi Yossef Gikatillia (co-author of the *Zohar* with Rabbi Moshe de Leon in the thirteenth century in Spain) affirms in his book *Guinat egoz* that "the circle is built from the name *shadai*." He is referring in particular to the episode that ends the story of the Garden of Eden: He stationed the cherubim and the fiery revolving sword, thus tracing the circle of the universe (Genesis 3:24). If we use *gematria*, the numerical value of *shadai*, as we have seen, is 314 (*shin* = 300, *dalet* = 4, *yod* = 10).

Strange coincidence: 314 represents the proximate value of π, multiplied by 100

On this, Manitu (Leon Ashkenazi), one of the last great contemporary Kabbalists, makes the following comment: "π is precisely the relationship between the forces that make possible the delimitation in the physical world, a delimitation that exists through the name *shadai* at a metaphysical level."

The word and the number π

The rational value of π is 22/7. For the Kabbalists, this number suggests the articulation of the letters of the Hebrew alphabet (of which there are twenty-two) and the numeral 7, whose first meaning is the rhythm of time in biblical thought.

Thus, π (22/7) means the ratio between the alphabet and time, i.e. the word. Indeed, what it does is to put the alphabet in motion, thanks to the combination of the letters.

$$\text{word} = \frac{22 \text{ letters}}{7} = \frac{\text{alphabet}}{\text{time}} \cong \pi$$

The meanings of π, be they mathematical, philosophical, or kabbalistic, join together toward a common direction: the relationship of the forces that make the void possible and the world as void. An entire exciting perspective opens up here, about man as speaking breath. Is it by chance, then, that in Hebrew π means "my mouth"?

The harmony of the world and the number π

The Kabbalists use many metaphors to state their ideas. In the Kabbalah, there are numerous allusions to fire, trees, the earth, and water. Water is the symbol of life and movement, The river appears in certain texts as the privileged image to express life and particularly the transmission from generation to generation. We find this image of the river in the prophets, especially in Ezekiel. We find in these authors something we may call a "river metaphysics"; π is no stranger to this metaphysics.

Einstein himself was one of the first to be interested, from a physical point of view, in the phenomenon of the meanders of a river. Professor Hendrik Stølum, a specialist in earth science at the University of Cambridge, calculated the ratio between the length of the rivers, from their sources to their mouths, including their meanders, and their real length as the crow flies, i.e. their mathematical length.

Hans-Hendrik Stølum made an extraordinary discovery in this regard. Although the ratio varies from one river to another, the average value is slightly greater than 3; in other words, the real length is approximately triple the direct distance. In fact, the ratio is close to 3.14, and therefore close to the value of the number π.

$$\frac{\text{real length with meanders}}{\text{mathematical length}} \cong 3.14$$

This ratio of π is found most often in the rivers that flow slowly through rather flat plains, like in Brazil or in the Siberian tundra (cf. Singh, *op. cit.*).

In other words, one is tempted to offer the following hypothesis: The ratio that exists between, on the one hand, a tendency toward entropy, deployment, and expansion—known by the kabbalistic name of *hessed*—and, on the other hand, a tendency toward order and limitation—*din*—is on the order of π.

Or else: The ratio that exists between chaos and cosmos tends toward the value of π, i.e. 3.14 or, in kabbalistic language, *shadai*.

Something to think about…

$$\frac{\text{chaos}}{\text{cosmos}} \cong 3.14$$

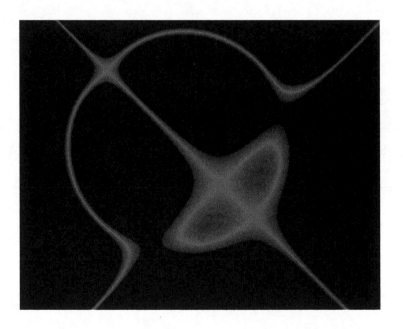

Brian Meloon, *Happy Henon*, 1993.
Image obtained by iteration of Henon's application.

3

Fermat and the Kabbalah

The secrets of the tetragrammaton

I turn toward you, in bed or in life,
and discover that you are
made of the impossible.

Then I turn to myself
and I see the same thing.

It is for this that even while loving
the possible, we will finish by shutting it in,
so that it will no longer prevent
this impossible
without which we cannot live together.
Roberto Juarroz

Concerto for four consonants without vowels

The name YHVH is given as purely visible, four ineffable consonants, without vowels. A name made to be hidden. A name that withdraws while giving itself out. An essential paradox affirming a relationship with God that cannot be reduced to the knowledge that classifies, defines, or synthesizes. By this withdrawal into silence, the revelation keeps the transcendence of what is manifested. The absence of vowels, which makes the name impossible to pronounce, creates an unbridgeable distance that rules out the possibility of considering God an object. The tetragrammaton is like a hole in language, from which language itself draws meaning, a name written not to be pronounced according to its own letters, but to be commented on, translated by other letters or other names.

The name offers the unthinkable.

Seeing the four-letter name means plunging into the void of meaning, penetrating into a voidance of knowledge, experiencing the void.

Note on the two names *yhvh* and *adny*:

Commenting on verse 15 in the third chapter of Exodus, "This is my name forever, and this is my memorial unto all generations," the Talmud explains that the "name" is the tetragrammaton YHVH, also called *Shem-Havaya*, and that the "memorial of the name" is the "name of the name," so-called *Shem-Adnut*, which is written *aleph-dalet-nun-yod*.

There is the ineffable written name

YHVH (*Shem-Havaya*).

There is also the spoken name, which is written

ADNY (*Shem-Adnut*).

The simple *gematria* of *Shem-Havaya* (YHVH) is 26:

yod	=	10
he	=	5
vav	=	6
he	=	5
total		26

Shem-Adnut is called "palace of the name" (*hekhal*). It has a simple numerical value of 65.

aleph	=	1
dalet	=	4
nun	=	50
yod	=	10
total		65

Tree of light with seven branches written with the letters of Psalm 67,
crowned by the inscription: "The tetragrammaton is always before my eyes."
Present in prayer books and on the walls of synagogue,
this illustration helps one to meditate and concentrate on the permanent presence of God.

The enigma of the number 26

We can wonder about the specificity of the *gematria* of the tetragrammaton *Yod-He-Vav-He*, which is 26.

According to certain authors, especially Baal Shem Tov, the meditation based on the alphabet and the names of God consists of always keeping in mind the tetragrammaton and its numerical value 26, and finding this numerical structure in all other letters and, if possible, in all other objects in nature.

Fermat's mathematical discovery
that could revolutionize the Kabbalah

One day, Fermat noticed that 26 is between the number 25, a square number ($25 = 5^2 = 5 \times 5$) and the number 27, a cubic number ($27 = 3^3 = 3 \times 3 \times 3$). By trying in this fashion other numbers found between a square and a cubic number, he could not find any, and he wondered whether 26 was the only one of its kind.

During several days of intense effort, Fermat was able to build a complex reasoning that showed that, indeed, 26 is an exception, and no other number resembles it.

"The number 26 is a unique number in the entire mathematical universe."

Pierre de Fermat

Fermat announced this unique property of 26 to the scientific community, then challenged the community to demonstrate it. He admitted that he had the proof, but the issue was knowing whether others had enough imagination to match him.

In spite of the simplicity of the postulate, the proof is extremely difficult, and Fermat felt a special pleasure in defying British mathematicians Wallis and Digby, who had to admit they had been defeated.

The challenge is now launched to the Kabbalists: How can one translate this discovery in *gematria* terms, and beyond that, into mystical terms.

The fourth dimension

But what is the importance of this situation of a number between 25 and 27, between a square and a cube?

From a geometrical viewpoint, the square corresponds to a surface and the cube to a volume. Such being the case, 26 would represent a dimension other than the surface or the volume. More precisely, it must be a dimension that would let us switch from the surface to the volume.

For mathematicians, the powers note various stages of the development of matter in space.

The point is noted "0."

The line is noted "1."

The plane is noted "2."

The volume is noted "3."

The number 26 would therefore correspond to a fourth dimension that allows switching from the second dimension to the third. Is it not also the time needed to switch from 0 to 1 and from 1 to 2?

Perhaps it would be possible to define the Kabbalist as someone who, referring to the unique property of the tetragrammaton, wrote one day, as a marginal note in one of the books of the Kabbalah he was reading or writing:

Cuius rei demonstrationem mirabilem sane detexi hanc marginis exiguitas non caperet.

Which means:

"I've found a truly remarkable proof of this fact, but his margin is too narrow to contain it."

"This was the note scribbled by Fermat in the margin of the Latin version of *Arithmetica*, by Diophantus of Alexandria, who lived circa 250 B.C.E.

Diophantus specialized in problems whose solutions were integers, today defined as Diophantine equations. He spent his career in Alexandria, collecting known problems and inventing new ones, which he gathered in a treatise titled *Arithmetica*. Of its thirteen books, only six survived the Middle Ages and inspired the mathematicians of the Renaissance and Pierre de Fermat. The other seven books were lost under dramatic circumstances."

(S. Singh, *op. cit.*, p. 77.)

26, the cube, and Solomon's seal

This number 26 is found in two geometric figures. In one of them, it is found in the structure itself; and in the other, it is found in the numerical organization the figure may be bearing.

The first is the cube, whose elements give the sum of 26. Indeed, it has 8 (corners), 6 (faces), and 12 (edges), three numbers whose sum is 26.

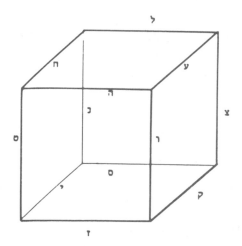

The second figure is Solomon's seal, a six-pointed star whose numbers borne by the apexes and whose intersections are organized so that each line has a total of 26.

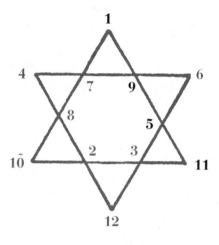

Example: $1 + 9 + 5 + 11 = 26$

Book Three

Shapes

Magic squares and other talismans

Part One

Magic squares

Lines, columns, and diagonals

Chinese origins

How do you build a magic square?

Faust, Goethe, and the magic squares

Melancholia

Some extraordinary magic squares

1

Lines, columns, and diagonals

*I want this work to be written
in a style of my own invention,
which will permit me
to marvelously go and come
from the bizarre to the everyday,
from fantasy to extreme rigor,
from prose to verse,
from the flattest truth to ideals,
the most...the most fragile ones...*
Paul Valéry

293

The *magic square* is a method consisting of entering numbers in a given frame to obtain equal sums, regardless of the lines (or rows), columns, or diagonals. The simplest magic square is of the order 3.

– The "order" of a square is the number of entries in a column, line, or diagonal. A square of order 3 contains nine numbers. A square of order 5 contains twenty-five.
– Squares built on an even number, such as 4, are even squares; squares built on an odd number, such as 5, are odd squares.
– Odd squares have a central symmetry number called the "center" or "reference." Even squares have four central numbers.
– In magic squares of an odd order, the number in the middle of the series of numbers used is placed in the center of the square.

– We call the "constant" of a square the identical sum given by each line, each column, and each diagonal, and sometimes the center of the even square (see the example at the bottom of the page).

– We call the "sum" of a square the sum of all the numbers found in it. It is always equal to the triangular number of the last number of the series used, if it is of the type (0, 1, 2, 3, 4, 5, etc.).

Example:

$$4 \quad 9 \quad 2$$
$$3 \quad 5 \quad 7$$
$$8 \quad 1 \quad 6$$

Odd square of order 3.
The center is marked 5, which is the center of the series of numbers 1, 2, 3, 4, **5**, 6, 7, 8, 9.

– Each column or line or diagonal has three numbers, and therefore, it is of order 3.
– The sum of the numbers of each row, each column, and each diagonal is 15. Consequently, it has a constant of 15.
– The sum of the numbers of this magic square is 45 and corresponds to the sacred number or triangular number 9.
– In the Kabbalah, this number symbolizes "man" and his inquisitive nature, since 45 means "*what?*" It is also one of the gematric developments of the tetragrammaton of God (*Yhvh*).

$$1 \quad 16 \quad 11 \quad 6$$
$$13 \quad 4 \quad 7 \quad 10$$
$$8 \quad 9 \quad 14 \quad 3$$
$$12 \quad 5 \quad 2 \quad 15$$

An even square of order 4. Here the constant of the square is 34.

Magic squares most often have remarkable properties. Thus, for the first squares, one of the simplest and best known (in a later chapter, we will see its relationship to alchemy), we can note that:

$$4^2 + 9^2 + 2^2 = 8^2 + 1^2 + 6^2$$

$$\text{and}$$

$$4^2 + 3^2 + 8^2 = 2^2 + 7^2 + 6^2$$

The trajectory of the internal dynamics of a magic square produces a diagram in which the geometric equilibrium is always surprising.

Note:

There is only one magic square of order 3 that uses the first nine numbers. The others play on rotation or symmetry.

(See the example of the Lo Shu square, p. 299.)

Beautiful harmony

Looking at the world, we find it beautiful because of its colors, its shapes, its movement, and often because of the grace of the dynamic interactions of geometric figures that produce harmonies and bring us aesthetic pleasure.

But there are also harmonies that are more abstract, designed to bring joy to the intelligence, rather than to move the senses.

In the previous chapters, we have encountered many of these harmonies that create links between numbers and that constitute the theory of numbers. In a sense, magic squares fall into this category. Indeed, the magic square is a complex of numbers gathered in a square structure, where the often-playful intelligence of their remarkable links awake and amaze us. We say "intelligence" stressing one of the word's etymological meanings, derived from *intellegere*, which may mean "to bind together."

Why are these squares magical? According to a passage in Goethe's *Faust*, which we cite a little further on, they seem to have had magical powers, such as the ability to make potions of all kinds effective, including the elixir of youth. We will see other examples. Magic numbers have been talismans worn around the neck or simply hidden in the pocket of a garment, written on parchment, or embroidered on a piece of fabric.

The magic square of order 3, which is the simplest one, has in its primary form a center of 5. A version derived from this magical and protective number can be seen in various amulets, especially in Muslim countries and among the Jews, in the representation of the "hand" of Fatima often associated with one or several fish that protect against the evil eye.

This 5, as a talisman or amulet, is also frequently found in the representation of a five-pointed pentagon inscribed in a circle, which was one of the fundamental symbols of the Pythagoreans.

It also constitutes the seal of Solomon, whose value is 15, the same as the constant of the square of 3.

$$1 + 2 + 3 + 4 + 5 = 15$$

Chinese mathematician Li Shanlan (1811–1882),
author of *The Impact of Western Mathematics on China.*

2

Chinese origins

Dreams came up the river.
We stop and talk to them.
They know many a thing,
but not where they come from.
Franz Kafka

The Chinese origins of magic squares are considered relatively certain, but we will show later on the possibility of a Greek provenance.

The oldest traditions concerning these squares actually go back to Chinese texts, which offer numerous variations of a founding myth, including this legend from the twenty-third century B.C.E.: A turtle comes out of the river Lo, thus revealing to Emperor Yu a magic square engraved on its back.

This square became famous under the name of the square of Lo Shu (the "writing of the river Lo"). It serves as the basis of Chinese numerology, as well as various derivative, simplified systems of numerology.

$$\begin{array}{ccc} 4 & 9 & 2 \\ 3 & 5 & 7 \\ 8 & 1 & 6 \end{array}$$

Female and male: *yin* and *yang*

In China the binary principle is represented by *yin* and *yang*: in a circle two shapes are interlocked together.

The one is black, the other white, and each has a small core of the other color. Their shape and position evoke circular movement, the alternation of day and night, summer and winter, auspicious and inauspicious. *Yin*, which is black, is considered passive and female, while *yang*, which is white, is considered active and male.

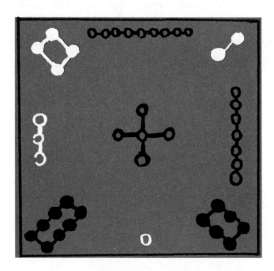

In its original form, the Lo Shu square was written in ancient Chinese numerals. Even numbers are female and are called *Yin*. They are represented by solid dots, linked by lines.

Odd numbers are male and are called *Yang*. They are represented by small empty circles linked by lines.

We must note the cross-shaped 5, which is precisely the center of the square. This cross shape reveals that the graphic form of the numerals originates from the magic square of order 3 with a reference of 5.

Although the numbers are either male or female, we can still stress their compound nature: male *and* female (*Yang* and *Yin*). With 5 playing, in a way, the role of a base, we obtain the following equivalences:

$$6 = 5 + 1$$
$$7 = 5 + 2$$
$$8 = 5 + 3$$
$$9 = 5 + 4$$
$$10 = 5 + 5$$

For example, 6 in itself is even and female. But it becomes male and female when we read it with the "center-base": 5 + 1 = 6.

This is the metaphysical meaning of addition, and it is revealed by the square called Ho Tu.

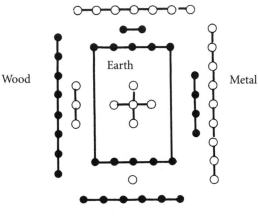

Fire

Wood

Earth

Metal

Water

We can clearly see here that each side of the square, each orientation, bears two numbers: 2 and 7 are together, the same as 1 and 6, 3 and 8, etc.

And we can also clearly see that Ho Tu works like a table that offers the rules of addition: 5 + 1 = 6, 5 + 3 = 8, etc.

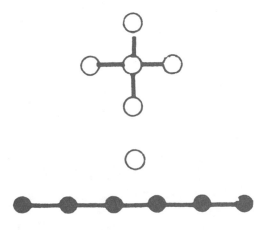

The Lo Shu Square

In Chinese numerology, the Lo Shu Square is an important aid in the interpretation of character and of the "lines of destiny." Each square corresponds to a year in a cycle of 9; every nine years, the same square repeats. Each month and each day, as well as each hour, has a link with the square.

We will give an example at the end of this chapter.

To obtain the nine Lo Shu squares, it is enough to move the numbers within the square according to a very simple logic, namely:

Starting from the basic Lo Shu square,

1 goes to 2, 2 to 3, 3 to 4, 4 to 5, 5 to 6, 6 to 7, 7 to 8, 8 to 9, and 9 to 1, which gives a new square:

$$3 \quad 8 \quad 1$$
$$2 \quad 4 \quad 6$$
$$7 \quad 9 \quad 5$$

This new square, in turn, becomes a third square by moving the numbers in the same way. This continues until the return of the basic square. In all, this gives us nine Lo Shu squares.

The place of each number is called the "house," and the number in the center of the square is called the "reference." The reference in the basic square is 5, the reference of the second derivative (obtained by moving the numbers) is 4, and so forth until you get the square in which the reference is 9.

These nine squares form the basis of a Chinese numerology that, like other popular types of numerology, allows us to highlight the characteristics of the personality, its strengths and weaknesses and the broad lines of an existence.

9	5	7
8	1	3
4	6	2

Reference 1

1	6	8
9	2	4
5	7	3

Reference 2

2	7	9
1	3	5
6	8	4

Reference 3

3	8	1
2	4	6
7	9	5

Reference 4

4	9	2
3	5	7
8	1	6

Reference 5

5	1	3
4	6	8
9	2	7

Reference 6

6	2	4
5	7	9
1	3	8

Reference 7

7	3	5
6	8	1
2	4	9

Reference 8

8	4	6
7	9	2
3	5	1

Reference 9

3

How do you build
a magic square?

*Once written, there is no book
that isn't books, nor word that isn't words...*
Edmond Jabès

The construction of a square of order 3

The magic square of 3 is easy to construct. By laying out the series of the first nine numbers in a row, Theon of Smyrna noticed that the two numbers that are symmetrical in relation to the axis represented by 5 give a sum equal to 10.

$$1\ 2\ 3\ 4 \quad 5 \quad 6\ 7\ 8\ 9$$

What could be more natural than to place the 5 in the central spot of a square made up of nine spots, and then place 1 and 9, for example, in the central column?

x	1	x
x	5	x
x	9	x

The sum of the column is 15. If we try to complete the lowest line by two numbers such that the sum of this line would also be 15, only 2 and 4 work.

$$
\begin{array}{ccc}
x & 1 & x \\
x & 5 & x \\
2 & 9 & 4
\end{array}
$$

In that case, we must write 6 and 8 in spots that are diagonally symmetrical in relation to the central axis.

$$
\begin{array}{ccc}
6 & 1 & 8 \\
x & 5 & x \\
2 & 9 & 4
\end{array}
$$

Finally, there is only one way of placing the two remaining numbers, 3 and 7, so that the sums of the corresponding columns are also 15.

$$
\begin{array}{ccc}
6 & 1 & 8 \\
7 & 5 & 3 \\
2 & 9 & 4
\end{array}
$$

How do you build an odd magic square?

There is a way to build an odd magic square. (See the definition of an odd square on page 293. For this chapter, we were inspired by the works of F. X. Chaboche, *Vie et mystère des nombres*, Albin Michel, Paris, 1976, and A. Jouette, *Le Secret des nombres*, Albin Michel, Paris, 1998.)

Place the elements like this:

```
            1
        4       2
    7       5       3
        8       6
            9
```

Apply the grid, and place each element outside the frame at its antipode.

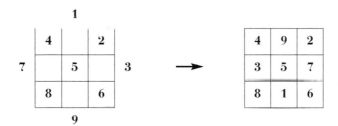

Another example:
Place the elements like this:

```
                    1
                6       2
            11      7       3
        16      12      8       4
    21      17      13      9       5
        22      18      14      10
            23      19      15
                24      20
                    25
```

Apply the grid, and place each element outside the frame at its antipode.

11	24	7	20	3
4	12	25	8	16
17	5	13	21	9
10	18	1	14	22
23	6	19	2	15

Note:

A square remains magical if we increase or reduce all the elements by the same number. The square below is made with the elements of the square of order 4 (see earlier in chapter 1, page 293) plus five units, with the constant increasing from 34 to 54.

6	20	19	9
17	11	12	14
13	15	16	10
18	8	7	21

Equally, the square remains magical if we multiply all the elements by the same number.

As we saw in the definitions of the first chapter, in a magic square of odd order, the number in the center of the series of numbers used is placed in the center of the square. (In the case of the square in our second example, 13 is in the center of the series and of the square.)

4

Faust, Goethe,
and the magic squares

A recipe for kouglof:
Mix 1/2 pound of sugar
with the zest of an orange and a lemon.
Sift the sugar to remove all the lumps.
Add six egg yolks and mix delicately
for a half hour
Add a little lemon juice and mix in an
amount of flour equivalent
to the weight of two hard-boiled eggs.
Add six egg whites
that have been beaten stiff
and bake the mixture in a buttered pan
that has been sprinkled with flour.
Anna Pouzovna

A magic potion that makes you thirty years younger

In his drama *Faust*, Goethe speaks of the significant series represented by the first ten numbers, even though he does it in a manner quite far from the usual observations. Faust is led by Mephistopheles into the kitchen of the witch to receive a potion that should make him thirty years younger. While preparing the potion, the witch recites these verses that she reads from a big book:

"Make no mistake!

From One make Ten

And leave Two alone and do the same with Three. You're rich!

Lose Four, from Five and Six, the witch tells you,
Makes Seven and Eight. It's done!
And Nine and One and Ten is nothing."
This is the witch's "One times One."

These enigmatic words have been interpreted every possible way, but without paying attention to the fact that Goethe puts them in the mouth of a witch. The charm that must be found in the potion when it is prepared must first of all be put there by all kinds of spiritual operations. Such a charm, such witchcraft, must therefore be contained in the witch's "One times One."

A magic square?

Let's try to read Goethe's text line by line to discover whether this may be a magic square.

First line

We enter the numbers 1 to 9 to form, according to a numerical sequence:

$$\begin{matrix} 1 & 2 & 3 \\ 4 & 5 & 6 \\ 7 & 8 & 9 \end{matrix}$$

We then apply to it Goethe's words: first of all, from 1 make 10 ("From One make Ten"); we keep 2 ("And leave Two alone"); we do the same with 3 ("and do the same with Three").

Then, the first line of the square is no longer 1, 2, 3, but 10, 2, 3. This already gives the partial sum of 15. In this way, we have become rich ("You're rich!").

Second line

Now it's the turn of the numbers 4 through 9. 4 must be eliminated, hence the appearance of an empty place whose numerical sign is 0 ("Lose Four"). The numbers 5 and 6 must be replaced by the pair 7 and 8 ("Lose

Four, from Five and Six, the witch tells you, Makes Seven and Eight"). Thus, the former second line 4, 5, 6 becomes the new 0, 7, 8, whose sum is again 15.

Third line

For the new third line, we already know the first two numbers, 5 and 6. To get the sum 15 here too, the last number must be 4, which was therefore lost from its original place at the beginning of the second line. Thus, what we lose has not completely disappeared, but took another place that was not expected.

When Goethe puts the tenth verse after the first nine with the words "It's done," it comes out that the last line of the square must be 5, 6, 4.

Concerning the interpretation of the two final verses: "And Nine and One/And Ten is nothing" it means that the witch made the two regular numbers 9 and 1 disappear and, in their place, brought by artifice the two irregular numbers 10 and 0 (nothing). 9 must have had the same fate as 1, namely it was not taken into account. 9 is like 1. Equally, 10 is like 0: Both of them should not have appeared at all, but they found a place because 9 and 1 were thrown out. The modified square is then:

$$
\begin{array}{ccc}
10 & 2 & 3 \\
0 & 7 & 8 \\
5 & 6 & 4
\end{array}
$$

An imperfect square

In the last square, the sums by lines, and also by columns, give indeed the same value: 15. One of the diagonal sums also gives this result, but not the other. This defect of form distinguishes the square from the true traditional magic square, which gives the sum 15 on both diagonals.

Dürer's magic square, with constant 34: detail from the work *Melancholia* (reproduced on page 268 of this book). The date 1514 appears at the bottom.

5

Melancholia

Suns-threads
Above the gray-black desert.
A thought as high as a tree
catches the sound of light:
there still are songs to sing
beyond man.
Paul Celan

The most famous of magic squares is that included by the painter and engraver Albrecht Dürer in the print titled *Melancholia*.

Albrecht Dürer (1471–1528), an outstanding personality of the German Renaissance, traveled to Italy twice to be initiated in a tradition rediscovered thanks to the arrival of Byzantine scholars fleeing from Constantinople after it was conquered in 1453 by the Turks of Mehmed II. A first trip took place in 1494. The young artist had just finished his training with Michel Wohlgemuth, and then with the Schongauer brothers from Colmar. He met the Neo-Platonist Jacopo de Barbari, who disclosed to him only fragments of what he knew. Dürer wrote about it: "Jacopo did not want to tell me clearly about his proportions.... Still, he showed me a man and a woman drawn according to certain measurements. At the time, I was less intent on visiting unknown countries than on penetrating his theories."

At the height of his talent, the German artist returned to the peninsula a second time. He was 34. We know that he then met the Franciscan Fra Luca Pacioli di Borgo, and we can suppose that Fra Luca taught him Plato's and Pythagoras's "divine proportion."

Indeed, four years later, Fra Luca published a book with this title. (See the chapter on the golden number, page 263.)

From Dürer as an engraver, we know the fifteen plates of *The Apocalypse*, engraved on wood (1598) and also splendid bronzes, such as *The Knight and Death* and *Melancholia*. We can stress how, in the latter work, the pensive angel is inscribed in a five-pointed pentagon (Pythagoras's pentagon). One can contemplate the curious cut stone placed at the foot of a ladder with seven steps (the traditional "ladder of the sages"). (See the illustration reproduced on page 268.)

A magic square of order 4 and constant 34 is engraved on the wall. Albrecht Dürer was pleased to arrange it so that the date of his work, 1514, appears clearly in the square—in the two middle spots on the last line.

Albrecht Dürer, *The Four Horsemen of the Apocalypse*, 1498.

6

Some extraordinary
magic squares

God doesn't exist,
and we are his chosen people.
Woody Allen

The first six numbers may be placed differently. For example, Bernard Frenicle de Bessy (1605–1675) showed that there were 878 arrangements suitable to produce a square of order 4 with the first sixteen numbers.

315

$$
\begin{array}{cccc}
1 & 16 & 11 & 6 \\
13 & 4 & 7 & 10 \\
8 & 9 & 14 & 3 \\
12 & 5 & 2 & 15
\end{array}
$$

The sum of the numerals of the central square is thus equal to the constant of the square: 34.

Magic squares and geometric figures

If we try to figure out the path taken by one number substituting for another within the magic square, we notice that the resulting graph is extremely precise and very beautiful, from a geometric viewpoint.

Here is a square of order 4 and constant 34, in which the elements were laid out according to a certain design:

1	15	14	4
12	6	7	9
8	10	11	5
13	3	2	16

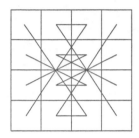

The magic square of order 6
Each alignment totals 111.
This square is interesting because 111 is the numerical value developed from the letter *aleph. Aleph-lamed-pe*: $1 + 30 + 80 = 111$.

6	25	24	13	7	36
35	11	14	20	29	2
33	27	16	22	10	3
4	28	15	21	9	34
32	8	23	17	26	5
1	12	19	18	30	31

The oldest magic square
An Indian square
In Khajuraho (India) there is a temple, built in the eleventh and twelfth centuries, in which one pillar bears a grid around it that, flattened out and translated into our numerical script, would be:

7	12	1	14
2	13	8	11
16	3	10	5
9	6	15	4

The total of the lines, columns, and diagonals is 34. It is probably the oldest magic square.

Diabolical squares

The square of silence, or the square of the master, or the square of the sanctuary

Certain magic squares are called "diabolical" and have interesting particularities. For example, in the square below, the sum of each row, column, or diagonal is 65.

If we cut this diabolical square by a vertical line between any two columns and we move around the two pieces, we still obtain a magic square. By cutting with a horizontal line, we will get the same result.

We can thus notice that in any diamond (9 are possible) cut from the diabolical square, the sum of the elements is again 65.

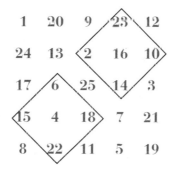

A magic and kabbalistic square

It is also possible to build a square with constant 65 containing a central magic square with constant 39.

23	8	5	4	25
20	14	15	10	6
19	9	13	17	7
2	16	11	12	24
1	18	21	22	3

This square seems particularly important because the numbers revealed in it are fundamental numbers in the Hebrew Kabbalah.

The constant of this square, 65, is the numerical value of the name *adonay* (see the chapter on the names of God, p. 273), and 39 is the value of the expression *Yhvh ehad*, "God is one." The number 65 is also the numerical value of "silence" (*hass*) and "sanctuary" (*hekhal*). In this sense, this magic square would have a talisman value close to the Jewish *mezuzah*, the little parchment one places at the entrance of houses and on doors. The kabbalistic character of this square is confirmed by the fact that the difference between the two constants is:

$$65 - 39 = 26$$

since 26 is precisely the numerical value of the holy tetragrammaton *Yhvh*.

The ultra-magic square

Here is an ultra-magic square, in which the total 40 is obtained in twenty-two different ways according to the four horizontal rows, the four vertical columns, and the two diagonals. (We must remember that 22 is the number of letters in the Hebrew alphabet, as well as the number of blades of the tarot, without implying any possible connection between the Torah and tarot.)

1	15	20	4
18	6	7	9
8	16	11	5
13	3	2	22

Furthermore, the addition of the elements entered in the four corners of twelve quadrilaterals also gives the sum of 40.

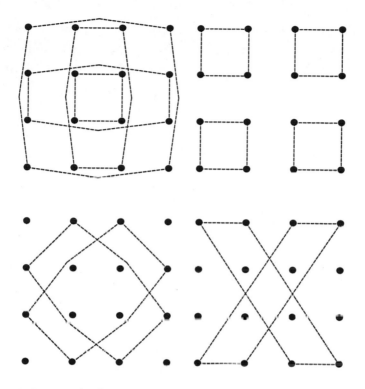

An interesting particularity

Dürer's square, *Melancholia*, presents the same properties, plus the arrangement:

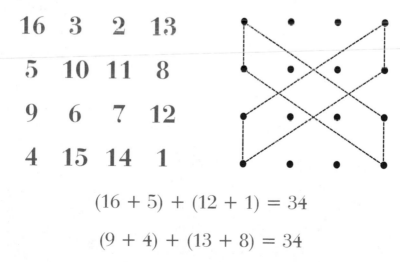

$$16 \quad 3 \quad 2 \quad 13$$
$$5 \quad 10 \quad 11 \quad 8$$
$$9 \quad 6 \quad 7 \quad 12$$
$$4 \quad 15 \quad 14 \quad 1$$

$$(16 + 5) + (12 + 1) = 34$$

$$(9 + 4) + (13 + 8) = 34$$

Euler's magic square

This very great German mathematician combined, just to amuse himself one day, the following magic square in which the sum of all the numbers on a horizontal or vertical line is equal to 260.
The sum of each half-line is equal to 130.

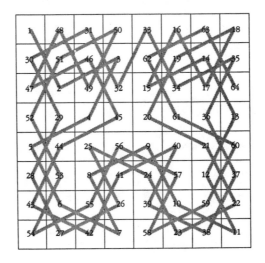

From a kabbalistic point of view, these numbers are important. 260 is the differential *gematria* of *shem*, the "name," and 130 is the simple *gematria* of *sulam*, which means "ladder," as in the biblical passage of Jacob's dream. In addition, if we start from 1, advancing like the knight in the game of chess to go to 2, then to 3, and so on, we draw the symmetrical network shown above.

Magic stars

There are also magic stars. They can be made in star-shaped polygons. The idea is to place the numbers so that the sums of those that appear on any side of the star are always equal between them. Thus, it is possible to build star-shaped heptagons. For example, this one (at right) has a constant of 30:

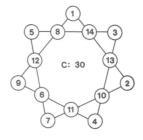

Based on the hexagram, there are perfect magic stars. Some of these stars are called "Solomon's Seal," and others are called "David's Shield." Their constant is often 26, the numerical value of the tetragrammaton YHVH.

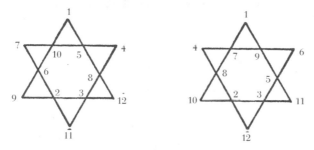

If there are numbers only at the ends of a star, the sum is 21, the triangle of 6, and the numerical value of the name of God, *Ehye*.

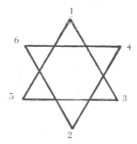

The magic hexagon of Clifford W. Adams

It took Adams forty-seven years to discover this hexagon in 1957 (with constant 38), but since he lost the paper where he had noted the solution, he tried again for five years before finding...the paper.

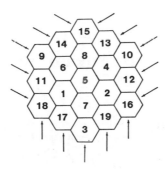

Part Two

Alchemy and talismans

Alchemy

The Bible and magic squares

Healing and relaxation

"The erotic affair between the straight line and the circle"

Theseus and the Minotaur in *The Story of the Myth of Theseus*, by Cassoni Campana, circa 1510.

1

Alchemy

One must not touch the idols
because the gilding sticks to the fingers
Gustave Flaubert

The alchemists who searched for the philosopher's stone defined magic squares based on the planets and the materials used in their various experiments. We present them here, each time with a brief commentary.

The Square of Saturn

(order 3)
This is the most widely known. We find it under the names of Lo Shu and Solomon's Square. Its constant 15 corresponds to the name of God Yah (YH).

4	9	2
3	5	7
8	1	6

The material that corresponds to this Square of Saturn is lead, because in general these squares are written on lead and sometimes on new fabrics or new parchment. They were known as magic talismans that made childbirth easier. Thus, they were inscribed on a piece of fabric or parchment that was placed at the feet of the woman in labor.

Medallion talisman bearing the Square of Saturn.

Odd and even

We can add here a property to this beautiful magic square. The odd numbers form a cross:

$$4 \quad 9 \quad 2$$
$$3 \quad 5 \quad 7$$
$$8 \quad 1 \quad 6$$

The Square of Jupiter
(order 4)

$$4 \quad 14 \quad 15 \quad 1$$
$$9 \quad 7 \quad 6 \quad 12$$
$$5 \quad 11 \quad 10 \quad 8$$
$$16 \quad 2 \quad 3 \quad 13$$

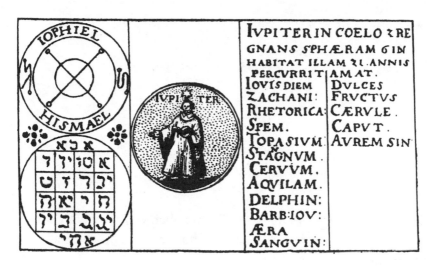

Amulet bearing the Square of Jupiter with an inscription in Hebrew and Latin.
The square itself is in Hebrew numeral-letters.

This square has a constant of 34. The corresponding material is tin. It is engraved on coral, to protect against curses.

Another one (below) is made up of a combination of 8, 6, 4, and 2. It is placed under the wing of a white dove, and has the property of convincing a young woman to accept a marriage proposal.

8	6	4	2
4	2	8	6
2	4	6	8
6	8	2	4

The Square of Mars
(order 5)

11	24	7	20	3
4	12	25	8	16
17	5	13	21	9
10	18	1	14	22
23	6	19	2	15

The constant of this square is 65. This number, which we will find in the names of God, also means "silence" and "sanctuary." The sum of this square is 325. The corresponding metal is iron.

The Square of the Sun
(order 6)

6	32	3	34	35	1
7	11	27	28	8	30
19	14	16	15	23	24
18	20	22	21	17	13
25	29	10	9	26	12
36	5	33	4	2	31

Its constant is 111 and the sum of the square is 666, a mythical number whose meaning is still enigmatic. This square has 36 places, a number we have found earlier, and that is also the number of the hidden wise men in the Kabbalah.

The center, or "heart," of this square gives 2 times 37, which is the "number of man" ($n^2 + 1$) of 6 ($6^2 + 1$). We note that 666 divided by 37 is 18, a number in which we find 666, as well as 6 + 6 + 6. 18 is also the number of life in Hebrew. It is pronounced "hay" and is often worn around the neck as a talisman.

The Square of Venus
(order 7)

22	47	16	41	10	35	4
5	23	48	17	42	11	29
30	6	24	49	18	36	12
13	31	7	25	43	19	37
38	14	32	1	26	44	20
21	39	8	33	2	27	45
46	15	40	9	34	3	28

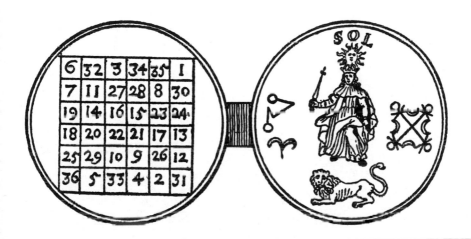

Medallion-talisman with the magic square of the Sun.

The constant of this square is 175. The sum of the square is equivalent to the triangular number of 49 (49 + 48 + 47... + 1 = 1,225).

It is also called the Seal of Abraham, because according to the biblical text, Abraham lived to the age of 175.

As we have shown several times, magic squares offer an internal geometry of great harmony that emphasizes their structured character. Here is the internal geometry of the Seal of Abraham, or the Square of Venus. This square is a talisman that brings a long, happy life.

The Square of Mercury
(order 8)

The Square of Mercury has the constant 260, a number we will find as the differential value of the word *name* in Hebrew (*shem*), and the first two letters of Moses' name.

The total sum of this square is 2,080. The metal attributed to it is the silver alloy. In its structure, this square corresponds to the chessboard, 8 by 8. It is also equivalent to 2 times 32 (the 32 paths of wisdom). Its heart has diagonals that each add up to 65, one of the numbers we have seen (see the Square of Mars, p. 326). This is the square of wisdom and intelligence.

8	58	59	5	4	62	63	1
49	15	14	52	53	11	10	56
41	23	22	44	45	19	18	48
32	34	35	29	28	38	39	25
40	26	27	37	36	30	31	33
17	47	46	20	21	43	42	24
9	55	54	12	13	51	50	16
64	2	3	61	60	6	7	57

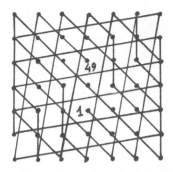

Geometry and internal dynamics of the Seal of Abraham.

The Square of the Moon
(order 9)

The total sum of the square is 3,321. Its constant is 369. This number 369 is equivalent, according to its numerical value, to the Hebrew expression "golden horn," *keren hazahav*. Consequently, it can be considered a talisman for success and luck. In spite of the "gold" we just mentioned, silver is its corresponding metal. Perhaps this number suggests a highly alchemistic manner of transforming silver into gold.

37	78	29	70	21	62	13	54	5
6	38	79	30	71	22	63	14	46
47	7	39	80	31	72	23	55	15
16	48	8	40	81	32	64	24	56
57	17	49	9	41	73	33	65	25
26	58	18	50	1	42	74	34	66
67	27	59	10	51	2	43	75	35
36	68	19	60	11	52	3	44	76
77	28	69	20	61	12	53	4	45

The Square of the Earth
(order 10)
The constant of the square is 505 and its total sum is 5,050.

1	99	98	4	95	6	7	93	92	10
90	12	13	87	16	85	84	18	19	81
80	22	23	27	75	76	74	28	29	71
31	69	68	34	36	65	37	63	62	40
50	49	53	47	45	46	57	58	59	41
51	52	48	54	55	56	44	43	42	60
61	39	38	64	66	35	67	32	33	70
30	72	73	77	26	25	24	78	79	21
20	82	83	17	86	15	14	88	89	11
91	9	8	94	5	96	97	3	2	100

2

The Bible and magic squares

Malicious gossip appears as a refusal of
the complexity of the real, such is
its gravity...
dysfunction of the word...
expression of a religious word gone astray,
which would demand that knowledge
always be true or always be false
objectively—and that someone be
either completely right
or completely wrong.
In this either is contained
an inability to withstand the relativity
of human things. As if the universe
removed its veil in the form of a
simple affront
between good and evil. It is in fact
a propensity of fundamentalism to think
itself capable of responding to all demands
and of breaching all the gaps in meaning.
To explain the unexplainable, justify God.
And yet, the Talmud's vocation is to speak of
the ambiguity of the world and
educate man to a wisdom which is that of
uncertainty, to a spirit which is that
of complexity.
Gilles Bernheim

331

The breastplate of the high priest

Although the Chinese origin of the magic square is stated in traditional texts, we think that the square's imaginative developments, such as the fact that it caught the attention of wizards, of alchemists and Kabbalists, has its source in a passage of the Bible concerning one of the "habits" of the high priests.

To officiate in the sanctuary of the desert (*mishkane*) and later in the holy temple of Jerusalem, the high priest wore eight sacerdotal garments, described in the biblical text of Exodus (28:2 and following). According to the Talmud, these garments had the power of correcting faults. It is interesting to note that the cloak, for example, corrected malicious gossip.

The outer garment was the breastplate (in Hebrew, *hoshen*), a square plate, measuring a half cubit by a half cubit (approximately 10 by 10 inches) made of gold, azure, and crimson, which was set in twelve precious stones engraved with the names of the twelve tribes of Israel (Exodus 28:15).

The serpent, the diviner, and the Messiah

The verse insists on the word *square*: *Ravoua yihyé kafoul, zérèt orko ve zérèt rohbo*—"Square it will be, double, a half cubit long by a half cubit wide."

The word *hoshen*, which designates this square, is important because its three letters mean, in a different order, "to guess" (*nahosh*), and the man who uses this square becomes a *diviner*. Also remarkable is the fact that the verb *to divine* means "the serpent" (*nahash* in Hebrew). This serpent appears several times in the biblical text with different functions. At first glance, they seem paradoxical; the serpent of original sin, the serpent of the miracles of Moses and Pharaoh's magicians, the serpent that bites and kills in the desert, the serpent that heals in the same desert—hence the origin of the caduceus.

Also important is the numerical value of this word, which is 358—the same value as the word *Meshiah*, which means "Messiah."

Reading, combining, interpreting, and foreseeing

This square is really "magical" to the extent that it had an oracular function. The high priest, the king, or the prophet asked a question, and the stones lit up and blinked to inscribe the answer depending on the letters of the names engraved on the precious stones. Then there was substantial interpretation work to be done, because each name had several letters; it was necessary to make a choice, then combine the letters chosen to make words and phrases with them. Be that as it may, the idea of a square with magical powers emerged, we think, starting from that period.

The number of the Beast: 666

The Apocalypse, the last book of the New Testament, is a prophetic message from Jesus addressed through his servant John (1:1) to the seven churches of Asia Minor. It is noteworthy that the word *apocalypse* means "unveiling," not "final destruction at the end of time."

This revelation-unveiling of John is made in the form of a sumptuous and dramatic poem announcing the reign of divine justice on earth. The images are symbolic rather than descriptive, and John, who had great arithmological knowledge that he derived directly from kabbalistic *gematria*, constantly refers to the language of numbers and colors.

The number of the Beast, the famous 666, is the best known of all this arithmology. John was certainly initiated intellectually and must have known perfectly well the entire arsenal of Pythagorean numbers. At the end of chapter 13 of his poem, John poses one of the most famous riddles ever posed, in the way that Plato, a few centuries earlier, had posed to Greek philosophers the riddle of the Soul of the World, which reflected musical connections.

After saying that nobody can buy or sell, except for the one who has the mark, the name of the Beast or the numeral of his name, John formulates it as follows:

> "Here is wisdom. He that hath understanding, let him count the number of the Beast. For it is the number of a man, and the number of him is 666."
> Apocalypse 13:18.

Why 666? An enigma to think about…

333

We finish this chapter with this mathematical miracle: the magic square of the Apocalypse—a rather strange magic square that is 6 by 6, in which all values are prime numbers (divisible only by themselves and by 1), and in which the sum of each line, column, and diagonal is equal to 666, the number of the Beast.

3	107	5	131	109	311
7	331	193	11	83	41
103	53	71	89	151	199
113	61	97	197	167	31
367	13	173	59	17	37
73	101	127	179	139	47

3

Healing and relaxation

What do we call a classic?
A book everyone talks about
and no one has read!
Ernest Hemingway

The question that we are often faced with when we explain how magic squares work is: What are they for? The answer is that they are for nothing; they help nothingness happen.

The magic square has a relaxing, soothing function, a meditative side that we find in all Far Eastern meditation practices, in which the idea is to reach, at one time or another, the "no mind," according to a commonly used English expression. This space of nothingness or "no-mind-land" may be called a "zero degree of the senses," or "parallel zero," which opens man up to a deep and sometimes difficult de-signification.

It liberates all the elements that make up language and the spirit. A new life is created within the rhythms and the entire linguistic and numerical material of thought. The words, syllables, consonants, vowels, measures, rhymes, the various forms of scansion, everything starts being exchanged, starts speaking and responding. They are offered for exchange (and this process is a joy). There is in it a zero degree of the senses, which is not a freezing of the senses but of life, movement, and time. This movement calls into play vital energies and also creates balance and well-being. By the play of numerals and letters involved in magic squares, there is a mobilization of all psychic processes, which also takes place in the analysis of the working principles of these squares.

The constants of magic squares, or certain numbers that constitute their intimate structures, are numbers we find in the Kabbalah: 45, 65, 111, etc. Consequently, we offer a few elements of reflection that join the magical science of the squares and the spiritual experience of the Kabbalah or one of its aspects. If we follow the example of the breastplate of the high priest, according to certain commentators, the magical side of this talisman is based on the combination of letters and their interpretation.

This is not a passive magical power; it is the fact of having access to the letters, the combination, and the interpretation that opens new psychological possibilities and unties the knots of language and difficult situations.

One must understand that the magic of the squares does not essentially come from the existence of the square and the positioning of the numerals and numbers in it, but from all the possible play and reflections this positioning allows one to create: For example, from the primordial importance of the calculation that verifies the correctness of the constant in each line, each column, and each diagonal, to the introduction of the thought in a movement whose subtle turns and returns have therapeutic virtues.

A poetico-analysis

To analyze these numbers and letters, one could speak along with Gaston Bachelard of a poetico-analysis: The images open up the dream world. The poetics of the image represent a different way of approaching man. As Bachelard says, "Philosophers and psychologists don't know everything. Poets understand man differently."

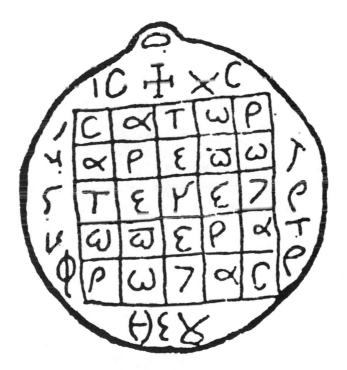

Medallion bearing the Sator-Rotas magic square—one of the most famous magic squares. At left: its other face, with small lucky-charm fish.

Sometimes, the existential truth of being is seized in a much more refined way by the imagination than by statistics, tests, and other data in which the quantifiable, no matter how precise, does not reveal the lived experience.

Poetico-analysis, along with philosophy and other human sciences, offers a way by which the image makes us dream and therefore reinvent and recover the dynamism of creation.

By poetico-analysis, man rids himself of preconceived ideas and images to enter a charged, creative modality of intelligence.

Hollow isodecahedron, attributed to Leonardo da Vinci.

4

"The erotic affair of the straight line and the circle"
As a conclusion and a beginning

I am looking only for thoughts that tremble. There is blushing that belongs inside the soul. In Jin Ping Mei's sixth book, there suddenly appears Wen Bigu, a man of letters. He isn't yet 40 years old. He is dressed and his hair is done up like a man of letters, white teeth. Xen Qing salutes him. He asks him up to the reception room. He invites him to sit down. He offers him a drink, and finally he bows: "What is your name?" Wen Bigu replies: "My humble first name is Bigu (Need-to-imitate-the-elders). My personal name is Rixin (To-renew-one self-day-by-day)." They drink tea to the light of a torch.
Pascal Quignard

A little story

There was a famous scholar in ancient Greece who traveled everywhere and lectured. These kinds of men were called Sophists. As this famous Sophist was returning to Athens one day after a lecture tour in Asia Minor, he met Socrates in the street. Socrates used to stand in the street and talk to people, for example, discussing what a shoe is with a shoemaker. Socrates' only topic was: What is the nature of things?

– "Are you still doing that?" asked the irritated Sophist arrogantly, "and are you still saying the same thing about the same thing?"

– "Yes," answered Socrates, "that's what I do. But you who are so especially clever, you certainly never say the same thing about the same thing."

What is "the same thing about the same thing"?

The formula is strange. The analysis of the origins of mathematics will enable us to answer this question.

The meaning of the word *mathematics*

The history of mathematics covers almost 2,500 years. Its center of gravity has often moved, concerning both its substance and its venue.

We see, from the beginning of this story and especially in the Greek period (this fact will still be very visible much later, since Pascal and Descartes were great mathematicians and philosophers), that mathematics and philosophy are closely related, and our task is to stress the pertinence of this relationship.

One of the main aspects of this connection can be seen in the evolution of the meaning of the word *mathematics* itself over the centuries, from its Greek invention to our days. The underlying question is the meaning given by each mathematician to this word that designates his profession. This is a difficult question, just as difficult as the question "What is philosophy?" for a philosopher or "What is literature or poetry?" for a writer.

Does *mathematics* mean the same thing for Thales and Pythagoras, or for Fermat and Evariste Galois, for example? Counting, classification, enumeration, grouping, division, multiplication, all these movements of the spirit are not neutral. Behind the way of cutting and organizing the world there is a series of presuppositions that we must try to decipher and that let us understand the evolution and mutations of a science.

A mental revolution

Progress toward ideality

What is mathematical?

If this science was born at a certain moment in the history of man, it is because it corresponds to a mutation, a new way of seeing the world and of analyzing it. Consequently, it is necessary to understand the before and after of this epistemological cut, as philosophy says.

Mathematical? The simplest and most correct way to proceed is to question words. We must remember that the word *mathematics* comes from the Greek *ta mathemata*. It means "what can be learned," and therefore also "what can be taught." *Manthanein* means "to learn," and *mathesis* means "lesson," with the double meaning of "that which one learns" and "that which ones teaches." Teaching and learning are used here in a broad sense and also in an essential sense, not in the ulterior, narrow, and derivative sense of school and the erudite.

We said that *mathesis* means the act of learning; *mathemata* means what can be learned. According to what has been said, then, this designation refers to things to the extent that they can be learned. Learning is a way of apprehending, of appropriating.
But to take is not always to take in. We can take a thing, a stone, for example, carry it with us, and put it in a collection of minerals, and we can do the same with plants. The cookbook says *take* and this means "use it." *Taking* means entering into possession of a thing and using it.
But *learning*? What is taken from things, and how is it taken? What is taken is the "idea of..."

In philosophy, starting with Plato, this was called "the essence of things"— the idea of the thing. It is the body as body-ness, the plant as plant-ness (Heidegger's neologism), the animal as animal-ness, like the idea of the shoe. (On this topic, see Martin Heidegger, *What is a thing?*, Rowman & Littlefield, 1985.) This way of seeing the world—based on the *idea* of things and not things on their own—created the era of mathematics.

The revolution of mathematics
Understanding mathematics, and especially the birth of mathematics, means understanding how this science is revolutionary.
What is new about it?

The Babylonians and the Egyptians preceded the Greeks but were also their contemporaries. The Greeks already had a well-developed technical and numerical/numbering knowledge. Why did this knowledge not constitute the birth date of mathematics? Why was it just a form, sometimes very sophisticated, of mathematics, but only a foreshadower.

Answering this question is essential, and we are going to try to do so taking as an example the case of Thales.

Mathematics started in Greece with geometry

This term comes from the Latin *geometria*, borrowed from the Greek *geometria*, from *ge*, "the earth," and *metria*, "the technique and science of measuring." We are in the seventh century B.C.E., in Anatolia. While in Sardes, the capital of the empire of Lydia, King Gyges reigned, in nearby Ionia, no king reigned over Miletus. The town is one of the first city-states: a free city. Thales was born there in around 620. We owe to him the famous phrase "Know thyself." He was one of the Seven Wise Men of Greece and the first to define general results concerning mathematical objects.

Thales did not work a lot with numbers; he was mainly interested in geometric figures—circles, straight lines, triangles. He was the first to consider the angle as a full-fledged mathematical entity, calling it the fourth dimension of geometry, thus joining the already existing trio of length, area, and volume.

The erotic affair of the straight line and the circle

The story takes place on a plane, and the characters are a straight line and a circle. What can happen to a straight line and a circle? Either the straight line cuts through the circle or it does not cut through it. It can also touch it. If it cuts it, it necessarily divides it into two parts. How should the straight line be situated for the two parts of the circle to be equal? Thales gave the answer: For the straight line to divide the circle into two equal parts, it must pass through its center. The line is a diameter! The diameter is the longest segment the circle contains within it: The line crosses the circle throughout its length. This is why we can say that the diameter "measures" the circle.

Thales' remarks are certainly important and interesting, but how are they a basis for the birth of mathematics?

In fact, we started suggesting it on the preceding page, when we said that he was the first to propose general principles. Thus, Thales' answer does not concern a particular circle, but any circle. Thales did not propose a numerical result established on the basis of an individual object, as was the case before him for the Egyptians and the Babylonians. His ambition was to pronounce truths concerning a whole class of entities—an infinite class. He wanted to affirm truths for an infinity of objects in the world. It was an entirely new endeavor. To achieve it, Thales was obligated by his way of thinking to conceive of an ideal entity, the circle, which in a sense represents all the circles in the world.

Because he was interested in all the circles of the world, and not just some of them, and because he claimed to affirm about them truths that have to do with their nature as circles, we can give Thales the title of "the first mathematician in history." It was an extraordinarily new way of seeing things.

In our story of the circle and the straight line, the act of stating a phrase like "any straight line that passes through the center of a circle bisects it into two equal parts" is an intellectual revolution of such magnitude that it opened up the scientific and philosophical world to a new era.

Toward the general formula

We can now understand the meaning of Socrates' phrase "the same thing about the same thing." It is what remains identical no matter what the object is. It is its general properties that do not depend on one object or another. Thus, by pointing out mathematical laws, we find each time the same thing, the same law in the same category of objects made up of all individual circles. Whether they are traced with chalk on the ground or on the blackboard, in red or in green, etc., the laws will always be the same.

This is how mathematics was born.

343

Book Four

Apendixes

Ideas and men

Glossary
of common nouns

This glossary was written on the basis of several bibliographic sources, including, in particular, Stella Baruk, *Dictionnaire de mathématiques élémentaires*, Le Seuil, Paris, 1992, and Bertrand Hauchecorne, *Les mots et les maths*, Ellipses, Paris, 2003.

Abacist: Person using the abacus. See Algorist.

Abacus: Calculation board with pieces called *apices*.

Abundant number: Number lower than the sum of all its divisors. Example: 12 is the first abundant; indeed, $1 + 2 + 3 + 4 + 6 = 16$.

Aleatory: The word *aleatorius* already existed in Latin, and it concerns the game, an adjective made from *alea*, which refers to the game of dice. *Aleatory* appeared in the sixteenth century and meant at the time "subject to chance." It was only in the nineteenth century that it took on the meaning of "uncertain." In mathematics, it appeared at the beginning of the twentieth century with the formalization of calculation of probabilities in the term *aleatory variable*.

Aleph: Aleph is the first letter of the Hebrew alphabet. It represents the sound "ah," like *alpha* in Greek, which has the same Phoenician origins. This letter was used by the Hebrews to note the numbers 1 and 1,000. In 1811, Wronski, a mystical mathematician of Polish decent, used it to designate certain functions. It was only in 1895 that Cantor named transfinite cardinal numbers with this letter. This notation replaced Peano's.

Algebra: *Algebra* comes from the Arabic word *al-jabr*, which we find in the title of the book *Al-jabr wa muqabala*, by Al-Khuwarizmi Kitab. It means "putting back in its place." In this work, it consists of changing, on one side of an equation, the terms with negative signs so as to make them positive. Long ago in Spain, on the signs of certain healers one could read *algebrista y sangredor*. They set bones and did bloodletting. During the Renaissance, algebra designated an extension of the calculation methods, generalized to include negative numbers with the utilization of unknowns and parameters. At the beginning of the nineteenth century, algebra was still considered a type of arithmetic with symbols. The construction of the complex numbers in the early nineteenth century, as well as Hamilton's quaternions in 1843, led to the introduction of hyper-numbers. These new structures became too remote from our conception of the number. Then a new structure called "algebra" was defined. In the eighteenth century, the French adjective *algébrique*, concerning algebra, replaced the term *algébraïque*, which had appeared two centuries earlier.

Algebraic number: A number is algebraic if it is the solution to an algebraic equation with whole coefficients. $\sqrt{2}$ is one of them, for example, because it is the solution of $x^2 - 2 = 0$.

Algorist: Name given in the Middle Ages to a person who used the new Indo-Arabic figures in his calculations. Algorists were opposed to the abacists, who still used boards (*abaci*) and pieces (*apices*). We speak of the dispute between abacists and algrists.

Algorithm: *Algorithmus* in Medieval Latin, then turned into the French *algorithme.* Deformation of the name of the Persian mathematician Al-Khuwarizmi. The ending is influenced by the Greek *arithmos*, "number," which we find in both arithmetic and logarithms. This term means a series of operations that are necessary to go through in order to obtain a certain result.

Apices: Small pieces of wood or horn on which numerals were written, and which led to the introduction of Indo-Arabic numerals in the West in the early eleventh century.

Arithmetic: Body of knowledge that has to do with the study of whole numbers and the numbers that are deduced from them. The Greek word *arithmos* (number) gave *arithmetike* in Greek and *arithmetica* (science of numbers) in Latin. The Greeks differentiated logistics from arithmetic. Logistics was the art of calculation—in other words, handling the operations; arithmetic was more theoretical (today we would say "theory of numbers"). Intellectuals had contempt for logistics, and it was mainly used by merchants, which is probably why only the second term survived to our era.

Arithmo-geometry: Pythagorean knowledge that deduced arithmetic properties from geometric considerations, especially in figurative numbers.

Arithmology: Utilization of the symbolic meaning of numbers.

Automorphous number: Number that, multiplied by itself, gives a product that contains it as its last numerals. Example: 25 x 25 = 625. 5 and 6 are the smallest known and possible automorphous numbers.

C

Cabala: Christianization during the Renaissance of the traditional Hebrew Kabbalah, by synthesis with Pythagorean and Platonic ideas rediscovered thanks to the conquest of Constantinople and the flight of Byzantine scholars to Italy. For the definition of the Hebraic Kabbalah, see Kabbalah.

Calculus: For the Romans, the word *calculus* referred to a pebble. It certainly came from the Greek *khalix*, which has the same meaning, and not *calx* (lime), as some people believe. Roman children learned to count with pebbles. In classical Latin, "to count" was *computare*, which became the English "computer." In low Latin, the word was *calculare*. French comes from low Latin, and *calculer,* which as early as the fourteenth century, meant at the time "to determine using operations." In the sixteenth century, a *calculator* was "somebody who knew how to calculate." Two centuries later, the word meant "one whose actions are premeditated," and in the next century, it meant a "calculating machine."

Cardinal: The Latin *cardo*, "hinge" or "pivot" of a door, gave the Latin adjective *cardinales*. This word appeared in French in the twelfth century. It qualifies something that serves as support, both literally and figuratively. By extension, it soon started meaning "principal." In the thirteenth century, there were already mentions of the four "cardinal virtues" (those on which morality is based) and of the four "cardinal points." Then the Church used this word to designate the most important priests. The adjective *cardinal* was not used in mathematics until the seventeenth century, when it was opposed to *ordinal*. A number may indicate a quantity (number of), a place, or it may be a numerical ideality (it is the theoretical number, the number we find in "number theory"). When a number indicates a place, a sequential number in a series, it is an ordinal number. When it is not ordinal, the number is cardinal, whether it indicates a quantity or is a theoretical number.

For example, the month of December has thirty-one days. The number 31 indicates the total number of days in this month; consequently, it is a cardinal number. If, on the contrary, we consider an expression like "the thirty-first of December," then the number 31 is not used in its cardinal aspect. It is the "thirty-first" day of December: it means the rank of a well-defined element (in this case, the last) of a series that has thirty-one days; so it is indeed an ordinal number.

Chaos: The Greek *khaos* means the state of confusion that reigned in the universe before the appearance of the gods. Bible translators used it to translate the *Tohu-va-Vohu* of the Hebrews, with the same meaning concerning their god. Introduced into French, it means something in a state of great confusion, *tohu bohu*, especially a mess of rocks. It also means an absence of structure.

Comma: [Used in French and elsewhere in place of the decimal point] In Latin, *virgula*, which has the same root as the French word *verge*, designated a small branch. The introduction of this punctuation sign in the sixteenth century, named after its shape, gives a new sense to the word *virgule* (in French), which would soon eliminate the literal meaning. In general, it is believed that decimal fractions were introduced by Stevin in 1585, even though we find their rudiments earlier, but without an understanding of the problem. There were many notations to designate the separator between the whole part and the decimal part. The first appearance of the comma in this role dates from the early seventeenth century, but it only became common practice on the Continent a century later.

Compound number: Number that is not prime.

Computer: [French: *ordinateur*] *Ordinator* existed in Latin. It designated the one who puts order, who settles things. The first Christians used it to designate the leader of ceremonies. This is why we are still speaking of the *ordination* of priests. *Ordinateur* was introduced in French around 1600 with similar meanings, but remained rare until 1954. In 1955, Jacques Perret, an IBM engineer, resuscitated this word to replace in French the English *computer,* formed from the Latin *computare* (to calculate). The French use of the word *ordinateur* gives a broader sense to the terminology, since the role of the "ordinator" exceeds by far the role of the "calculator"—it orders and manages many activities.

Conjecture: Mathematical hypothesis that can be verified but that cannot be demonstrated, or that has not yet been demonstrated.

Constant: In mathematics, it designates, in a magic square, the sum of the lines, which is always identical.

Cosmos: Name used by Pythagoras to designate the universe as a harmonious whole comprehensible through numbers.

Cube: From the Greek *kybos,* whose meaning extended to any cube-shaped object, but also to everything that is related to chance. Through Latin, the word *cube* appeared in French at the end of the fourteenth century. Of course, it designates the geometrical figure. Plato related it to the element of earth. The cube is also a power of a number raised to the cube—in other words, multiplied three times by itself, noted "n³," e.g. $2^3 = 2 \times 2 \times 2 = 8$.

Decade, sacred Pythagorean: This is the number 10, resulting from the sum of the sacred Tetraktys $1 + 2 + 3 + 4$.

Decimal: Word formed from the Latin *decimus,* "tenth." In the Middle Ages, it qualified the amount of the tithe, the one-tenth tax that was levied on income. To *decimate* a herd or an army meant to kill one-tenth of it. *Decimal* became outdated at the same time as the tax. Following the introduction of the current notation of non-whole numbers using numerals placed before and after a separator (in our times, a point), the adjective *decimal* reappeared by 1680. There was a need to give a name to the numerals after the point. The word became a noun, and we now speak of decimal(s); for example, the decimals of the number π.

Deficient number: Number larger than the sum of all its divisors. Example: 8; indeed, $1 + 2 + 4 = 7$.

Diameter: In Greek, the *diametros* refers to the diagonal (*diagonalis* for the Romans). It is formed from *dia* (across) and *metron,* which designated the measure, but also the space measured. Introduced into French, it first was applied to the circle, then to the sphere, starting from the seventeenth century.

Diophantian: The diophantian equations owe their name to Diophanthus, a Syrian mathematician of Greek culture, who lived in Alexandria in the third century C.E. He searched for solutions to a certain number of equations. His work spread in the seventeenth century thanks to the Latin translation of Bachet de Méziriac, which was used by Fermat.

Dodecahedron: Regular polyhedron whose faces are twelve pentagons. Plato used it as his model of the cosmos.

Emptiness: In various forms, the adjective *empty* (in which we no longer recognize the Latin ancestor *vacuus*) is old in our language. As with zero, it appeared long after the other numbers. One had to wait until the first half of the twentieth century to sense the need to name a whole without an element.

Equation: For the Romans, *quatio* meant "equalization," "equal distribution." Medieval Latin uses the word *equation* in the sense of "equality." Descartes was the first, in 1637, to use this word in its current mathematical meaning. Its meaning has not changed since, even though the terms of the equation considered have diversified in their nature. The use of the word *equation* in chemistry dates back to the nineteenth century. The word is used

in psychology in the expression *personal equation*, a term that is misused in common language.

Even: Made up of two equal parts. By addition with itself, the even can generate only the even. The principle of the even is the number 2.

Factorial: Written "n!"—this is the product of all whole numbers up to "n" inclusive. Example: $4! = 1 \times 2 \times 3 \times 4 = 24$. It is the number of combinations of a word or a number of n different letters or numerals.

Factorion: See Narcissistic numbers.

Fibonacci series: Regular series of numbers in which each is the sum of the two preceding ones. This series is made up of the numbers 1, 1, 2, 3, 5, 8, 13, 21, 34, 55, 89, etc. See Golden number.

Fifteen: Constant of the smallest magic square. Numerical value of the name of God, written *yod-he*.

Figurative number: A group according to a regular geometric shape (polygon or polyhedron) of units whose sum is the value of the figurative number.

Fraction: This word is formed from the late Latin *fractio*, which in turn comes from *frangere*, meaning "to break." In the twelfth century, *fraction*

351

was used only in religious language and meant "to break the host." The word *fraction* appeared in mathematics with Pelletier in 1549. It was only in the nineteenth century that, in French, it took on the meaning of "part of an organization." At first, the fraction was not considered a number. For a long time, *three-fifths* meant "three out of five," without conceptualizing the number we write as 0.6 today.

Friendly numbers: Pairs of numbers in which each is equal to the sum of all the other's divisors. Example: 220 and 284.

G

Geometry: All knowledge that has to do with the study of figures traced on the plane and in space.

Googol: Very large number written as a 1 followed by a hundred zeros.

Googolplex: Square of a googol. It is written as a 1 followed by a thousand zeros.

Gematria: These are the series of calculations that are possible on the basis of the numerical equivalence of the letters of the Hebrew alphabet. Since each Hebrew letter (and according to numerology, each letter in general) is a number, any word and any phrase have a numerical value. The combination of several words that

have the same numerical value and the analysis of these values and combinations constitute gematria. See Kabbalah and Logo-rhythm.

Golden number: Value of the proportion resulting from dividing a segment of a straight line in a way that is both asymmetrical and harmonious. It is equal to 1.618.

Grid of Eratosthenes: Simple procedure to generate the suite of prime numbers by eliminating successive integers from 2 to 2, from 3 to 3, etc.

H

Hazard: This word was widely used in the first exchanges of letters in the beginning of the calculation of probabilities. The Arabic word *az zar* refers to the game of dice. *Az* corresponds to the article *al*, in which the last letter is sometimes assimilated to the first letter of the word. The word *hasard* entered into the French language and means "game of dice." The meaning of "random chance" dates from the sixteenth century.

Hexagon: Regular polygon with six sides.

Hexagram: *Hexa* means "six" in Greek, and *gramma* means "the thing traced." A hexagram is an assembly of six letters. This word was introduced into mathematics by Blaise Pascal. It designates the figure of the famous theorem concerning six points, written with letters, inscribed in a cone. It is also a geometric figure in the form of a six-pointed star made up of two intertwined equilateral triangles that mean the harmonious union of what is down and what is up, of the microcosm and the macrocosm. It is also called a Star of David or Solomon's Seal in esoteric traditions. Numbers associated with the peaks and intersections of this star sometimes give a "magic" star, in which the sum of the numbers in each line is identical to the sum of the other lines (often 26) (see Magic squares). This name is also given to Chinese divinatory combinations.

Hypotenuse: The right angle of a right triangle was placed at the top of the arrangement by the ancients. This explains the formation of the word *hypotenuse* from the prefix *hypo-* (underneath) and the Greek verb *teinein* (to tend). Thus, for the Greeks, the hypotenuse retains the two sides of the right angle by catching them underneath. The word *hypotenusa* already existed in Latin. It was picked up in French in the form *hypoténuse* since the early sixteenth century, with the first geometric works written in French.

Hypothesis: This word is formed from the Greek prefix *hypo-* (underneath) and the word *thesis* (the act of placing). The hypothesis is in a way what one places underneath. The word *supposition* is a Latin version of *hypothesis*. Indeed, it is formed from the prefix *sub-* (underneath) and the verb *ponere* (to place). For the Greeks,

the hypothesis is the basis of reasoning, its root. It is symbolically placed underneath. *Hypothèse* entered the French vocabulary during the Renaissance with the development of the study of the sciences.

Icosidodecahedron: Regular polyhedron whose faces are formed by twenty equilateral triangles. Plato related the element of water to it.

Imaginary: From the Latin *imaginarius*, which designates the images simulated by the spirit. René Descartes used, apparently for the first time, the term *imaginary* in 1637 in the "*Géometrie,*" an appendix to the *Discourse on Method*. He used this term as a common word. He explained that one can imagine roots, but they do not correspond to quantities that exist. Not until Euler in 1749, in his article "Research on the Imaginary Roots on the Equations," did one obtain a definition: "We name imaginary quantity that which is neither greater than zero nor smaller than zero nor equal to zero; it would be something impossible."

Incommensurable: This adjective already existed in Latin to designate "that which has no common measure." We must remember that, by the example of Eudoxus, the ancients differentiated between *number* and *measure* of magnitude. For them, a magnitude was, for example, a length, a surface, a volume, or a weight. Measuring a magnitude consisted of repeating it, perhaps mentally, a certain number of times to obtain the same measurement as a whole number of times the standard magnitude. When this was possible, the magnitudes were commensurable between them. Otherwise, the magnitudes were incommensurable. The Pythagoreans showed that the diagonal of a square and its side are incommensurable. It is certainly to Diderot that we owe the use of "incommensurable" in common language to designate that which is too large to be measured. It is obviously a misnomer.

Irrational number: It can be constructed geometrically (for example, the diagonal of a square), but it is not possible to express it by a fractional value, no matter how complicated. Irrational numbers are solutions of algebraic equations of a degree higher than 1.

Iso-: The Greek prefix *iso-* has served to construct many scientific words since the early nineteenth century. It comes from the adjective *isos*, which meant "equal in number," and then, more generally, "equal."

Isosceles: In Greek, *isoskeles* means "that which has two legs." By extension, it describes a triangle that has two equal sides or an even number—in other words, a triangle that can be divided into two equal numbers.

Kabbalah: Mystic Hebraic doctrine transmitted traditionally from master to disciple. The word means precisely "reception," and its purpose is to let man in on the secrets of the terrestrial world and the superior worlds through knowledge and practice obtained by a series of techniques for the interpretation of texts, including gematria. Kabbalah is, at the same time, a theology, a life philosophy, mathematics, and the geometry of language.

Linear number: Figurative number built on the straight line. Linear numbers are none other than the sequence of natural integers: 1, 2, 3, 4, etc.

Logarithm: When he defined logarithms for the first time in 1614, John Napier also gave them their name. This word is constructed from the Greek words *logos* (in the sense of "ratio") and *arithmos* (number). To understand this etymology, one must remember that Napier defined a logarithm as the ratio of the distance to be traveled from two moving objects, one traveling at constant speed and the other at a speed proportional to the distance that remains to be traveled.

Logometry: Word that we introduce to translate gematria and emphasize that it is a measure of language and not a measure of the reality of physical objects.

Logo-rhithm: The term *logo-rhithm* was introduced for the first time in recreational mathematics by L. Sallows in an article published in 1994 (in *The Lighter Side of Mathematics*). By logo-rhithm, Sallows simply means the number of letters that make up a word. For example, the logo-rhithm of *mathematics* is 11. According to Sallows, these logo-rhithms play a role in the creation of magic squares that use words and not simply numerals and numbers.

Logo-rhythm or logorythm: This is an extension of the meaning of Sallows's *logo-rhithm*. First of all, it is the essential relationship that exists between letters and numbers (as in gematria, for example), which allows us to establish numerical equivalencies between various words and to reflect on the proximity and articulation of their meanings. Then, it is the series of external or internal vibratory manifestations, captured and analyzed, whose presence and efficacy in daily life are rarely perceived and that, precisely, "logo-rhythmic analysis" allows us to reveal.

Long squares: Rectangles made up of two adjacent squares. If the side is equal to 1, the diagonal of the long square is equal to $\sqrt{5}$.

Magic numbers: Sequence of the numbers 2, 8, 20, 28, 50, 82, 126, which governs the structure of particularly stable atom cores.

Magic squares: Arrangement of n^2 numbers set up in the boxes of a square with side n, so that the partial sums of the lines, columns, or diagonals are always the same, equal to what is called the "constant" of the square. We can cite, for example, the so-called "magic square of the Apocalypse," whose side is 6 by 6, in which all values are prime numbers and whose constant is 666, the so-called "number of the Beast," cited by John in the Apocalypse.

Mathematics: The word comes to us from the Greek *mathema*, or rather from its plural, *mathemata*. This plural designated both the fact of learning and its result: knowledge, science. Under the influence of Plato and Aristotle, according to whom mathematics was fundamental knowledge, the word became specialized in what we call mathematics. The Romans, and then the Scholastics, designated by the name *ars mathematica* everything that concerns calculable magnitudes. In the seventeenth century, people spoke of mathematics, certainly with the idea that this subject included disciplines that have become separate, such as geometry, algebra, or even branches that today, would be classified under physics.

In Auguste Comte, we find the idea of pointing out the unity of the subject by speaking of mathematics at a time when the separation from physics became clearer. The former is based on abstract concepts, while the latter describes our world. This idea gathered new momentum in the 1960s, with the introduction of so-called "modern mathematics," which is intended to be detached from reality.

. **Narcissistic numbers**: Numbers equal to the sum of their n numerals, each raised to the power of n. Examples: 153 = 13 + 53 + 33; 370 = 33 + 73 + 03. The largest narcissistic number has thirty-nine numerals: 1 1 5 , 1 3 2 , 2 1 9 , 0 1 8 , 7 6 3 , 992,565,095,597,973,971,552,401. Each numeral must be raised to the power 39.

Natural numbers: The expression *natural number* appeared around 1675. That was the time when negative numbers were fully accepted. It was then necessary to qualify the numbers considered more in accordance with reason. This is why some call them "natu-

ral." Others prefer to consider them part of the numbers and call them "affirmative" or, later, "positive," by opposition to numbers that not so long before were called "negative."

Negative numbers: The word *negative* came from the Latin adjective *negativus*, which in turn came from the verb *negare*, which meant "to deny." In French, it exists as early as the thirteenth century in the sense of "that which serves to deny," then "that which expresses negation." In the sixteenth century, a number smaller than zero was often called a "denied quantity" without really being considered a number.

The word *negative* appeared in mathematics with the current use of numbers lower than zero. It is attested for the first time in 1638. Negative numbers were used at the time to express a debit. The difference between subtraction and the intrinsic notion of a number lower than zero gradually appeared at that time. However, these new numbers did not fully have their place in the minds of those who handled them. This explains the use of a term with negative connotation to name them. It is as opposed to positive, meaning that the latter is based on something.

Novena Reduction or theosophical reduction: Every time the total of the numerals of a number reaches two numerals, they are reduced by adding them up. Example: 538 = 5 + 3 + 8 = 16 = 1+ 6 +7. This process is also called a "theosophical reduction."

. **Number**: *Numerus* in Latin originally indicated quantity. However, it was used to translate the word *arithmos*.

The latter corresponded more or less to the Latin word, but also designated what we call a whole number. Introduced in old French in the twelfth century, it kept, above all, the Latin meaning. It expresses a large quantity. An expression such as "in large numbers" comes from it. The first proof of the word in mathematics dates back to the mid-twelfth century in connection with the golden number, in the sense of perfect quantity. Then *number* was increasingly used to designate an entity. The word *numeration* is from the same family. It comes from the Latin verb *numerare* (to count, to enumerate), and appeared in French in 1435. Today, we distinguish between *number* and *numeral*, the latter representing the tools of the notation of numbers.

Numeral: Curiously, the word *zero* and the French word *chiffre* (numeral) have the same origin. The Arabs adopted zero around the ninth century under the name of *sifr*, which means "empty" or "number" (we find the same root in Hebrew, SFR, pronounced *sefar*, which became *mispar*, "number"). This word is transcribed as *cifra*. In Medieval Latin, it was pronounced *tchifra* in the Italian style. Modern numerals appeared in France around the year 1000, under the influence of the mathematician-pope Gerbert of Aurillac. Still, it was only during the Renaissance that their use became generalized with the development of trade and the printing press. By extension, these new symbols are all called "numerals" in contrast to Latin notations.

Numerology: Numerology is the art of the interpretation of numbers to relate them with destiny and its changes. Numerology requires know-how and great subtlety to avoid falling into the trap of simplicity or inappropriate statements. The great majority of existing numerologies use as support the first and last names of the person who comes for a "numerological consultation," as well as various dates, such as the birth date of the person or that of his parents, etc.

In fact, all the supports (personal) are valid, because, basically, numerology operates on a system of associations of ideas whose letters and numbers are the transmission belts.

Octahedron: Regular polyhedron whose faces are eight equilateral triangles. Plato related the element of air to them.

Odd: Number that cannot be divided other than into two unequal parts. Example: 3, which is the first odd number among natural integers. By adding it to itself, the odd number generates its counterpart, the even number, and therefore appears to be more powerful than it. Example: 3 + 3 = 6; 3 is odd, 6 is even. The principle of the odd number is 3. According to Pythagorean and Chinese esoteric traditions, even numbers are female and odd numbers are male.

Ordinal: See Cardinal.

Ordinal number: Corresponds to classification, order, the smallest and the largest. Examples: sevenths, twelfth.

P

Pentacle: Talisman in the shape of a five-pointed star. It symbolizes the microcosmos because its shape suggests that of a human being with his arms extended and legs spread.

Pentagon: Regular polygon with five sides. The word *pentagonos* existed in ancient Greek. We find the prefix *penta-*, which means five, in *pentathlon* (a sports competition with five events) and Pentateuch (the first five books of the Bible).

Perfect number: Equal to the sum of all of its divisors. Example; Indeed, 28, indeed $1 + 2 + 4 + 7 + 14 = 28$.

Permutation: In Latin, *permutare* meant "exchange" and *permutatio* designated a change, a modification. In the Middle Ages, a *permutation* was a barter or an exchange. By the fifteenth century, the word came to mean the exchange of two elements. Leibniz gave the name of "variation" to what today we call "permutation". At the beginning of the nineteenth century, coming close to the Latin meaning, *permutation* in

mathematics meant the modification of the order of n letters. Some mathematicians, however, used it in the sense of "arrangement." We find it often in Lagrange, Cauchy, and Galois, especially when they work on the roots of a polynomial equation. See Tzeruf.

π or Pi: The British mathematician William Jones was the first to use the letter π, in 1706, to designate the ratio between the circumference of a circle and its diameter. Jones wrote in Latin, a language in which the circumference was called *peripheria*. However, he preferred to use the Greek initial of this word, rather than the letter π, as various other mathematicians did. This notation was generalized when Euler adopted it in 1737, closely followed by Nicolas Bernoulli.

Platonic bodies: See Regular polyhedron.

Poly-: The Greek prefix *poly-* comes from the word *polos* (numerous). It is used to form many scientific words, and is also used in common language; think of *polyglot* or *polygamy*, which came from Christian Latin. In mathematics, we find it in *polynom, polyhedron, polygon*.

Polygon: *Polygon* is formed from the prefix *poly-* (numerous) and *gonia* (angle, corner). The Indo-European root *gon* or *gen* designates both what has to do with birth and what forms a curvature, an angle. Apparently, we find it in the French word for knee, *genou*, but also in the names of the cities Geneva, Genoa, and the old Orléans, Genabum. These three cities are all in a place where the coast or a river makes an angle. The adjective *polygonos* (that which has many angles) already existed in ancient Greek. After becoming *polygonius* in Latin, the word was borrowed by the French as soon as the interest in geometry was revived.

The name of a polygon is obtained by replacing in the word the prefix *poly-* with the Greek name of the corresponding number. Thus, we speak of a pentagon or an enneagon. Only the triangle and the quadrilateral are exceptions.

Polyhedral number: Figurative number constructed in space, using as supporting skeleton one of the five regular polyhedrons. Polyhedral numbers were studied systematically by Descartes.

Polyhedron: The suffix *hedron* comes from the Greek word *hedra* (base, face). It is found in *cathedra*, the high-back chair inspired the French word *chaire* (chair) and *cathedral* (the seat of the bishop). The word *polyhedron* did not exist in ancient Greek. It is a creation of the seventeenth century. Based on the model of polyhedron, specific names were forged, corresponding to the number of faces. *Poly-* was replaced by the name of the numbers in Greek: *tetra* for four, *octa* for eight, *dodeca* for twelve, and *icosa* for twenty. We must note that we do not speak of a hexahedron but of a cube.

Polyhedron of Archimedes: Volume whose peaks are located on a sphere and whose faces are regular polygons in which the edges are of the same size. Two or three different poly-gons are used. There are only thirteen Polyhedrons of Archimedes.

Positive: The expression *positive number* appeared by 1750. It came after *negative number* and *natural number*. Numbers higher than zero were named only by reference to negative numbers. In addition, *positive* has been the antonym of *negative* only since that time. In the previous century, the phrase used was *affirmative numbers*.

Postulate: This word was introduced in the eighteenth century by mathematicians working on Euclid and his fifth postulate. It was forged from the Latin verb *postulare* (to ask, to wish) and designated a proposition, not necessarily evident, that was assumed without being able to be demonstrated. At the time, it was differentiated from *axiom*, a truth obvious by itself, but which could not be demonstrated. In our times, this difference no longer makes sense. A theory is based on axioms; they are its basic principle. Their evidence depends on what they are supposed to represent and is no longer the domain of the theory itself.

Prime number: It is divisible only by itself and the unit.

Product: From *duire*, which meant "to lead, to steer"; "to produce" would literally mean "leading forward" and, by extension, "to cause, to bring." The verb took its current meaning with the development of the merchant society at the end of the Middle Ages and the Renaissance. At the time, numerous works appeared to familiarize the increasingly numerous merchants in the handling of Arabic numerals. The result of a multiplication often corresponds to the number of objects sold multiplied by the unit cost. This is the product of the sale. The two terms of the multiplication are involved, they make the product; they are called "factors."

Progression: Sequence of whole numbers generated so that each is equal to the preceding one, plus a constant integer (arithmetic progression) or to the preceding one multiplied by a constant integer (geometric progression). The constant integer is called the "ratio" of the progression.

Pythagorean triangle: Right triangle in which the three sides are measured by whole numbers. The most famous is the 3-4-5 triangle, sometimes called the "triangle of Isis" because it was known to the Egyptians.

Quadrature: In classical Latin, the adjective *quadratus* meant "square." *Quadrature* was borrowed circa 1400 from the low Latin *quadratura* to designate the operation that allows us to build, with a ruler and compass, a square with the same area as a figure delimited by a closed curve. In particular, this allows us to calculate its area. At that time, the "quadrature of the circle" was already discussed as something impossible to achieve. However, it was only in 1881 that Lindemann demonstrated the transcendence of π, to justify its impossibility. During the Renaissance and until the introduction of integral calculus just before 1700, achieving the quadrature of a curve meant calculating the area it encompassed.

Ratio: Comparison of two numbers arising from their subtraction (arithmetic ratio) or their quotient (geometric ratio).

Rational: In current language, rational qualifies "everything that has to do with reason." Just like the word *reason*, it designates what has to do with the ratio of two numbers. This is why fractions are rational numbers. We must note, however, that in the first uses, fractions were not considered numbers per se. The word *rational* also indicates the relationship between two numbers, but in its adjective form, it already designates a number. In our mind, 3/5 is synonymous to 0.6. It does not make us think of three objects among five. In this way, 3/5 and 6/10 are equal; in other words, they designate exactly the same thing. *Rational* appeared in mathematics by 1550, at the same time as its antonym, *irrational*. An irrational number was sometimes called at that time a "deaf number," meaning vague, a figurative meaning taken on by this adjective. It would seem that this name is a poor translation of the words *rational* and *irrational* in Arabic at the time of Al-Khuwarizmi, which was retranslated into Latin.

Rational number: Expressed in the form of a ratio of two whole numbers; it is also called a "fractionary number." Example: 21/8 or 32/422.

Regular polygon: Geometric figure consisting of the segments of a straight line connecting a series of points regularly arranged on a circle. Examples: equilateral triangle, pentagon. There is an infinity of regular polygons.

Regular polyhedron: Volume in which all peaks are located on a sphere and whose faces, all identical, are regular polygons. There are only five regular polyhedrons.

S

Star polyhedron: Volume deduced from a regular polyhedron by methods similar to those that allow switching from regular polygons to star polygons. Thus, there is a star octahedron, three star dodecahedrons, and fifty-nine star icosidodecahedrons.

Tetrahedron: Regular polyhedron whose faces are four equilateral triangles. Plato related the element of fire to it.

Tetraktys: Summarized in the formula of the fourth triangular number (10 = 1 + 2 + 3 + 4), the Tetraktys represents the cosmos, because it summarizes the unit, the even (2), the odd (3), and the measure (4).

Thirty-six: 36 is the square of the number 6, the first perfect number, the product of the squares of the integers 2 and 3, which, in the Pythagorean tradition, had a sacred character. In the Kabbalah, there is a tradition of thirty-six hidden wise men on which the world rests.

Transcendent number: Irrational number that is not the solution to any algebraic equation with whole or fractionary coefficients. For example: π.

Transfinite number or current infinite: The first is the number of all whole numbers; the second is the number of all the points of a line; the third is the number of all intersections, one by one, of all the curves traced on a plane.

Triangular number: Figurative number constructed on a triangle. The most famous are 10 (Tetraktys), 28 (perfect number), 153 (in the Gospel of John), and 666 (Beast of the Apocalypse).

Twin number: Prime numbers that are different by only two units. Example: 641 and 643.

Tzeruf: Hebrew term that designates the combination of numerals or letters. Example: 123, 321, 231, 213, etc.

Tzimtzum: Hebrew word that, in the Kabbalah, designates the withdrawal of God before creation to make room for the world.

that survive when they are multiplied, battling within the vampire number. Example: 27 x 81 = 2,187. Another vampire number is 1,435, which is the product of 35 and 41. True vampires must respect three rules: They must have an even number of numerals, each of the two original numbers must contain half of the numerals of the vampire, and finally, a true vampire cannot be obtained by simply adding zeros at the end of the numbers, like in 270,000 x 810,000 = 218,700,000,000.

Undulating number: Number with the form abababababababab. For example: 696 969 or 171 717. We find undulating decimals in the periodicity of rational numbers. Example: 135/11 = 12.2727272727272727...

Vampire numbers: There are "vampires" in the world of mathematics, numbers that look like normal numbers but have a hidden difference. In fact, they are the product of two numbers

Women: In spite of horrible prejudices in earlier times, several women fought against the institutions and persevered in mathematics. Until the twentieth century, women who received an education were rare and the path to more in-depth study was generally closed to them. Many of these women had to go against the wishes of their own families if they wanted to learn. Some even had to take on a false identity, study under terrible conditions, and work in intellectual isolation. Consequently, very few women contributed to mathematics. Many of these women came from families of mathematicians. Emmy Noether, Hypatia, and Maria Agnesi, among others, never married, partly because it was not socially acceptable for a woman to pursue a career in mathematics, and therefore, men were reluctant to marry such controversial young women. The mathematician Sofia Kovalevskaya was an exception to this rule: She entered into a marriage of convenience with a man who agreed to a platonic relationship. For Sofia and her husband, marriage meant escaping their families and concentrating on their respective work. Marriage also gave Sofia greater freedom to travel, because at the time, traveling through Europe was more convenient for a married woman than for a single one.

zero in numbers, in the twentieth century, the word started to signify more generally the neutral element in the addition of a body, as well as the elements that cancel a function. Thus, one speaks of the zeros of a polynomial. Zero entered common language to designate an attitude or a person who is totally worthless. It is surely this meaning of the word that prevents the elision in the French phrase *des héros et des héroïnes.*

Zero: A numeral that, by itself, has no value, but that increases ten times the numeral that precedes it. The Hindus invented the zero at the beginning of the Middle Ages. At first, it designated the absence of an object, then the absence of tens or hundreds in position numeration. Arab mathematicians used it in turn and called it *sifr*, a word that designates emptiness. This word was transmitted, on the one hand, to Medieval Latin (in which most scientific tests were written at the time) in the form of *cifra* and, on the other hand, into Italian in the form of *zefiro*. The latter was adopted into the French language in the contracted form *zero* in 1485. Used to designate

364

Glossary
of proper names

This glossary was written on the basis of several bibliographic sources, including, in particular, Stella Baruk, *Dictionnaire de mathématiques élémentaires*, Le Seuil, Paris, 1992, and Clifford A. Pickover, *Wonders of Numbers*, Oxford University Press, 2003, and *Oh, encore des nombres!*, Dunod, Paris, 2002.

Agnesi, Maria (Milan, 1718 – *id.*, 1799): During her adolescence, she studied, on her own, the mathematics of Descartes, Newton, Leibniz, and Euler. At 20, Agnesi published a treatise of philosophy. When her book was published in 1748, she was elected member of the Academy of Science of Bologna. In 1749, Pope Benedict XIV awarded her a gold medal and, the next year, appointed her at the University of Bologna to teach mathematics; this was an extremely rare situation, because very few women were even authorized to take courses at the university. But she turned down this position to dedicate the last forty-seven years of her life to tend to sick and dying women.

Archimedes (Syracuse, -287 – *id.*, -212): One of the greatest scientists of Antiquity. Hieron, king of Syracuse, would have given him the task of uncovering a possible fraud in the composition of a gold crown while being careful not damage the precious object. While taking a bath, having observed the apparent reduction in the weight of his body, Archimedes discovered the fundamental principle of hydrostatics as well as a way to satisfy the king. This is when he shouted his famous "Eureka!" ("I've found it!") Even though the Roman general Marcellus would have ordered that Archimedes be spared, he was killed during the conquest of Syracuse by a Roman soldier who had not recognized him. Because of this, certain mathematicians have said that the only contribution of Roman culture to mathematical science was Archimedes' head.

Aristotle (Stagira, -384 – Chalcis, -322): At the age of 28, he came to Athens, was the student of Plato, and did not leave the Academy until the death of his master (-348). In -343, Philip of Macedonia called Aristotle to his court to become a tutor to his son Alexander, then 13. Six years later, when Alexander took power, Aristotle went back to Athens, where he founded the Lyceum.

Cantor, Georg (St. Petersburg, 1845 – Halle, 1918): German mathematician. Founder of set theory, which led him to define the concept of power and to introduce a hierarchy among infinites. He defined countable sets, derivative sets, transfinite cardinal and ordinal numbers, and built an arithmetic wisdom. His theories, revolutionary for his time, caused a true crisis of mathematics and led to a revision of its foundations.

Copernicus, Nicolaus (Torun, 1473 –Frauenburg, 1543): Polish astronomer. His book *De revolutionibus orbium caelestium libri sex* was the first treatise of heliocentric astronomy capable of rivaling the system of Ptolemy, presented fourteen centuries earlier in Almagest. According to Copernicus, the sun occupies the center of the universe. The Earth and the planets travel on circular orbits around the sun in a uniform movement. The Earth makes a complete revolution in twenty-four hours. Beyond planetary orbs, there is the immobile sphere of stationary stars.

D

Dedekind, Richard (Braunschweig, 1831–*id.*, 1916): German mathematician. In 1850, he was admitted to the University of Göttingen, where he studied under mathematicians Moritz Abraham Stern and Carl Friedrich Gauss and physicist Wilhelm Weber. In 1852, he defended a doctoral thesis before Gauss on Eulerian integrals. In 1857, he was appointed professor at the Polytechnicum in Zurich, and in 1862, he became professor at the Superior Technical School of Braunschweig, where he remained until his death. He was a friend of Cantor's, and through their correspon-dence, he contributed to building the theory of sets.

Descartes, René (La Haye, 1596– Stockholm, 1650): French philosopher and scientist. After being trained at the Jesuit College of La Flèche, he enlisted in several princes' armies and traveled through Europe for many years. Then he abandoned his military career. Descartes lived for twenty years in Holland. He was invited by Queen Christina to come to Sweden, where he fell victim to a fatal cold. His work, which had considerable influence on Western thinking, touches numerous fields: philosophy, mathematics, physics, medicine.

Diophantus (third or fourth century): Greek mathematician from the Alexandrian school, known for his innovative theory of first- and second-degree equations. Out of the thirteen books of his *Arithmetics*, only the first six remain. His influence on Renaissance algebrists was significant.

367

Erdös, Paul (Budapest, 1913– Warsaw, 1996): This legendary mathematician, one of the most prolific in history, was so devoted to mathematics that he lived like a nomad, without a home or a traditional career. In the last year of his life, at 83, he continued turning out theorems and giving conferences, upsetting the conventional idea that mathematics is a sport for the young. In this regard, Erdös said that "the first sign of senility in a man is when he forgets his theorems, the second is when he forgets to button up his fly, and the third is when he forgets to open it."

Euclid (third century B.C.E.): Greek geometer, theoretician of numbers, astronomer, and physicist, famous for his treatise *Elements of Geometry*, an extravaganza in thirteen volumes, which is the oldest substantial Greek treatise of mathematics that has survived.

Euler, Leonhard (Basel, 1707–St. Petersburg, 1783): Swiss mathematician. His work, which covers all of the branches of the mathematics of his time, is considerable. He is the most prolific mathematician in history. He was a student of the mathematician Jean Bernouilli, and became friends with his sons, Nicolas and Daniel, whom he joined in St. Petersburg in 1727, at the invitation of Empress Catherine. He died in 1783 of apoplexy. Euler published more than 8,000 books and articles, most of them in Latin, on all the aspects of pure and applied mathematics, physics, and astronomy.

Fermat, Pierre de (Beaumont-de-Lomagne, 1601–Castres, 1665): French mathematician. The scion of a bourgeois family, he learned Latin, Greek, Spanish, and Italian very early on. In 1631, he purchased a seat in the Parliament of Toulouse which led him to a seat in Castre, in the Chambre de l'Edit, made up of both Catholic and Protestant Parliament members. Along with Descartes, Fermat is the founder of analytical geometry. He made a substantial contribution to the theory of numbers and may be considered a precursor of differential calculus. Along with Pascal, he was the founder of the calculation of probability. His works are mainly known through the correspondence he exchanged with Pierre de Carcavi and Father Mersenne.

Fibonacci, Leonardo, a.k.a. Leonardo of Pisa (Pisa, v.1175–*id.*, after 1240): See the chapter dedicated to him.

G

Galileo (Pisa, 1564–Arcetri, 1642): Italian astronomer and physicist. Galileo Galilei is considered one of the founders of the experimental method and dynamics. By dropping marbles from the top of the tower of Pisa, he discovered that all bodies fall at the same speed, and then determined the general laws of their movement by using an inclined plane. He stated the law of the composition of speeds and the principle of inertia. In 1638, he established that the trajectory of a projectile in a vacuum is a parabola. We owe to him one of the first microscopes. With the help of the telescope, which he built in Venice in 1609, he observed the solar system and the Milky Way. Because he had adopted Copernicus's system, he was barred from teaching. The work he published in Florence in 1632, in which he confirmed Copernicus's ideas, took him before the court of the Inquisition. To escape prison, he had to recant before the Council of the Sacred Congregation in 1633. It was at that time that he would supposedly shouted, "*Eppur' si muove!*" ("And yet it moves!")

Galois, Évariste (Bourg-la-Reine, 1811–Paris, 1832): Author of the Galois theory. Famous for his contributions to group theory, he created a method of determining the solvability of general equations by radicals. When, one day, he was challenged to a duel, he accepted, knowing that he would be killed. Preparing for his end, he spent the day feverishly noting his mathematical ideas and his discoveries as completely as he could. The next day, Galois received a bullet in his stomach. He lay on the grass, helpless. There was no doctor to tend to him, and the winner carelessly left, leaving Galois agonizing in pain. It was only after 1848 that group theory progressed enough for his discoveries to be appreciated. His reputation as a mathematician is based on less than one hundred pages of extremely original work, published posthumously.

Gauss, Carl Friedrich (Braunschweig, 1777–Göttingen, 1855): He worked in a variety of fields in mathematics and physics, including algebra, probabilities, analysis, differential geometry, geodesics, magnetism, astronomy, and optics. His work had a huge influence in many domains. As a child, his great precocity in mathematics attracted the attention of the Duke of Braunschweig, who financed his studies. A notebook kept by Gauss in his youth was discovered in 1989, showing that, as of the age of 15, he had made conjectures that included many remarkable results, including the prime number theorem and ideas of non-Euclidean geometry.

Germain, Sophie (Paris, 1776–*id.*, 1831): She made major contributions to number theory, acoustics, and elasticity. At the age of 13, she read an account of the death of Archimedes at the hands of a Roman soldier. She was moved by this story and decided that she too must become a mathematician. She obtained lecture notes from many courses at the École Polytechnique. After reading lecture notes on analysis by Joseph-Louis Lagrange, she used the pseudonym M. Leblanc to submit to him a paper whose originality and depth made Lagrange desperately search for its author. When he discovered that "M. Leblanc" was a woman, his respect for her work remained and he became her sponsor and mathematical counselor. Sophie proved that if $x^5 + y^5 + z^5 = 0$, then one of the three relative integers x, y, or z is divisible by 5. The Germain theorem was an important step toward the proof of Fermat's Last Theorem.

370

Hilbert, David (Königsberg, 1862–Göttingen, 1943): German mathematician and philosopher, often considered the most important mathematician of the twentieth century. He contributed to the study of algebra, number fields, integral equations, functional analysis, and applied mathematics.

Hopper, Grace (New York, 1907–Arlington, 1992): She taught mathematics at Vassar and in 1944 worked with mathematician Howard Aikin on the Mark I computer at Harvard. At the time, she invented the word *bug* for a computer error. (The original bug was actually a night butterfly that had caused a material error in Mark I.) She left the American navy with the rank of rear admiral in 1966, but continued participating in the standardization of her programming languages. In 1991, she received the National Medal of Technology.

Hypatia (Alexandria, 370–*id.*, 415): She was the first woman mathematician, famous for her speeches, among the most popular in Western civilization, and for her capacity to solve problems better than anyone else. She was the first woman to make a substantial contribution to the development of mathematics. She was the daughter of the mathematician Theon, and in the end became head of the Platonist school at Alexandria. She came to symbolize learning and science, a study that, unfortunately, the early Christians identified with paganism. She was killed by a mob that dragged her out of her chariot and skinned her alive with oyster shells.

K

Kovalevskaya, Sofia Vassilievna

(Moscow, 1850–Stockholm, 1891): She made valuable contributions to the theory of differential equations and was the first woman to obtain a doctorate in mathematics. At a very young age, she fell in love with math. When she was 11, the walls of her room were papered with pages covered with calculations. In 1869, she traveled to Heidelberg to study mathematics, but discovered that women could not attend the university. Finally, she convinced the management of the university to let her attend the courses unofficially. She immediately attracted the attention of her professors by her brilliant mathematical talent. In 1871, she went to Berlin to study with the mathematician Karl Weierstrass. In 1874, she obtained her doctorate *summa cum laude* at the University of Göttingen. In spite of her degree and enthusiastic letters of recommendtion

from Weierstrass, she could not obtain an academic position because she was a woman.

Lambert, Johann Heinrich (Mulhouse, 1728–Berlin, 1777): French mathematician and physicist. In mathematics, he is known for having proved the irrationality of the number π in 1768 and for having founded spherical trigonometry in 1770. In physics, he is one of the founders of photometry.

Legendre, Adrien Marie (Paris, 1752–*id.*, 1833): French mathematician, whose most remarkable work was the creation of the theory of elliptical integrals. He tried several times to demonstrate Euclid's fifth postulate.

Lindemann, Ferdinand von (Hanover, 1852–Munich, 1939): German mathematician who gave a definitive answer to the problem of the quadrature of the circle by demonstrating the transcendence of the number π.

371

Nash, John F. (Bluefield, 1928): This brilliant mathematician received the Nobel Prize for economics in 1994. Nash's work that earned him this award had appeared almost a half century earlier in his thin doctoral thesis, written at the age of 21. In 1950, while a student at Princeton, John Nash formulated a theorem that allowed the field of game theory to obtain a great influence in modern economics. In 1958, *Fortune Magazine* distinguished Nash for his results in game theory, in algebraic geometry, and nonlinear theory, and named him "the most brilliant mathematician of the young generation." He seemed destined for a brilliant career, but in 1959 he was hospitalized and diagnosed with schizophrenia. Princeton and its management supported Nash and kindly let him wander in the department of mathematics for almost thirty years. There, he became a silent character who scribbled strange equations on the blackboards of the mathematics buildings and looked for secret messages in numbers. Unfortunately, Nash's son was also schizophrenic, but he was sufficiently adept at math for Rutgers University to give him a doctorate.

Newton, Sir Isaac (Woolsthorpe, 1642–London, 1727): Brilliant British mathematician, physicist, and astronomer. Newton and Gottfried Leibnitz invented differential calculus independently from each other. Newton was born fatherless on Christmas day, 1642. By the age of 20, he had already invented differential calculus, proved that white light is a mixture of colors, explained the rainbow, built the first reflection telescope, discovered the formula of the binomial, introduced polar coordinates, and demonstrated that the force that makes apples fall is the same one that conducts the movement of the planets and causes the tides.

Newton was also a fundamentalist in his reading of the Bible: He believed in the reality of angels, demons, and Satan. He accepted a literal interpretation of Genesis and believed that the Earth was only a few thousand years old. In fact, Newton spent much of his life trying to prove that the Old Testament is a truthful account of history. He compared himself to a little boy "playing on the beach and having fun from time to time looking for a smoother stone or a shell, prettier than the others, while the vast ocean of truth stretched unexplored before [him]."

Noether, Emmy (Erlangen, 1882–Bryn Mawr, 1935): She was described by Einstein as "the most significant creative genius in mathematics produced to date, since women have gained access to higher studies." She is especially well-known for her contributions to abstract algebra and in for her study of "ideals in any commutative ring with ascending chain condition." In addition, in 1915, she discovered a result of theoretical physics sometimes referred to as Noether's theorem. This basic result of the general theory of relativity was praised by Einstein. Noether's work on the theory of invariants led to the formulation of several concepts of Einstein's general theory of relativity. In 1933, in spite of her superb results, the Nazis caused her dismissal from the university of Göttingen, because she was Jewish. Later, she taught courses at the Institute for Advanced Study in Princeton.

P

Pascal, Blaise (Clermont-Ferrand, 1623–Paris, 1662): French geometer, statistician, physicist, and philosopher. Pascal and Fermat discovered the theory of probabilities independently of each other. Pascal also invented the first calculating machine, studied conical sections, and found important theorems in projective geometry. His father, a mathematician, was in charge of his education. He was not allowed to tackle a subject before his father thought he was able to easily master it. Because of that, at the age of 11, he studied by himself, in secret Euclid's first twenty-three propositions. At 16, he published essays on conics, and Descartes refused to believe that Pascal was a teenager. In 1654, he decided that religion was more to his taste, so he joined his sister in a convent and abandoned mathematics and social life.

Plato (Athens, -428–*id.*, -348): Born during the first years of the Peloponnesian war, Plato died when he was over 80, at a time when Philip of Macedonia had already embarked on his conquest of Greece. His father, Ariston, was a nobleman who claimed to descend from the last legendary king of Athens. Coming from an aristocratic family, Plato, like most young men in his circle, was a student of the Sophists. Following the example of his cousin Critias, his uncle Charmides, and their friend Alcibiades, he was one of Socrates' disciples. Plato certainly owes his surname (*Plato* means "the large one") to his master, since his true name was Aristocles. According to Diogenes Laertio, Plato first dedicated himself to painting, poetry, and tragedy before meeting Socrates at the age of 20. On that occasion, he burned all his poems. Mathematics occupied a privileged place in Plato's education system.

Poincaré, Henri (Nancy, 1854–Paris, 1912): Great French mathematician, physicist, theoretician, astronomer, and philosopher. He was the creator of algebraic topology and of the theory of analytical functions with several complex variables. In applied mathematics, he studied optics, electricity, telegraphy, capillarity, elasticity, thermodynamics, the theory of potentials, quantum theory, the theory of

373

relativity, and cosmology. In the field of celestial mechanics, he worked on the problem with three bodies, and on the theories of light and electromagnetic waves. He is recognized as the co-discoverer, with Albert Einstein and Hendrik Lorentz, of the theory of limited relativity. In his research on planet orbits, Poincaré was the first to consider the possibility of chaos in a determinist system.

Ptolemy, Claudius (ca. 85–ca. 165): Greek astronomer, geographer, and mathematician who lived in Alexandria. He is the most famous astronomer of antiquity. His great *Mathematical Syntax* (ca. 140), the *Almagest* of the Arabs, assembles all the astronomical knowledge of his time. Deriving inspiration from Hipparchus, Ptolemy developed a geocentric system that remained in use until the introduction of Copernicus's heliocentric system. Ptolemy certainly was the first to try to demonstrate Euclid's fifth postulate based on the first four. His astronomical research led to certain advances in trigonometry.

Pythagoras (sixth century B.C.E.): See the chapter dedicated to him.

Ramanujan, Srinivasa Aiyangar (Erode, 1887–Kumbakonam, 1920): Employed in the accounting department of the post office of Madras, he became India's greatest mathematical genius and one of the best mathematicians of the twentieth century. Ramanujan made substantial contributions to analytical number theory and worked on elliptical functions, continuous fractions, and infinite series. Coming from a poor family, self-taught in mathematics, he obtained a research scholarship at Madras University in 1903, but he lost it the next year because he dedicated all his time to mathematics and neglected the other subjects. G.H. Hardy, a professor at Trinity College, invited Ramanujan to Cambridge after reading a now historic paper that contained almost one hundred theorems. A few years later, weakened by his strict vegetarianism, he became severely ill with tuberculosis. Yet neither the physicians nor his family could convince him to stop his research. He returned to India in February 1919 and died in April 1920, at the age of 32. During this period, he wrote approximately 600 theorems on loose sheets. They were discovered only in 1976 by professor George

Andrews from Pennsylvania State University, who published them under the title *Ramanujan's Lost Notebook*. Numerous formulas of the mathematician now have a central place in modern theories on algebraic numbers.

Rasiowa, Helena (Vienna, 1917–Warsaw, 1994): She grew up in Warsaw; at the time, the 1939 German invasion of Poland made her pursuit of mathematics very dangerous. However, Rasiowa persevered in order to get her license. In 1944, when the Germans crushed the Warsaw uprising, her thesis burned along with her entire house. She survived with her mother in a cellar covered by the ruins of the building. Her 1950 doctoral thesis ("Algebraic treatment of the functional calculus of Lewis and Heyting"), presented at the University of Warsaw, concerned algebra and logic. Rasiowa was regularly promoted until she reached the rank of professor in 1967. Her main research concerned algebraic logic and the mathematical bases of computer science. In 1984, she developed techniques that are now central to the study of artificial intelligence.

Riemann, Bernhard (Breselenz, 1826–Selasca, 1866): German mathematician who made many significant contributions to geometry, complex variables, number theory, topology, and theoretical physics. His ideas on space geometry greatly influenced the general theory of relativity. His name is closely associated with Riemann's hypothesis, a famous unresolved problem concerning the function *zeta*, central for the study of the distribution of prime numbers.

Robinson, Julia (St. Louis, 1919– Oakland, 1985): She studied number theory and was the first woman elected to the American National Academy of Science and the first woman president of the American Mathematical Society.

Thales of Milet (Milet, ca. -625– *id., ca.* -546): Designated as one of the Seven Wise men of Greece by Diogenes Laertius, Thales was a man of many talents: merchant, diplomat, statesman, philosopher, mathematician, engineer. At the beginning of his life, he seems to have been a shrewd merchant.

Having amassed a great fortune, Thales was quite free to travel and dedicate himself fully to his research. During his travels, he acquired some knowledge of algebra and astronomy when he came in contact with the Babylonians, and of geometry when he visited Egypt. Back in Milet, he became famous because of his many talents. According to the Greek historian Herodotus, who lived in the following century, Thales predicted a solar eclipse in -585. And there are many other legends about him. One night, when he was out walking and looking up at the stars, he did not see an open ditch in front of him. His servant, who witnessed the episode, berated him vehemently. This story has since traveled over time and

375

taken various forms, until it reached La Fontaine (fable of *The Astrologer Who Stumbled into a Well*):

To an astrologer who fell
Plump to the bottom of a well,
"Poor blockhead!" cried a passerby,
"Not see your feet, and read the sky?"

Wiles, Andrew (Cambridge, 1953):
See the chapter dedicated to him.

Bibliography

ADAMOFF, Georges, see PEIGNOT, J.

ALLENDY, René, *Le Symbolisme des nombres: essai d'arithmosophie*, Éditions traditionnelles, Paris, 1984.

BALL, Walter William Rouse, *Mathematical Recreations and Essays*, MacMillan, 1960.

BARUK, Stella, *Doubles jeux: fantaisies sur des mots mathématiques*, Le Seuil, Paris, 2000.

BARUK, Stella, *Dictionnaire de mathématiques élémentaires*, Le Seuil, Paris, 1992.

BAUDET, Jean, *Nouvel Abrégé d'histoire des mathématiques*, Vuibert, Paris, 2002.

BERTEAUX, Raoul, *La Symbolique des nombres*, Edimaf, Paris, 1998.

BINDEL, Ernst, *Les nombres et leurs fondements spirituels*, Éditions anthroposophiques romandes, Genève, 1985.

BREZIS, Haïm, *Un Mathématicien juif*, conversations with Jacques Vauthier, Beauchesne, Paris, 1999.

BRUTER, Claude Paul, *La Construction des nombres*, Ellipses, Paris, 2000.

CHABOCHE, François-Xavier, *Vie et mystère des nombres*, Albin Michel, Paris, 1976.

CHRISTIN, Anne-Marie (ed.), *A History of Writing: From Hieroglyph to Multimedia*, Flammarion, 2002.

DANTZIG, Tobias, *Number: The Language of Science*, MacMillan, 1966.

DATTA, Bibhutibhusan and SINGH, Avadhesh Narayan, *History of Hindu Mathematics*, Asia Publishing House, Bombay, 1962.

DELAHAYE, Jean-Paul, *Le Fascinant Nombre Pi*, Éditions Pour la science, Paris, 1997.

DELAHAYE, Jean-Paul, *Merveilleux nombres premiers: voyage au cœur de l'arithmétique*, Belin, Paris, 2000.

DUVILLIÉ, Bernard, *Sur les traces de l'Homo mathematicus*, Ellipses, Paris, 1999.

FÉVRIER, James G., *Histoire de l'écriture*, Payot, Paris, 1948.

FERMIER, Jean-Daniel, *ABC de la numérologie chinoise de Lo-Chou*, J. Grancher, 1993.

FERNANDEZ, Bastien, *Le Monde des nombres*, Le Pommier, 2000.

FILLIOZAT, Jean, see RENOU, L.

FILLIOZAT, Jean, "Écriture *nâgari*," in *Notices sur les caractères étrangers et modernes*, Imprimerie nationale, Paris, 1948.

FISZEL, Roland (ed.), *Les Caractères de l'Imprimerie Nationale*, Imprimerie Nationale, Paris, 1990.

FRÉDÉRIC, Louis, *Dictionnaire de la civilisation indienne*, Robert Laffont, "Bouquins," Paris, 1987.

FRÉDÉRIC, Louis, *Le Lotus*, Éditions du Félin, Paris, 1988.

FREITAS, Lima de, *515, le lieu du miroir: art et numérologie*, Albin Michel, Paris, 1993.

GHYKA, Matila Costiescu, *Le Nombre d'or*, Gallimard, "La Nouvelle Revue Française," Paris, 1931.

GOBERT, M.-H., *Les Nombres sacrés et l'origine des religions*, Stock, Paris, 1998.

GOLD, Robert, *Dieu et le nombre Pi*, Éditions Otniel Bène Kénane, Jerusalem, 1997.

GUEDJ, Denis, *Numbers: The Universal Language*, Harry N. Abrams, 1997.

GUEDJ, Denis, *The Parrot's Theorem: A Novel*, St. Martin's Press, 2002.

GUITEL, Geneviève, *Histoire comparée des numérations écrites*, Flammarion, Paris, 1975.

HAKENHOLZ, Christian, *Nombre d'or et mathématique*, Chalagam, Marseille, 2001.

HAUCHECORNE, Bertrand, *Les Mots et les Maths*, Ellipses, Paris, 2003.

JOUETTE, André, *Le Secret des nombres*, Albin Michel, Paris, 1996.

JOUVEN, Georges, *Les Nombres cachés: ésotérisme arithmologique*, Dervy, Paris, 1978.

KARPINSKI, Louis Charles, see SMITH, D. E.

LAHY, Georges, a.k.a. VIRYA, *Paroles de nombres*, Lahy, Roquevaire, 2003.

LAURA, Marc, *Extraits littéraires et empreintes mathématiques*, Hermann, Paris, 2001.

LE LIONNAIS, François, *Les Nombres remarquables*, Hermann, Paris, 1983.

LÉVY, Tony, *Figures de l'infini: les mathématiques au miroir des cultures*, Le Seuil, Paris, 1987.

MANKIEWICZ, Richard, *The Story of Mathematics*, Princeton University. Press, 2001.

MENNINGER, Karl, *Number Words and Number Symbols: A Cultural History of Numbers*, MIT Press, Boston, 1969.

MOLK, Jules (ed.), *Encyclopédie des sciences mathématiques pures et appliquées*, J. Gabay, Sceaux, 1991.

Nancy, Jean-Luc, *L'il y a du rapport sexuel*, Galilée, Paris, 2001.

Needham, Joseph, *Science and Civilisation in China*, University Press, Cambridge, 1959.

Noël, Émile (conversations), *Le Matin des mathématiciens*, Belin, Paris, 1985.

Peignot, Jérôme, *Du chiffre*, J. Damase, Paris, 1982.

Peignot, Jérôme and Adamoff, Georges, *Le Chiffre*, P. Tisné, Paris, 1969.

Péré-Christin, Évelyne, *L'Escalier: Métamorphoses architecturales*, Alternatives, Paris, 2001.

Perelman, Yakov, *Expériences et problèmes récréatifs*, Mir Publishers, Moscow, 1974.

Perelman, Yakov, *Mathematics Can Be Fun*, Mir Publishers, Moscow, 1985.

Perelman, Yakov, *Oh, les maths!*, Dunod, Paris, 1992.

Pézennec, Jean, *Promenades au pays des nombres*, Ellipses Marketing, Paris, 2002.

Pickover, Clifford A., *Wonders of Numbers*, Oxford University Press, 2003.

Pickover, Clifford A., *Oh, encore des nombres!*, Dunod, Paris, 2002.

Pihan, A. P., *Exposé des signes de numération usitée chez les peuples orientaux anciens et modernes*, Imprimerie orientale, Paris, 1860.

Pihan, A. P., *Notices sur les divers genres d'écriture des Arabes, des Persans et des Turcs*, Paris, 1856.

Pinault, Georges-Jean, "Writing in Continental India," *in A History of Writing: From Hieroglyph to Multimedia*, Flammarion, 2002, see Christin, A.-M.

Prinsep, James, "On the inscriptions of Piyadasi or Ashoka," *in The Journal of the Asiatic Society of Bengal*, Calcutta, 1838.

Rachline, François, *De zéro à epsilon*, First, Paris, 1991.

Renou, Louis and Filliozat, Jean, *L'Inde classique: manuel des études indiennes*, École Française d'Extrême-Orient, Paris, 1985, reprinted 2001.

Salomon, Richard, *Indian Epigraphy: A Guide to the Study of Inscriptions in Sanskrit, Praktit and the Other Indo-Aryan Languages*, University Press, Oxford, 1998.

Sauvaget, Jean, "Écritures arabes," *in Notices sur les caractères étrangers et modernes*, Imprimerie Nationale, Paris, 1948.

379

SEIFE, Charles, *Zero: The Biography of a Dangerous Idea*, Penguin, 2000.

SESIANO, Jacques, *Une Introduction à l'histoire de l'algèbre*, Presses Polytechniques et Universitaires Romandes, Lausanne, 1999.

SINGH, Avadhesh Narayan, see DATTA, B.

SINGH, Simon, *The Code Book: The Science of Secrecy from Ancient Egypt to Quantum Cryptography*, Anchor, 2000.

SINGH, Simon, *Fermat's Last Theorem*, Fourth Estate, 1998.

SMITH, David Eugene and KARPINSKI, Louis Charles, *The Hindu-Arabic Numerals*, Ginn, Boston, 1911.

SMITH, David Eugene, *History of Mathematics*, Ginn, Boston, 1925.

SMITH, David Eugene and GINSBURG, Jekuthiel, *Numbers and Numerals*, National Council of Teachers of Mathematics, Washington, 1937.

SMITH, David Eugene, *Numbers Stories of Long Ago*, Ginn, Boston, 1919.

SMITH, David Eugene, *Rara Arithmetica*, Ginn, Boston, 1908.

STEWART, Ian, *Nature's Numbers*, Basic Books, 1997.

STRUIK, Dirk Jan, *A Concise History of Mathematics*, Dover, New York, 1987.

TATE, Georges, *The Crusades and the Holy Land*, Thames and Hudson, 1991.

THOMPSON, John Eric Sidney, *The Rise and Fall of the Mayan Civilization*, University of Oklahoma Press, 1973.

WARUSFEL, André, *Les Nombres et leurs mystères*, Le Seuil, Paris, 1961.

WOEPCKE, Franz, "Mémoire sur la propagation des chiffres indiens," in *Journal asiatique*, 6th series, volume I, January–February, Imprimerie impériale, Paris, 1863.

Acknowledgements

This book, just like the previous ones, owes very much to the teachings and advice of my father, the great rabbi Jacques Ouaknin (I salute in passing his love at first sight for magic squares and stars) and to the attentive, joyous, and dynamic encouragements of my mother, Eliane Sophie Ouaknin (saluting in passing her passion for study and teaching, always present for her Monday class). May both of them find here the pleasure and happiness I feel because I can give them, as I do every time, a modest homage of love and admiration.

This great trip into the universe of numerals would not have been possible without all the researchers who preceded me, many of whom belong to the last two centuries. I am thinking in particular of Genevieve Guitel and her *Histoire comparée des numérations écrites,* a true bible on the matter, as well as of Menninger and Smith, Dantzig, Renou, Filliozat, and all the others, the veterans of this research.

I am also thinking of the young researchers, who belong to the generation of the second half of the twentieth century. And although they are all present in the bibliography, I would like to acknowledge my debt to one of them, Denis Guedj, who succeeded in transmitting to me (by mathematics!) the passion of these numerals and numbers, with his works, both in specialized research and those written for a broader public.

I would like to thank all those who welcomed me, offering a place for study and friendship: Michèle and Claude Kaminsky from the Spinoza Course, with the friendly and efficient complicity of Monique and Gérard Sander (seminars of the Aleph Center), Joel Abisror and Lazare Kaplan (Mary Kaplan Study Circle, Zal), Helene Attali (Youth Aliah, Synagogue on rue Copernic), Mirjam Zomersztajn and Raphaëlle (CCLJ, Brussels). May all of them find here the expression of my warm friendship.

The time for study, research, and writing is always a good time for dialogue as well. Ideas are shared, exchanged, taught, verified when comparing notes with other researchers, with students and friends, always the first to hear the ongoing work. May each of them be warmly thanked here for their friendship, their comments, and their *hidushim,* which let the course of thought become deeper, and open new paths for research.

Special thanks:
To Françoise-Anne Ménager, who, thanks to our lengthy studies on all the issues developed in this book, allowed me to discover and refine certain aspects, philosophical, literary, and mathematical—a precious companionship of study and friendship that not only often gave me the energy to continue this large work, but also gave this book a tonality for which I am grateful to her;

To Danielle Carassik, who, under Edmond Rostand's kind eyes, was one of the first readers of this book and the first to experience the "teaponchic" effects of the logo-rhythms;

To Richard Rossin, always there and available for all the most unexpected poetic adventures, each one always more Ulipian than the next;

To Katia and Sidney Toledano, who, during an "Indian" dinner, opened up significant prospects for research on the issue of mathematical abstraction, prospects that were decisive for the reflections and writing of this book;

To Mitchélé and Jeanoël, for the chants and the music of the rain;

To Lalou, Dvora Zeèv, Radu, Laura, Davis, Aurélia, Anne, Alain, Fabienne, Alain D.-W., Dominique, B. Richard, Leïla and Hughes, for the happiness of the images, voices, lights, humor, and boardwalk;

To Joëlle for the painful blessings, Marc P. Paollo, Daniel and Nadia, Stéphane and Marie, Chams, Danielle, Mariette, Andre, Claudine, Greg, Claudine, Clémence, Ion, Nicole, Lelia, Dan, for the imagination and passion of the dance, of the breath and the "young girls in flower" of our friend Marcel;

To Pierette, Denis, Ariane, Jean-Nicolas, Suzanne, Favio, Carine, Armand, Rachel, Jérôme, Paul, Steeve, Patrick, Sylvain, for the piano and for the encounters with the depths of the soul;

To Lazare, Coco and Pierre, Isabelle, Jean-Hughes, Célia, Alain, Marie, Roger, Vanina, Richard, Gérard and Antoine, for the high-soaring Tuesdays;

To Claudine Hazout, Laurence Dreyfus, and Mathieu Briand, for the mysteries of 23;

To Jean Daviot for the sky within reach;

And to Sophie Clavel for her generosity and the precision of her glance.

Aharon, Aharon haviv… I also thank Itshaq, "Grand Master of Hidush" (I also salute Pierrette), Aldo and Jeanne Naouri, Georges Pragier, Nathalie Seroussi, Gérard and Élisabeth Garouste, for always having new colors and shapes for the passion of study.

Thanks to Valérie Solvit and Gisèle Franchomme, who had the talent of giving this book all the audience it hoped for.

This new version owes very much to the reactions of readers who were kind enough to send me their comments, remarks, and criticisms, so that I could correct and improve both the text and the iconography. Thanks to all.

I also wish to thank the entire team of Assouline Publishers, whose welcome and know-how let this book see the light of day, Francesca Alongi, Christine Claudon, Julie David, Mathilde Dupuy d'Angeac, Charles Frischer, Kay Guttmann, Clement Humbert, and Nelly Riedel. Thanks to all.

Finally, I must express here my very deep gratitude to Martine and Prosper Assouline, who, more than ever, showed me that it is possible to join together without fault the art of the book and friendship.

Photo credits

Page 22: © Sami Briss; page 31: © photo and collection from the National and University Library of Strasbourg, Ms. 4,602; page 38: © French National Library, Sanskrit Ms. 67, folio 19b-20a; page 39: © D.R./after Amulyachandra Sen, *Asoka's Edicts*, The Indian Publicity Society, Calcutta, 1956; page 41: © French National Library, Pali Ms. 715a; page 43: © Imprimerie nationale; page 45: D.R./after Klaus Ludwig Janert, *Abstande und Schlussovkalverzeichnungen in Asoka-Inschriften*, Franz Steiner Verlag, Wiesbaden, 1972; page 49: © D.R./after Judith M. Tyberg, *First Lessons in Sanskrit Grammar and Reading*, East-West Cultural Center, Los Angeles, 1964; page 61: © Guimet Museum, Paris; page 71: © Jean Louis Nou/AKG Paris; page 82: © The Art Archive/Victoria and Albert Museum London/Eileen Tweedy; page 84: © G. Dagli Orti, Paris; page 86: © British Library; page 87: © The Archive/British Library; page 93: © G. Dagli Orti, Paris; page 94: © Rue des Archives/The Granger Collection NYC; page 96: © Bayerische StaatsBibliothek, Munich; page 103: © The Art Archive/French National Library; page 108: © Roland and Sabrina Michaud/ Rapho; page 109: © Chester Beatty Library, Dublin; page 110: © Mashhad Shrine's Library, Mashhad, Iran; page 112: © British Library; page 114; © Rue des Archives, Paris; page 128: © AKG Paris; page 131: © The Art Archive; page 132: © Palais de la Découverte, Paris; page 133: © Bettmann/Corbis; page 134: © Giraudon/Bridgeman Art Library; page 137: © National Library of Florence; page 142: © British Library; page 144 (top): © École des Beaux-Arts, Paris; page 144 (bottom): © Imprimerie nationale; page 149: © Palais de la Découverte, Paris; page 150: © Jean-Claude Matzloff and Jean-Claude Venet; page 151 (top): © Pour La Science; page 151 (middle and bottom): © Annick Horiuchi; page 152: © Museo della Civilta Romana, Rome; page 172: © Photo RMN/Ch. Larrieu; page 176: © Bettmann/Corbis; page 179: © Sophie Basouls/Corbis Sygma; page 185: © Photo RMN/J.-G. Berizzi; page 201: © Bettmann/Corbis; page 265: © AKC, Paris; page 256: © The Art Archive/Museo del Prado Madrid/Album/Joseph Martin; page 268: © AKC, Paris; page 282: © The Geometry Center; page 312: © AKC, Paris; page 322: Giraudon/Bridgeman Art Library.

The images for which no attribution is mentioned come from unidentified sources. All the research that was done to identify the beneficiaries, and the errors or omissions indicated to the publisher, will be corrected in the following editions.